British Housebuilders

History & Analysis

Fred Wellings

To Robert,

With thanks for your
invaluable contribution.

Fred.

Blackwell
Publishing

© 2006 Fred Wellings

Blackwell Publishing editorial offices:
Blackwell Publishing Ltd, 9600 Garsington Road, Oxford OX4 2DQ, UK
  Tel: +44 (0)1865 776868
Blackwell Publishing Inc., 350 Main Street, Malden, MA 02148-5020, USA
  Tel: +1 781 388 8250
Blackwell Publishing Asia Pty Ltd, 550 Swanston Street, Carlton, Victoria 3053, Australia
  Tel: +61 (0)3 8359 1011

First published 2006 by Blackwell Publishing Ltd

ISBN-10: 1-4051-4918-3
ISBN-13: 978-1-4051-4918-1

Library of Congress Cataloging-in-Publication Data
Wellings, Fred.
British housebuilders : history and analysis / Fred Wellings.
    p. cm.
Includes bibliographical references and index.
ISBN-13: 978-1-4051-4918-1 (pbk. : alk. paper)
ISBN-10: 1-4051-4918-3 (pbk. : alk. paper)
1. Construction industry–Great Britain–History–20th century.   2. Housing development–Great Britain–History–20th century.   3. Housing–Great Britain–History–20th century.   I. Title.

HD9715.G72W39 2006
338.4′769080941–dc22
2006000403

A catalogue record for this title is available from the British Library

Set in 10/13 pt Trump Mediaeval
by Graphicraft Limited, Hong Kong
Printed and bound in India
by Replika Press Pvt Ltd, Kundli

For further information on Blackwell Publishing, visit our website:
www.blackwellpublishing.com

The Royal Institution of Chartered Surveyors is the mark of property professionalism worldwide, promoting best practice, regulation and consumer protection for business and the community. It is the home of property related knowledge and is an impartial advisor to governments and global organisations. It is committed to the promotion of research in support of the efficient and effective operation of land and property markets worldwide.

Real Estate Issues

Series Managing Editors

Stephen Brown   RICS
John Henneberry   Department of Town & Regional Planning, University of Sheffield
David Ho   School of Design & Environment, National University of Singapore
Elaine Worzala   Real Estate Institute, School of Business Administration, University of San Diego

Real Estate Issues is an international book series presenting the latest thinking into how real estate markets operate. The books have a strong theoretical basis – providing the underpinning for the development of new ideas.

The books are inclusive in nature, drawing both upon established techniques for real estate market analysis and on those from other academic disciplines as appropriate. The series embraces a comparative approach, allowing theory and practice to be put forward and tested for their applicability and relevance to the understanding of new situations. It does not seek to impose solutions, but rather provides a more effective means by which solutions can be found. It will not make any presumptions as to the importance of real estate markets but will uncover and present, through the clarity of the thinking, the real significance of the operation of real estate markets.

Books in the series

Adams & Watkins *Greenfields, Brownfields & Housing Development*
Adams, Watkins & White *Planning, Public Policy & Property Markets*
Allen, Barlow, Léal, Maloutas & Padovani *Housing & Welfare in Southern Europe*
Ball *Markets and Institutions in Real Estate & Construction*
Barras *Building Cycles & Urban Development*
Beider *Urban Regeneration & Neighbourhood Renewal*
Ben-Shahar, Leung & Ong *Mortgage Markets Worldwide*
Buitelaar *The Cost of Land Use Decisions*
Byrne and Ong *Real Estate Investment*
Couch, Dangschat, Leontidou & Petschel-Held *Urban Sprawl*
Couch, Fraser & Percy *Urban Regeneration in Europe*
Dixon, McAllister, Marston & Snow *Real Estate & the New Economy*
Evans *Economics & Land Use Planning*
Evans *Economics, Real Estate & the Supply of Land*
Guy & Henneberry *Development & Developers*
Jones & Murie *The Right to Buy*
Leece *Economics of the Mortgage Market*
McGough & Tsolacos *Real Estate Market Analysis & Forecasting*
Monk & Whitehead *Affordable Housing and the Property Market*
Newell & Sieracki *Property Investment & Finance*
O'Sullivan & Gibb *Housing Economics & Public Policy*
Seabrooke, Kent & How *International Real Estate*
Wellings *British Housebuilders: History & Analysis*

Contents

List of Figures and Tables

Preface

British Housebuilders: History & Analysis is not a history of the economics of the industry, nor its architecture, nor its sociology. Instead, it remedies a major gap in the supply side analysis of the housebuilding industry: who the housebuilders were and how their behaviour has affected the corporate structure of the industry. Merrett wrote in his standard work on owner-occupation that 'A systematic treatment of speculative housebuilding would be a massive work in itself and at the time of writing no such volume has been produced'.[1] I would like to think that his sentence could no longer be written. *British Housebuilders* is the first comprehensive account of the corporate history of the twentieth-century speculative housebuilding industry – the firms that 'supplied' those houses and the entrepreneurs who created those firms. As any history should, it is hoped that this volume will also enable current practitioners to avoid at least some of the errors of the past, not the least of which would be to 'stick to their last'; and it challenges the received wisdom that economies of scale have driven the creation of national housebuilders.

The book was originally started in the late 1990s, at the end of a stockbroking career which largely centred on writing about the building industry. I was aware that many of the firms that had been leaders in the housebuilding industry had passed on with little written record, and I embarked on what was intended to be a series of mini-corporate histories. In a sequence of events which are now fading from my memory, I found myself adapting and extending the work as a doctorate at my old university, a process somewhat more distant than the writing of stockbrokers' circulars. After a passage of four years, work on the book resumed and it has become a revised version of the thesis. The company histories which underpin this work, 141 of them, are being separately published by myself in a companion volume, *A Dictionary of British Housebuilders*.[2]

British Housebuilders has two objectives, drawn from areas of the economic history spectrum that are rarely connected. The economic history of the twentieth-century housebuilding industry has been written with little reference to the firms that supplied the industry's output: it was almost as if houses appeared by themselves, products of economic laws and social

---

[1] Merrett, *Owner Occupation in Britain*, p. 159.
[2] ISBN 0-9552965-0-1. See www.fredwellings.co.uk for order details.

considerations, but untouched by human hands. To address this important gap, Part I of this book presents a supply side matrix of the housebuilding firms from the 1930s onwards, identifying all the larger housebuilders at key stages in the industry's development, and tracing the growth in concentration from the local developers of the inter-war period to the national housebuilders that dominated the industry at the end of the century. Part II uses the data to analyse the reasons for both the growth and decline of housebuilding businesses. Above all, the book rejects the contention that increased size is *necessitated* by economies of scale and scope, the former scarcely relevant and the latter largely offset by the managerial diseconomies of regional structures and dilution of entrepreneurial flair. Corporate decline is examined next and where this has happened – and it has happened a lot – this is attributed to succession issues, lack of focus and the severity of the 1974 and 1990 recessions. It is in these chapters that the lessons of history shine most brightly.

The book concludes with an alternative explanation for the emergence of national housebuilding organisations. If economies of scale do not necessitate the creation of large housebuilders, the driving forces must lie elsewhere. Here, they are considered to be, in no particular order: financial, with the stock market playing a key role both in facilitating acquisitions and in demanding growth from its constituent companies; second, the personal ambition that motivates some businessmen to seek growth and size for their own sake; and finally, the quality of judgement that allows some housebuilders, but not others, to avoid over expansion ahead of a major downturn in the housing cycle. In doing so, they create a 'pool of survivors' that are able to take full advantage of the next upwards phase of the housing cycle. As well as providing a better understanding of the specific problems facing housebuilders, it is hoped that the book adds to the understanding of the theory of firms' behaviour by concentrating on a peripatetic industry, which possesses no physical economies of scale and which is peculiarly dependent on entrepreneurial flair and judgement.

Footnote references use author and short title; the full work can be found in the Bibliography. The *Private Housebuilding Annual*(s) written by this author and published since 1980, have been abbreviated as *PHA*(s).

Acknowledgments

The book has been based on extensive research on individual housebuilders and the analysis is supported by some 141 corporate histories. The compilation of a corporate history is not an isolated process and I am indebted to the 180 people, frequently founders and invariably senior directors, who granted me interviews or corresponded between 1998 and 2002, some of whom gave extensively of their time, others who helped to clarify particular points. Thanks are also due to the many librarians who helped me track down obscure corporate data. In particular, I would like to record the considerable help received from Rosemary Ackland, the librarian of the then Credit Lyonnais Securities who provided several hundred microfiche records and gave invaluable assistance in tracing companies. I am also grateful to John Bundock who generously provided me with his housebuilding interview notes from the early 1970s.

Throughout the preparation of the manuscript I received both encouragement and guidance from Professor Robert Lee. He gently steered me down academic avenues that I did not know existed and his contribution to the development of the analysis has been invaluable.

This book has been many years in gestation and has been written at home. The support and encouragement I have received from my wife, Catherine, has been invaluable throughout this period, and it is to her that this book is dedicated.

Several of the individuals mentioned in the book have been knighted during the course of their career, occasionally being raised to the peerage. For simplicity, their original names have been used throughout, except where the individual was already titled at the time of the interview or first mention.

Fred Wellings

Part I   The Supply Side

1

Introduction

Housebuilding is one of the largest industries in the country and one that touches us all directly. There is a substantial body of literature to interest the historian: on its role in the economy, its social history, demography, planning control, the materials and building techniques. In all this, the diligent historian has been assisted by an abundance of statistics relating to the stock of houses, annual completions, the number of households, housing condition and house prices. But nowhere do we find the history of the housebuilders themselves, the men and the firms that gave us, for better or worse, the twentieth-century speculative housebuilding industry. The standard works on the industry make virtually no mention of the individual housebuilders and their role in the development of the housebuilding industry for the simple reason that little was known about them. Writing in 1982, Ball described the problem:

> 'It is very difficult to give a broad outline of the speculative housebuilding industry as little national data on it is published . . . no such thing as a minimum list heading, common for virtually every other industry, exists for construction . . . the number of volume builders . . . cannot be discovered.'[1]

The remarks of Merrett, writing in the same year to the effect that no systematic treatment of speculative housebuilding has been produced, were noted in the Preface. The author's own *Private Housebuilding Annual*, published since 1980, has begun to address that imbalance and is increasingly being used in academic articles,[2] but it covers, at most, the last two decades.

Why has there been so little corporate coverage of the housebuilding industry? Is it because the individual companies have tended to be small and

---

[1] Ball, 'The Speculative Housebuilding Industry', p. 31.
[2] Starting, ironically, with Ball, *Housing Policy and Economic Power*.

often of relatively recent origin, that there have been no substantial corporate histories? Even where there are histories, as for Laing, Alfred McAlpine and Taylor Woodrow, the treatment of the housebuilding element of the business languishes beside that of the more glamorous construction side. Other housebuilders have to make do with a few corporate brochures or privately circulated mini-histories. As for any work that attempts to pull the threads together and consider issues across the corporate spectrum, there are a number of books and articles covering the inter-war period but it is rare to find more than a passing mention of individual companies.

The treatment of the speculative housebuilder contrasts with the world of the Victorian contractor, particularly the civil engineer: books on Abernethy, Arrol, Brassey, Brunel, Cubitt, Farbairn, Gibb, Myers, journal articles on Gooch, James Young, Joliffe & Banks, and so on. There are also histories of many of the major building materials companies, but compared with other sectors of the construction industry there is, for housebuilders, little material available from which either historians or contemporary commentators can judge the characteristics of the successful speculative housebuilder, place them in a quantitative context, or answer such critical questions as: why they grew; why diversification failed; why there was such difficulty with succession; and why they declined. It cannot be stressed enough how limited is the documentary record of the housebuilders. Already, well known names have come and gone with scarcely a word to remember them by, including 20 companies that have been, at one time or another, among the country's ten largest housebuilders: names such as Broseley, Comben, Costain Homes, Ideal Homes (the largest before the war), William Leech, McLean (the largest a decade ago) and Whelmar, not to mention the well known pre-war names of G.T. Crouch, Davis Estates, Janes and Metropolitan Railway Country Estates.

There have been some 130 companies listed on the Stock Exchange that have, at one point or another, been totally or predominantly housebuilders, and as background to this book all these companies have been researched to provide the bedrock upon which the general conclusions rest. Many of the quoted firms were small, but there are 72 housebuilders that appear in the league tables compiled in Part I; these include all companies thought to have built over 500 units a year in the inter-war and early post-war periods and, as firms became larger, over 1000 units a year from the 1970s.

The book's structure

British Housebuilders divides into two parts: the first describes the changing corporate structure of the housebuilding industry, centred around housebuilders 'league tables' from the 1930s onwards; the second part analyses the reasons for the growth and decline of the housebuilding firms. The body of this opening chapter begins by defining the distinctive economic nature of the speculative housebuilding industry, including the development process, the wholesaling function and the capital risk. The substantial economic differences between speculative housebuilding and the physically similar construction of local authority housing are stressed. It outlines the sources of information for the individual companies that are at the heart of the book, the methodology used in determining which were the leading housebuilders and contains a more detailed explanation of the sources for the housebuilders' unit volume statistics.

To provide a basis for an analysis of the supply side of the speculative housebuilding industry from its emergence in a recognisable form between the wars, a matrix of the leading housebuilders has been constructed for five key periods in the industry's history, ranging from the 1930s to the end of the century. As background for this data, some 141 individual company histories were prepared: these were based on public records, unpublished archival material from the inter-war period, interviews with many of the founders and entrepreneurs that ran the companies, and a further 40 written contributions, plus my own previous knowledge of the companies. Thus, Chapters 2 to 6 are structured chronologically beginning with the inter-war period, followed by the Second War and building controls, the post-war housing boom (1955–1973), and then two periods of recession and recovery, 1973–1988, and 1989–2004. With the exception of the war, each of these periods contains one or more tables that delineate the leading housebuilders at specific points in time, ordered by the number of houses sold, in order to generate a 'league table', and to show the change in market share of the top ten companies. It is believed that every housebuilder that has attained an annual output of at least 1000 units has been included, with a lower threshold of 500 units for the pre-war and early post-war periods. This matrix provides a much-needed context for the later analysis. It facilitates a greater understanding of the origins of individual firms and their founders' characteristics, and allows a more systematic analysis of the economies of scale, the increase in concentration, and the emergence of national housebuilders.

The inter-war period (Chapter 2), particularly the late 1920s and the 1930s, was a period of unprecedented growth in private housebuilding which saw the emergence of the speculative housebuilding industry as it now exists. Provincial housebuilders moved to London, and by the late 1930s some London housebuilders were beginning to build outside London. Yet, although firms built on larger sites than today, for the most part they remained local businesses. How they would have developed remains unknown, for World War II and the post-war building controls (Chapter 3) created a 15-year period where there was practically no speculative housing and many of the pre-war housebuilders either vanished or substantially changed the balance of their business. For obvious reasons there is no table of leading housebuilders for this period, but the impact that this cessation of speculative development had on the subsequent structure of the industry was profound.

With building controls finally removed in 1954, the industry enjoyed a period of growth which lasted almost 20 years. The post-war housing boom described in Chapter 4 saw the emergence of a new generation of house-builders, a contrast with the inability or unwillingness of the pre-war housebuilders to reassert their position. The period also marked the start of the housebuilders' regional expansion. The industry's first major post-war recession started during 1973 and eliminated many housebuilders. The industry had to cope with lower demand for the rest of the decade but the emergence from recession and growth in the 1980s produced another generation of housebuilders (Chapter 5). The events outlined in Chapter 5 have their parallel in Chapter 6: the post-1989 recession was as severe as that of the early 1970s and similarly led to changes in the corporate structure of the industry, in particular allowing the increasing dominance of the national housebuilder.

For each of these time periods, market share statistics are prepared and Chapter 7 concludes with a summary of market share growth from the 1930s to the end of the century. The numbers can only be approximate but, in the 1930s, the 10 largest housebuilders had combined volumes of around 16,000 to 18,000 houses, or some 6–7% of the market. By the end of the century the 10 largest firms had combined volumes of 63,000 a year and accounted for over 40% of a much smaller industry output. Corporate change in the housebuilding industry through the twentieth century can be analysed for the first time.

Part II explores the factors underlying the consolidation process in the British speculative housing industry. Entrepreneurial flair is important in all businesses but the peripatetic nature of housebuilding production and the degree of speculation involved in acquiring land so far ahead of produc-tion made this especially important in the fortunes of the private house-builders. In view of the emphasis placed in this book on the entrepreneurial contribution, Chapter 8 describes the background of the founders and dominant characters who ran the larger firms. Perhaps surprisingly, by the end of the century there was an increase in the number of first generation founders running the larger companies, and the founders continue to include people with no post-school qualifications.

Chapter 9 addresses the housebuilders' arguments for growth, being in simple terms that size brings economies of scale. This chapter will argue that there is no overriding economic necessity to construct ever larger firms. If the housing site is taken as the production unit, there are minimal physical economies of scale and, in any case, the size of the site is not within the determination of the housebuilder, but is primarily determined by the planning process; he therefore has no control over the economies of scale. However, there are economies of scope that do accrue to the firm, and land acquisition, marketing and purchasing are addressed in detail. Against this, there are also offsetting managerial diseconomies and, perhaps even more important, a dilution of entrepreneurial flair as decision making is diffused across a regional network. A statistical analysis of profit margins provided no evidence to support the assertion that large housebuilders are inherently more profitable than small ones.

Devine et al. argued that 'analysing growth of firms is not a separate activity from analysing their decline',[3] so Chapters 10 and 11 explore the reasons why individual housebuilding entities have failed or just faded away. The chronological periods that provided the framework for Part I are used to show what happened to each of the larger companies. The dominant individual, once responsible for growing the business, frequently plays an important role in its decline, sometimes directly through aggressive over-expansion; sometimes indirectly through failure in handling succession. Lack of focus is invariably associated with decline. Housebuilders have frequently operated side by side with construction, commercial property development and overseas housing; they have also diversified into unrelated activities and, in turn, been part of conglomerate structures. Each one of these pairings is separately analysed and found wanting. Finally, whatever the structure that has been adopted by individual firms, all have been affected by the housing cycle. The cycle typically draws investment in towards the peak and the major recessions of 1974 and 1990 led all too often to sudden death; some 40 quoted companies left the industry as a result.

Having rejected any operational necessity for housebuilders to become national concerns, this book argues that the consolidation process within the housebuilding industry has been substantially driven by a three-pronged dynamic somewhat different to that envisaged by Chandler: financial

---

[3] Devine, *An Introduction to Industrial Economics*, p. 135.

opportunity and the influence of the Stock Exchange; personal motivation; and the apparently simple concept of avoiding firm-threatening mistakes. It is financially advantageous for owners to invest surplus funds in their own business: as their product cannot be physically delivered to the purchaser, reinvestment can only be made by extending geographical coverage. The ability to float on the Stock Exchange has provided an incentive for private companies to grow to a size where they can be floated; once there, the ability to issue shares has allowed companies to finance a faster rate of growth and to make acquisitions. Furthermore, they are not allowed to stop: the pressure from institutional investors on quoted company managements is to produce profits growth and consolidate into more marketable entities.

Rational economic man no longer holds sway and, as in all industries, personal ambition amongst the housebuilders remains a strong motive for corporate growth. The interviews even produced the occasional honest admission of personal ambition, but the behaviour of individual business leaders provides the strongest supporting evidence. It may also be argued that success in an entrepreneurial environment can occur by default if firms are able to grow merely because they are the ones that avoid firm-threatening mistakes. In the context of the housebuilding industry, this means the judgemental quality of entrepreneurs ahead of major cyclical downturns which enables them to withstand the acute financial pressure that ruins so many of their competitors. By default, the successful exercise of this judgemental skill (or instinct) creates a 'pool of survivors' who are able to use the recession to buy land (or competitors) at depressed prices, thereby being best placed to benefit from the cyclical upswing.

What is the speculative housebuilding industry?

The sector of the economy under review is variously described as private housebuilding, speculative housebuilding and estate development. It is viewed as a subset of the construction or building industry yet, despite its obvious physical similarity, the economics of private housing bears no relation to the rest of the construction sector. Indeed, it is the physical similarity between private housing and other building work that mistakenly gave some contracting firms the belief that private housing development can be undertaken as an integral part of their mainstream contracting business; observers of the industry have been known to make the same mistake.

The term 'speculative' that often accompanies what is otherwise known as private housebuilding is an interesting one. Its first use was attributed by

Ramsey to Thomas Cubitt whom he believed was the first reputable builder to offer houses completely ready for sale. However, the term came to be used more pejoratively than as a description of an economic process, or as Ramsey put it: 'Architects and superior people generally are apt to use the word "speculative" to imply a somewhat patronising contempt'.[4] Such attitudes persist today, yet it is hard to detect the logic. A wide range of other industries supplying the retail customer are also speculative in that the goods are produced and made available in advance of the consumer's decision to purchase, motor cars and the retail industry being examples, yet references to the speculative car industry or the speculative clothing industry are never made. Indeed, the opposite applies in that it is only when products are 'bespoke' that the economic nature of the transaction is appended as a prefix.

For obvious reasons, private and public sector housing appear similar: for some areas of macro-economic analysis the two are indeed interchangeable. However, for corporate analysis the contrast between the two is marked, and must be emphasised at the outset. Although local authority housebuilding is now virtually non-existent, for long periods of the twentieth century it was an important, sometimes even dominant, part of the total housing programme, yet the economic form is entirely different from the private sector. Local authority housing was all supplied on contract. The authorities provided the land and frequently the design specification; the contractor did no more than build the houses in accordance with the contract terms, usually at a fixed price, much as he would build a school or factory. In contrast, the private housebuilder is a developer rather than a builder. The land is purchased and much, or all, of the building work is done before there is a contract with the purchaser. Indeed, the operation of the estate developer is so far removed from the contractor that, over time, an increasing proportion of the physical construction work has actually been subcontracted out, leaving the developer with little more than a supervisory role over the production process.

The most common error in the description of the economic role of private housebuilders is one of omission: their wholesaling function is almost invariably ignored and the economics of the industry therefore frequently misrepresented. Thus can be found simple assertions which assume that housebuilders do nothing except walk on to a piece of vacant land and develop it immediately for a building profit or, alternatively, hold on to the land for 'speculative' profit. Gibb, et al. suggested only that 'Housebuilding

---

[4] Ramsey, 'Speculative House Building', p. 529.

firms have two ways of making a profit. They can make profit directly on their building activities, or indirectly through land-development profit or speculation'.[5] Similar comments were made by Smyth, while Lambert asserted that 'For companies that maintain the minimum land bank . . . the major source of profit will be on construction, and profits will be amassed predominantly on the volume of turnover.'[6] Another example of the failure to recognise the wholesaling and development function as an economic activity deserving of its own reward is the distinction made by Short et al. between housebuilders that derive substantial profits from increases in land prices whom they call 'landfinders' and those that earn their profits almost entirely from construction ('the constructors').[7] Even the Barker Report could not quite dismiss the concept of housebuilders as land speculators: when noting that housebuilders 'are often said to make their money from land', the statement was followed by a reluctant, 'This is not entirely true.'[8]

Even housebuilders who are able to acquire land and start work on the same day, in a period of total price stability, still merit far more than a construction profit. Wholesaling and land improvement are vital parts of the speculative housebuilder's activity. Although single plots can be found by putative house-owners, they are a rarity: individuals cannot obtain single building plots in the middle of green fields, miles from the nearest utility supplies. Land needs to be bought in bulk, roads constructed, drains laid and utilities supplied until the point where individual serviced plots are available. The end purchaser might at that stage arrange for his own house to be built but none of the earlier functions can be performed on a plot-by-plot basis. When it comes to high-rise urban development, the wholesale function must be taken even further: at the risk of stating the obvious, the customer cannot build one flat on the sixth floor. The wholesaling function requires the exercise of a diverse range of skills, and the fact that the individual plots are sold on to retail customers with the benefit of a completed house on top does not turn a developer into a contractor. The omission of the wholesaling function in commentary on housebuilders has, therefore, exacerbated the loose use of the term 'speculative' as a pejorative description, implying that land is acquired solely because it is expected to appreciate in value. That is not to dismiss the fact that some land may be bought to be held for appreciation, but wholesaling and land

---

[5] Gibb, 'Housebuilding in Recession', p. 1745.
[6] Smyth, *Land Banking, Land Availability and Planning for Private Housebuilding*; Lambert, *New Housebuilding and The Development Industry in The Bristol Area*, p. 93.
[7] Short, *Housebuilding Planning and Community Action*, pp. 58–9.
[8] Barker, *Review of Housing Supply, Final Report*, p. 106.

improvement remain an integral and necessary part of the development process.

The wholesaling function and the nature of the production process means that capital is tied up for long periods; it therefore necessitates high profit margins, in order that the housebuilder may achieve his desired rate of return on capital. In contrast, the contractor typically operates on low profit margins, say, 2–4%.[9] The regular payments from the client and the delays in paying their own suppliers often means that contracting requires little capital; sometimes it is even cash positive. Returns on capital are therefore high (or infinite) and the business risk centres around building within the price quoted. The estate developer, in contrast, employs substantial capital as it purchases the land and finances the growing working capital; its operating margins are high and may be 10% or 20% or more, but its capital is turned over slowly. Without wishing to minimise it, the housebuilder's risk is less related to the construction process but instead it centres on the possibility that land purchased may not obtain the desired planning permission, that houses do not sell, or that house selling prices differ from those originally expected: in other words, the housebuilder is vulnerable both to specific errors of judgement on his speculative land purchases, and to the vagaries of the housebuilding cycle.

High rates of inflation in house prices in the post-war era have produced periods of sustained growth and high returns for housebuilders, contributing to the frequent suggestion that inflation is the prime cause of high margins: without house price inflation, it has frequently been argued that housebuilders would only earn the rates of return typically earned by contractors. This view, however, pays too little attention to the three principal reasons why housebuilders earn higher profit margins even in periods of low inflation. The wholesaling function is capital intensive. Evans, also in this series, is but one of many authors to attribute the need for a land bank to delays in the planning system.[10] Even where land is bought with outline planning permission, it may take a year or two to obtain detailed consent, put in the infrastructure and build the first houses. Moreover, the land may have to be acquired in a size which is considerably larger than the optimum sales rate for that location, requiring the balance of the site to be held for a further period of years. The capital-intensive nature of the industry (the annual sales capital ratio has averaged around 1.3 over the last ten years) requires a profit margin to broadly equate with the desired return on

---

[9] Wellings, *Construction Equities*, p. 159.
[10] Evans, *Economics, Real Estate & the Supply of Land*, pp. 175–80.

capital. The unmatched nature of the transaction (in that purchases are made well before sales) also dictates a risk premium.

If the economic nature of the transaction makes private housing so different from construction, it should be no surprise that a similar distinction can be made about the operational methods and the management approach. A recurrent theme in Part II will be the extent to which the speculative housebuilding industry thrives on, indeed requires, entrepreneurial management. Although the claim is often made, no industry can describe itself as unique; there are always attributes that are common to other industries. However, many have particular features, each one perhaps shared with only a limited number of other industries which, when taken together, give that industry a distinctive character. For the speculative housebuilding industry, these characteristics centre around the transitory production location, labour supervision and the land buying decision. It is these which make the housebuilding industry so suited to, and so dependent on, entrepreneurial management.

Manufacturing industry, retailing and distribution, finance and most service industries operate predominantly from a fixed base (factory, store, warehouse) where systematic procedures can be established, routines followed, allowing day-to-day management to be systematised and therefore delegated. In contrast, housebuilders' operational locations are forever changing so that although generalised procedures and principles can be put in place, they are being applied in locations which are never the same, with planning requirements which differ from council to council, to products which may be specific to the site, and to ground conditions which certainly are unique to the site.

Most of the site trades are self-employed, with a recognised skill base and an independence that owes as much to temperament as to legal status. In the early stages of growth, site supervision will rest with the entrepreneur; decisions made on site require a strong personality. As the company grows, the entrepreneur needs to recruit, then motivate and supervise the senior management who now control the building operation. For the large company this culminates at the point where the team he leads contains people who, if they chose, could themselves be working as entrepreneurs.

Land is the housebuilder's raw material: it is rapidly exhausted and needs replacing. The entrepreneur who is adept at controlling building operations at a site level also requires the skills necessary to negotiate land purchases, often from owners whose social and professional status is far removed from that of the building site. He needs to visualise the transformation of raw land into a finished, customer appealing, housing estate. He is a dealer in land, every piece of which has unique physical and market related characteristics. Every purchase is a bargaining negotiation and the developer must be prepared to take a view on its future value, both in relation to alternative sites in the same area, to planning considerations and to future movements in land values.

It is the combination of natural personal authority, organisational skill, development vision and negotiating ability that characterises the successful housebuilding entrepreneur, to which one adds the determination and drive that are found in entrepreneurs throughout the business world. Although many of the successful housebuilding entrepreneurs use a related trade or professional qualification as a means of entry into the industry, most of these skills are inborn and honed in the real world. Few have been university educated, let alone had formal business training.

Sources of information

Published literature

Underpinning this book is the research that has produced the individual company histories that are included in the companion volume: they are used to determine the how, what and why of the industry's corporate history. Within that body of information is contained the specific data that is used in Part I to show both the growth in concentration from the 1930s to the present day, and the rise and fall of the individual firms, namely the number of houses sold (frequently termed unit completions) by individual firms. This section outlines the principal sources of information, starting with the most freely available, the published literature, and ranging through to the author's own research enquiries. In the middle lies information which is in the public domain, but is difficult to access and not previously subjected to comprehensive analysis – company accounts and other corporate filings.

As a generalisation, the body of literature on the speculative housebuilding industry concentrates almost exclusively on economic, social and political analysis: a comprehensive overview can be obtained from a handful of standard works. However, from the viewpoint of this book, the overwhelming lacuna in the literature on the supply side is that there is virtually no mention of the individual companies until the last 20 years. Indeed, one sometimes suspects that the analysis is conducted in the abstract, with authors being less than fully aware of the companies and people that generate the economic activity. The heyday of speculative building in Britain was in the 1930s yet works by Marian Bowley barely do more than mention the names of some half-dozen leading housebuilders, while other standards such as Richardson and Aldcroft, Parry Lewis, and Burnett do not manage even that.

There is the occasional journal article which recognises that the houses did not appear on their own: Miles Horsey does discuss Ideal, Laing and the much smaller Thomas Blade, but the historic data are no more than brief. In effect, snippets of information are gleaned here and there as some authors, not necessarily used to company analysis as a central part of their existence, select individual companies as illustrations for their more general statements. Isolated examples can be found, but nothing which even begins to provide a basis for constructing a profile of the industry's structure, or to show who were the leading housebuilders or what were their relative outputs. Even Nicholas Morgan's *A History of the NHBC and Private Home Building* gives only passing references to individual housebuilders and makes no use of the NHBC's extensive corporate data. Post-1980, work by Ball does as much as any to integrate the companies into his analysis of industry trends although access to earlier volume data would have provided a deeper perspective.[11]

There are exceptions to this peremptory dismissal of the industry literature, particularly Alan Jackson's very readable *Semi-detatched London* and John Bundock's thesis on speculative housebuilding in the London area during the inter-war period. Both provide an extensive discussion of the role of the individual housebuilder before the war although both are limited to the London area. Jackson contains brief biographical material relating to most of the London housebuilders but his numerical data are based only on the number of housing estates listed in the press advertisements. Bundock's work is the only one which consistently mentions the annual outputs of individual housebuilders and his text includes frequent short biographical descriptions of the London companies.

The American literature has been similarly criticised for its treatment of the housebuilding firms. Buzzelli mirrors the complaints of this book, arguing that the housebuilding industry had received 'little scholarly treatment' and commentators have often misinterpreted builders and their methods. Housing studies focused on demand to the neglect of supply and the housebuilders themselves 'have been understudied and

---

[11] Ball, *Rebuilding Construction*, pp. 175–80.

misunderstood';[12] he is perhaps unfair on Grebler and Eichler (whose father founded one of the larger housebuilders). Although discussing a market somewhat different to Britain, both authors provide excellent insights into the operation of the speculative developer, accompanied by a wider ranging discussion of individual firms than has appeared in British texts.

Sometimes, works have been based on interviews but, when conducted on any scale, the subjects are invariably not identified. Examples include Craven's thesis which contained many details about individual developers but they were all coded, and Drewett's study based on 28 interviews including six firms that built over 1000 units a year, but without identification it is impossible to know if his sample was typical. Even more of the literature describing the modus operandi of housebuilding firms does so without even reference to anonymous companies. There have also been generalisations that would have benefited from a closer examination of the industry's corporate structure: for example, Johnson's statement that by the 1930s the suburban speculative builder was either relatively large or defunct being a case in point.[13] The last 20 years has seen a more structured use of individual house completion data and corporate analysis. The source most frequently cited for the number of houses built by individual companies has been this author's *Private Housebuilding Annual*: Ball, already mentioned, has authored several papers on the structure of the private housebuilding industry over the last two decades, for example his *Housing Policy* in 1996; in the 1990s, Gillen made free use of both numbers and text from the *PHA*; Nicol and Hooper sourced units from the *PHA* in their 1999 study of change in the housebuilding industry; and, most recently, Adams and Watkins' *Greenfields, Brownfields* based the chapter on the speculative housebuilding industry on contemporary issues of the *PHA*.

Published company histories should be a fertile source of information, and the Bibliography looks reasonably extensive; unfortunately, the reality, as far as the housebuilding sector is concerned, is more limited. There are a few histories of the larger construction companies such as John Laing, Alfred McAlpine, Tarmac (for John McLean), Taylor Woodrow and, most recently, Bovis but even though these companies have, over the years, derived most of their profit from housebuilding, the treatment of the specific housebuilding element of the business takes second place to the power station and the motorway: the sins of the firm are visited upon their

12 Buzzelli, 'Firm Size Structure in North American Housebuilding', pp. 533–4.
13 Johnson, 'The Suburban Expansion of Housing in London 1918–1939', p. 157.

biographers.[14] Moreover, the histories tend to be more descriptive than numerical and only occasionally (for example Bovis and Redrow) do they give direct or indirect indications of housebuilding volumes.

Nevertheless, the histories are useful in that they provide points of reference and are usually very helpful in detailing the origin of the firm. The recently published history of Redrow is the only substantive history of a dedicated housebuilding business. Beyond that, many of the works cited are little more than corporate brochures, although Furnell's booklet on Ideal Homes (originally New Ideal Homesteads), or the Prowting, Wilson Connolly and Wimpey anniversary brochures are no less valuable than some of the glossier histories mentioned above. Many of what might be termed corporate pamphlets or booklets are not readily available – certainly not in the mainstream reference libraries. The unpublished histories of Hilbery Chaplin and A.J. Wait, for instance, were copies of the family descendants' only copies and Higgs & Hill, and Ward Holdings were dug out of company archives.

There are a few biographies, Coad's *Laing* probably being the best known. Autobiographies and reminiscences sometimes provide genuine insights into the development of the firm, as with Sir Albert Costain's *Reflections*, although sometimes they reveal more of the character of the individual, as in Nigel Broakes' *A Growing Concern* (Trafalgar House) or Fred Catherwood's *At the Cutting Edge* (Laing and Costain). Other books are of tangential use: Perry's *Movies from the Mansions* illustrates the diversity of Henry Boot's operations; Beaverbrooks' study of James Dunn describes the man behind the flotation of Ideal Homes and Taylor Woodrow; and John's *A Liverpool Merchant House: Being the History of Alfred Booth* discusses its one-time ownership of Unit Construction.

The trade press is an invaluable repository of company information and, from time to time, contains profiles on companies and individuals. Prime amongst the sources that have been regularly searched are *Housebuilder*, the journal of the Housebuilders Federation, first published in 1934 as *The National Federation of Housebuilders Monthly Report*, and *Building* (previously *The Builder*) from 1955 onwards. These magazines have what might be called phases of utility. After the war *Housebuilder* contained a number of speeches and reports about 'how things used to be before the war' while, from time to time, both magazines produced mini-profiles of

---

[14] These and the following titles are all listed in the company history section of the Bibliography.

individual companies. As the magazines widened their coverage to include City readership a more regular reporting of corporate and financial events was introduced. The financial background has been supplemented by the *Investors Chronicle*, particularly in the period 1964 to 1971, a crucial gap in the official corporate records (discussed in the next section).

The regional press was also searched for information, albeit at one remove. Some 33 of the largest regional libraries were approached, with a general enquiry as to what company material might be available. Local London libraries were also approached to try to trace what happened to some of the pre-war housebuilders. The librarians were invariably helpful in principle, but the result was disappointing as few appear to have had filing or indexing systems that readily accessed the information. Some of the information produced turned out to be on local companies that were too small to be of interest and sometimes ephemera. Occasionally, relevant information did materialise: Luton Library has an unpublished memoire of Herbert Janes; Blackburn produced press cuttings on Derek Barnes, founder of Northern Developments; Wakefield had press cuttings on Fell Construction. The London Borough libraries offered little more. Bromley library had a one-page history on Morrell Estates and Harrow an invaluable 1933 booklet on T.F. Nash. In contrast, the Epsom and Sutton local history department had no idea what happened to the dominant local builder (Berg) despite the librarian living in a Berg house. There may be more information available within the national and local newspapers but, without indexes, the task of collecting it would be Herculean and possibly with little additional benefit. The *Glasgow Herald*, for instance, is indexed but it produced virtually nothing on John Lawrence, the city's leading builder.

No references to individual company unit volumes before the war were located in the contemporary press, but there were some interesting reflections on what had been achieved in the pre-war period in post-war issues of *Housebuilder* magazine. Examples include references to Taylor Woodrow producing 1500 houses a year, Dare completing an average of about 800, Crouch 1000 houses a year on various estates in the south of England and Moss 3000 in total during the pre-war period.[15] As private housing resumed on a more substantial scale after 1954 there were numerous contemporary references to the size of individual companies' building programmes, for example Greaves 900 in 1969, Crouch 500 in 1971 and Francis Parker 1500 in 1972.[16] These statistical snippets proved invaluable in ranking those long departed housebuilders.

---

[15] *Housebuilder*, Nov. 1949, p. 253; Jan. 1950, p. 299; Oct. 1952, p. 215; Nov. 1949.
[16] *Housebuilder*, Sep. 1969; Dec. 1971; June 1973.

The most important publication for unit data over the last 20 or so years is the *Private Housebuilding Annual*, which was first written by this author in 1980, as part of a stockbroker's research output. It has gradually increased in coverage and was recently described as 'required reading and reference material for anybody who purports to take a professional interest in the housebuilding industry, the market, its structure, company details, the lot.'[17] The *PHA* provides volume and financial statistics for the larger companies, starting with the top ten in the first year and gradually expanding to a list of over 50 companies by the late 1980s, around 80 companies by the early 1990s and over 100 now. The *PHA* includes not only the data from the company accounts, but also unit numbers provided by private companies specifically for use within the publication. A handful of the company numbers is estimated, using either a combination of unofficial sources and published turnover. It is difficult to prove a negative, but is unlikely that any housebuilder currently building over 500 units a year is missing from the list. In total, the volume figures for some 140 of the larger companies that have operated over the last 20 years are on file, with perhaps a few gaps in the earlier years relating to companies that were then modest in size. Nearly all the companies have individually provided or verified the data each year of publication. Much of the research work for this book has involved extending that unit data from 1980 backward in time to the 1930s.

Company and accounting data

A prospectus is always issued when a company makes a public flotation; approximately 130 companies that have been quoted have been either wholly housebuilders, or where housebuilding has been a significant part of their business. A handful of these housebuilders have been 'reversed' into unrelated companies, for example Hallmark Homes into the New Bulawayo Syndicate, or Five Oaks Estates into Wilkes, thereby making the original prospectus irrelevant. There are others, typically construction companies, which diversified into housebuilding subsequent to flotation, for example Tilbury. That still leaves over 100 prospectuses of relevance, containing key dates, names and an increasing amount of company history as legislation and City practice required ever more disclosure. In addition, there are a number of public acquisition documents that can be particularly useful when unquoted companies are bought, for example the 1986 Walter Lawrence offer document for Poco Properties provided a five-year run of unit sales for the latter.

---

[17] *Housebuilder*, Sep. 2002, pp. 6–7.

Most flotations were post-1960 and the amount of detail provided has gradually increased over time. To illustrate how the unit volume disclosure has increased, the first dozen flotations (of companies that were primarily housebuilders at the time of the issue) were examined in each of the three decades, 1960s, 1970s and 1980s:

(1) For the 1960s, five of the twelve companies gave actual or approximate unit numbers; two gave the totals for the previous seven or eight years; and five gave no information.
(2) For the 1970s, eight gave the volume information; one gave the number of plots and the number of years they would last (allowing the annual output to be approximated); and the remaining three gave only the number of plots.
(3) Finally, in the 1980s, ten companies gave the specific unit volume information, one the total for the previous five years and only one gave no information.

Following on from the prospectuses come the company accounts, a massive, and potentially daunting, repository of information. Including unquoted companies, subsidiaries of larger concerns, and a few false trails, some 380 companies have been searched over time periods that, at the extreme, extend back to World War I. All listed companies were required to deposit a copy of their accounts with the Stock Exchange; these holdings were transferred to the Guildhall Library, but the accounts covered only the period up to 1964 and subsequent years have vanished without trace, an appalling loss of primary data. Since the early 1970s it has been a Companies Act requirement for all companies to file their accounts at Companies House, where each company is allocated a unique number. Not only are the accounts of quoted companies filed, but also accounts from the subsidiaries of quoted companies and from private companies. Naturally, the quoted companies contain the annual statements relating to the business of the year; private companies occasionally do the same but normally contain accounting information only.

Thus, there is a major gap in the public holding of quoted company accounts between the end of the old Stock Exchange Library series (*c.*1964) and the first filings at Companies House (early 1970s). Companies still extant will have master copies but for companies that have gone out of business there is no alternative source. There are some libraries (including the British Library) that have holdings of company accounts but they are far from comprehensive. The gap can be covered in a limited way by reference to the *Investors Chronicle* which briefly reviews the latest accounts of quoted companies in each issue. Private company accounts cannot be obtained prior to their first filings at Companies House in the early 1970s. However, even in those years prior to the filing of annual accounts, there will be a general file for all companies, private or public, which provides names of company directors, dates of appointment and share capital changes. They may also provide details of acquisitions. These provide limited reference points but the information is not always as comprehensive as might be expected nor is it always easy to follow.

Unpublished information

A trawl through the published literature produces some company-specific material but it covers only a small proportion of companies in the industry, and even the company histories can be light on hard factual content. The company information, therefore, has to be gleaned from a much wider array of different sources, outlined below.

The NHBC (National House-Building Council) has been supportive of this research and has provided some detailed information on the number of houses registered by companies in individual years. NHBC was formed at the end of 1936 (then named National House Builders Registration Council) but it was not until 1965 that virtually all new homes in the UK were covered. Until 1989, NHBC operated as the only registration scheme but an independent insurance company then entered the market. As a result, NHBC currently estimates its coverage to be approximately 85% of the market. In its internal records, NHBC maintains details of the number of applications made each year by each registered housebuilder. These have been made available for the period 1971 to 1985 for companies registering 250 or more units. Prior to 1971, the information is no longer retained and post-1985 it is considered too commercially sensitive to release.

The numbers recorded in each year are for registrations and these are not necessarily the same as either housing starts, housing completions or house sales. In practice, registrations will be closer to starts whereas the company figures in this book are for sales. There is another timing difference in that the registrations relate to calendar years whereas the sales figures are for companies' financial years. The registration figures may show more substantial differences from sales at turning points in the housing cycle: an expanding company in 1973 may well have increased its registrations only to find that in the ensuing recession its sales were half the anticipated level.

There are further practical difficulties: NHBC records its numbers by name of the registered builder. Some companies group their registrations together and others choose not to. Where registrations are ungrouped it can be difficult to identify registered subsidiaries and although in many cases it may be obvious (for example anything starting with the name Barratt) there are cases where the name of the registered company bears very little relationship to the parent company. Furthermore, all the companies are listed according to the latest name rather than the original name. Thus, some groups have in excess of 25 listed registered subsidiaries – and to match any one of those with an acquired company may require knowledge of several name changes since the acquisition.

To summarise, the NHBC list has been very useful in highlighting companies above a certain size operating in the 1970s, which might not have been picked up from other sources. It is also helpful in giving a possible order or size to the housebuilding programme of companies that went bankrupt in the mid-1970s and for which no other records survive. However, they are not a substitute for individual housebuilders' published sales figures. NHBC also publishes aggregate information on the number of houses built by groups of builders and the number of individual builders within certain size groups (for example building more than 2000 units a year). This information, which is summarised at the end of Part I, is useful in addressing issues such as industry concentration but there are problems in interpreting the data, and the information only dates back to 1979.

The most important resource for the inter-war period has been company archives, although they are by far the most sensitive and difficult to access as many of the companies are, of course, no longer in existence. It is the only source that requires permission and, for a non-commissioned history, one would not normally expect to obtain access to recent material, if any. On the basis that the pre-war period had the least information publicly available, and was likely to be the least sensitive to current management, access was requested to the archives of the larger companies that operated before the war and, if possible, to the early post-war period to see how these companies re-entered the private housing market. It was regarded as impractical and unproductive to ask for more recent access.

There was greater success in obtaining original archive material than initially expected but this has only been possible because of the personal contacts developed over a long period of years. Full access to pre- and early post-war minutes was granted for Laing, Taylor Woodrow and Wimpey. Through Persimmon, which acquired a number of old established housebuilders, the surviving records for Comben, Ideal, Leech and Metropolitan Railway Country Estates could be accessed. Unit Construction minutes were seen at the offices of (the then independent) Beazer. Henry Boot and James Miller have both conducted archive searches to provide relevant

Table 1.1   Pre-war housebuilders: archival access.

Company	Extant	Archive assessment
Henry Boot	Yes	Minute books searched by retired family member
Comben & Wakeling	No	Minute books at Persimmon – full access
Costain	Yes	Homes sold but not with archive. Failed to gain access
G.T. Crouch	No	No trace – company failed
Dares Estates	No	No trace – company failed
Davis Estates	No	Records destroyed
Ideal Homes	No	Minute books at Persimmon – full access
Janes	No	Acquired by Barratt – no access
Laing	Yes	Full access to pre- and early post-war minutes
William Leech	No	Minute books retained – little content
Mactaggart & Mickel	Yes	Published history
Miller	Yes	Pre-war material provided by company
Morrell Estates	No	No trace – company failed
N. Moss	No	No trace – company failed. No records survive except mortgage file at Companies House
T.F. Nash	No	Companies House records destroyed
Taylor Woodrow	Yes	Full access to pre- and early post-war minutes
R.T. Warren	No	No trace – company sold
Wates	Yes	No access but Bundock given access in 1970
Wimpey	Yes	Full access to pre- and early post-war minutes

material. British American Tobacco provided extracts from the minute books of its Dean Finance subsidiary which had floated, *inter alia*, Taylor Woodrow and Wimpey. There were, of course, disappointments. Costain initially offered access although it never materialised and there is some doubt as to what records have survived. When records were found, they were not always of the highest historical quality; the executive who had acquired the records of Davis Estates admitted after two years that he had probably thrown them away; there was a direct refusal from Wates although, ironically, this was the company which provided Bundock with the greatest access in 1970 and he has kindly provided his file notes. Table 1.1 covers the larger private housebuilders before the war and shows the extent to which archive access has been possible.

The content of what was available varied considerably. For John Laing, Taylor Woodrow and Wimpey there were several years when each board meeting sealed the legal transfer of every house, and those numbers can be totalled. Not all housing transactions are completed, however, and where the John Laing minutes gave a run of annual figures for sales, they did not fully agree with the individual totals. In some cases (Henry Boot and Miller Group) the archives were searched on the author's behalf. However, not all records survived and not all minute books recorded the optimum detail.

Companies like Ideal, Laing, Taylor Woodrow and Wimpey had extensive minute books, often containing strategic discussions. Most illuminating of all was Godfrey Mitchell's annual address to the Management Board, several closely typed pages of observations on the Company, the industry and life in general. At the other end of the spectrum, Leech had nothing of value. On a wider front, many companies (or founding families) have what might be called a 'history file' which contains the occasional relevant item, perhaps some unpublished notes on the company's formation, an article which appeared in the local newspaper, extracts from a house magazine or even a specially assembled fact sheet, Bellway being a helpful example.

Interviews

The interview process was the last, but in this case by no means the least, part of the research for this history of British housebuilders. The interview was partly concerned with filling the information gap about the individual companies, and partly with obtaining views on the strategic decisions which dominate Part II. The one specific piece of information sought was the unit completion data. Responses on the latter varied enormously from people who could remember almost exactly how many houses they had been building 20–30 years ago, or had kept records, to those who could barely suggest an order of magnitude. There were also occasional secondary information sources in that interviewees who started work in, say, the 1950s had memories of being told by colleagues what was built in the pre-war period. All the interview and media information is subject to errors of memory, self-importance and definition, and common sense needs to be used in its interpretation. As mentioned in the acknowledgements, I have also had access to Bundock's interview notes from 1969–1970 and they provide additional support for some of the pre-war numbers.

Interviews are an integral part of business research and have been a substantial, indeed indispensable, source for this book; the background to the interview process has, therefore, been given considerable weight in this introductory chapter. From a methodological perspective, Bornat has stressed the importance of the familiarisation process within the context of the interviewee's life and occupation.[18] The difference between a 'cold' interview and one where some form of relationship exists is, indeed, considerable, a point made by Redding in his study of the retail trade: 'I had the advantage of having been a supermarket manager for two years and of being associated with the industry for ten years previously, and this usually

---

[18] Bornat, 'A Second Take', p. 50.

allowed for the striking of quick rapport with the manager.'[19] This author's 'familiarisation' was considerably assisted by having interviewed senior housebuilding management since the 1960s: a handful in that decade, an increasing number in the 1970s, and from the publication of the first *PHA* in 1980 the contacts with company management have been extensive, approaching 200 companies. Additionally, formal or informal corporate advice has been provided to a number of the housebuilders. All of this, combined with the authorship of the *PHA* has provided an unrivalled entrée to management at the highest level: unusually for the academic/business interview process, I was well known to many of the interviewees and familiarisation was a two-way phenomenon.

It is surprising how simplistically the interview process is treated in business history, yet how much importance is then attached to the result. For the most part, the literature treats the comments of the interviewees as non-attributable which diminishes their utility. When questionnaires are used, the questions tend to be formulaic, apparently designed more for their ability to be processed in an appropriate statistical manner than to elicit meaningful information. Some authors were aware of the limitations of the questionnaire but carried on regardless: 'as it was apparent that the managers concerned would tend to be extremely busy the questionnaire was designed to be completed in only a few minutes.'[20]

For the original thesis, a total of 80 people were directly interviewed, some more than once, and often for up to two hours; a further 60 people were interviewed over the telephone; they were almost all conducted between 1998 and 2002. Although not part of the formal process, literally thousands of meetings have been held with housebuilding executives over the preceding decades in which strategy has been discussed and ideas have been exchanged. Many documentary records of these earlier interviews have survived; where they have not, their content has still permeated the memory bank and helped to create the conditions for the more focused interviews. For many of the direct interviews, and for every single one of the telephone interviews, they were preceded by the submission of a draft history of the company; this made it clear to the interviewee what was already known and, obviously, what mistakes or omissions there were. In this way, although the telephone interviews were relatively short, they became extremely focused. Even the occasional refusal to discuss matters long passed still produced the odd nugget of information.

---

[19] Redding, *The Working Class Manager*, p. 9.
[20] Clark, *The Industrial Manager*, p. 17.

The process of submitting drafts (and frequently second drafts) also led to extensive written responses both from those interviewed, and from others where an interview had either not been requested or not been granted. It is only fair to add that one or two expressed 'unhappiness' with what had been written, albeit without ever unburdening themselves on the source of their concern. Some of the responses were no more than minor factual corrections or clarifications; others were extensive and proved invaluable additional sources of information. In all, over 100 written responses were obtained of which some 40 were additional to those who had been interviewed. For the larger companies, a direct interview was always sought. Some 63 firms have built over 1000 units a year at some point in the twentieth century; for almost all of these there have been one or more interviews. In only six instances was it not possible to arrange an interview, four of which were for companies long since departed; for the top 30 companies (those building 2000 or more houses a year), all benefited from either an interview or correspondence, albeit that not every one came through official sources.

The contact at the larger companies was at a high level. Managing directors or chairmen were interviewed at some 25 of the top 30; in around half of these companies, the founder or a family member was interviewed. Sometimes those companies that did not wish to cooperate themselves were accessible in other ways. Thus, Lawrie Barratt does not give interviews but access was available to one ex-managing director, one ex-deputy chairman, one ex-company secretary and to others who had worked in the Company. Wates was another disappointment in view of its long-standing position in the industry but, again, several ex-directors were known. Of the 63 companies that have built over 1000 units, over 40 were already personally known before the start of the research, and all but four of the largest 25 housebuilders had been regularly interviewed.

The level of contact with the smaller, and often long departed, companies could be far removed from that of the larger concerns and required a different approach. The history has been traced, however briefly, of all those quoted companies that had been regarded as housebuilders at some point in their corporate history – all 130 of them. Many of the companies had failed or been taken over in the 1974 recession and its aftermath; some had vanished even before then. Thus, many of those in senior positions were no longer in the ranks of the active working: the search was for retired people, some of whom were not necessarily overjoyed when asked to cast their minds back to what had often been the failure of their business. Sometimes contacts still in the industry were able to point to the appropriate person. After that, the last recorded address on the Companies House file could be tried; individuals might still be on the list of directorships at Companies House by virtue of, say, a small family firm. At that point, an explanatory letter would be sent, with the appropriate draft history. Not infrequently there was no response: death, change of address, illness and genuine indifference all being contributory factors. However, more than half of the letters did produce a positive response and these were then followed up with a telephone call.

It is common for a research programme to have structured interviews in that the same questions are asked of each person. The interviews for this work have been far from structured in the formal sense of a standard approach with set questions; the starting point for each interview was rarely the same. When interviewees have been known personally for 20 or 30 years, the requirement was more to close knowledge gaps and explore selected strategic issues. In contrast, for companies that have never been quoted, the need might be to elicit the most basic information about the firm's history. Practical considerations have more of an influence on the form of an interview than is generally admitted. An 85-year-old is not interviewed in the same way as a 45-year-old; interviews in the home are different from in the office; and invitations to lunch, pleasurable though they might be, were always the most difficult interviews to structure. Telephone interviews required a more flexible technique, particularly when the return call came some weeks after the initial approach. Most of the formal interviews were tape recorded, as were some of the telephone calls; permission was rarely refused although from time to time one sensed that it would be wise to press the off switch.

The validation of the interview content is a well recognised problem. From the outset, one is contending with memory and Dunaway's comment was pithy: 'some subjects can't recall certain events; some do not wish to; some do not even pretend to try.'[21] Possessing a chronology of the individual company helped to provide a framework and factual inconsistencies could often be explored during the interview or checked later by both parties. Differences in interpretation present a greater test and it is inevitable that the interviewee's version of events will have a greater influence on the researcher than non-interviewees' – an oral history version of 'to the victor belong the spoils'. Amidst all the standard ways of checking facts and opinions (against published information, other interviewees, internal consistency) knowledge of the person, the subject and common sense were the best weapons. It is sometimes assumed that the more distant the event, the

---

[21] Dunaway, 'Method and Theory in the Oral Biography', p. 42.

less reliable will be the recall. While that may be true of factual matters, I found that distance lent honesty to judgement on strategic decisions. For instance, those who took their companies public tended to give entirely different reasons for floating than they had done originally; or, retired chief executives of national housebuilders appeared less convinced of the merits of size than those currently promulgating takeovers. All quotations were later checked with the interviewees as a matter of courtesy and although that led to occasional modifications of previously expressed views, there was only one occasion on which the interviewee requested that his remarks be non-attributable.

The disparity of approach between the various interviews should not be taken as an indication of a random process. The underlying objective in all the interviews was either to obtain from scratch, or to complement what is already available, sufficient information to prepare a short corporate biography of the company. For those companies that were already well known, the objective became the documentation and verification of existing hypotheses. For all companies there was a need to obtain as much detail as possible on housing volumes (if not already known) to satisfy the primary objective of establishing a matrix of housing volumes. That apart, much of the time was spent in exploring the origins and background of the founder or dominant individual – education, trade etc.; and the operational strategies of the business. Where the opportunities presented themselves, the interview also sought to record views on the success or failure of the business.

Methodology

Measuring corporate size

The remainder of this chapter outlines the alternative ways in which housebuilders might be classified. Accounting measures (turnover, profits) were considered but rejected as not being available for the whole of the period under review and being subject to considerable interpretational difficulties. Unit volumes (number of houses) are preferred as having a greater degree of consistency and for their comparability with industry statistics; they are also the measure used in all other analyses of the housebuilding industry. However, even though a physical rather than financial measure has been chosen, unit numbers are not without their own pitfalls, and the lack of homogeneity and the overlap with social housing are discussed.

The categorisation of companies, like all lists, has its own fascination but as raw material for business theory it provides the necessary data for the study of industrial (and commercial) concentration and the rise and fall in corporate leadership. The American business historian Chandler has been credited with stimulating the compilation of lists of large firms, ranked by varying measures of capital and labour, but it is hard to believe that the interest in classification would not have arisen spontaneously. The choice of measure varies. Wardley argued that employment measures tend to be chosen for simplicity and convenience, with business historians regarding them as being more intuitive, easier to find, and 'a less demanding concept from a theoretical perspective.'[22] In their search for the 'correct' universal measure of size, no one seemed to make the obvious point that the substantial capital and operational differences between industries means that there can be no such thing as a definitive measure of size that encompasses a national economy. Neither was the search for the unattainable helped by an unfortunate lack of 'feel' for the accounting concepts being used.

This book is concerned with the preparation of data on a single industry, rather than a national, ranking list. The comparability problems are therefore less acute than with national lists; nevertheless, in establishing a matrix of housebuilders covering a range of time periods, some of the comparability issues experienced in the national lists do occur and will be addressed in more detail. Fortunately, individual industries have one important advantage over the national lists in that they have an option to use a physical measure of output that is reasonably homogeneous – tons of coal, cement or steel, numbers of cars, barrels of oil and, in this case, the number of houses.

The analysis of corporate size and industry concentration requires data that can be measured and compared with reasonable consistency both across time and between companies. For all its drawbacks, these requirements lead inexorably to the use of physical data as the preferred measure of comparison for housebuilders: that measure being the number of houses sold or built.[23] The house (or flat) is a distinct physical entity remaining, if not exactly constant over time then, at the least, readily recognisable as the same product in any period under review. The use of a unit measure is also how the industry statistics are produced, which facilitates the calculation of concentration ratios; and the approach has a parallel with other sectors of the economy (as instanced above) where it is also normal to use a physical count of output. A similar discussion of measurement alternatives for

---

[22] Wardley, 'On the Ranking of Firms', p. 131.
[23] As output also includes flats, the expression 'units' is often used, but when a company's output of houses is mentioned, it can be taken to include flats as well, unless the context clearly suggests otherwise.

housebuilding by Short, et al. briefly reviewed financial and employment measures before concluding that despite its drawbacks 'the most suitable and illuminating categorisation of housebuilders is by number of annual completions'.[24] More recently, in their review of the literature, Nicol and Harper also pointed to the difficulty of classification of housebuilders by anything other than unit volumes.[25]

The alternative measures of size, primarily derived from company accounts, are monetary. The value of output, or company turnover, has the theoretical advantage that it gives the appropriate weighting to both large and small houses, differences in quality, and differences in location; it represents the totality of the business output. There are, however, considerable problems in obtaining consistent data over time. Pre-war financial information is only rarely available; only eight housebuilders were quoted in that period, most of them from the mid-1930s. Private company accounts have rarely survived. When accounts are accessible, they did not disclose turnover; indeed, company turnover was only required by the 1967 Companies Act and, in practice, it is only available from the early 1970s. For quoted companies, profits are available over the whole of the period but they are an unreliable indicator of a company's size, particularly before the 1948 Companies Act introduced consolidated accounts. Clearly, a large quantum of profit indicates a large company (although not how large); a low profit may only indicate poor returns, and a loss gives little indication of the size of the business. For private companies, or subsidiaries of larger groups, accounts data are, again, only available after the implementation of the Companies Act 1967.

It should not be assumed that even where turnover is available, it relates solely to speculative housebuilding; it is not necessarily the only activity within the company. Frequently, it is found in conjunction with construction which has the opposite financial characteristics to speculative housebuilding: construction is low margin, high sales to capital, whereas private housing is high margin, low sales to capital. Thus, for a given level of profit there will be a far higher construction turnover content than private housing turnover. Another typical mix of business is speculative housing with commercial property development. The last 20 or so years have seen an increasing amount of disaggregated information in quoted company accounts and, to a lesser extent, by unquoted companies. Many companies, of course, are solely speculative housebuilders so no disaggregation problem

---

[24] Short, *Housebuilding Planning and Community Action*, p. 279.
[25] Nicol, 'Contemporary Change and the Housebuilding Industry', p. 59.

exists, but even where turnover and profit do ostensibly relate only to private housing, financial data may include undisclosed land sales, occasionally part-exchange turnover,[26] and related property transactions (for example the ground floor of a block of flats may be retail premises).

Value-based accounting measures also suffer from the presentational difficulty that they encompass inflation so large that the comparisons over time are hard to grasp at first reading, necessitating frequent mental adjustments that cut across the flow of the narrative. A typical house price in the 1930s was around £600–£700 but the national average house price was more than one hundred times that by the end of the century. Taking company profits as another value-based comparison, the highest recorded inter-war profit is the £345,000 earned by Ideal Homes in 1933, less than the annual salary now demanded by today's managing directors. In fact, most of the larger housebuilders in the inter-war period only earned profits of the order of £100,000: by the end of the century many large housebuilders were making annual profits over a thousand times that. Although price deflators can be used, they are not without their own interpretational problems. There is no price series (as opposed to cost index) that extends back before the war and Fleming and Nellis, who established the modern indices used by the Nationwide and Halifax, argued that none of the data available could be regarded as providing a true measure of the movement of prices over time. If the objective of using value statistics deflated by a price index is to produce a proxy for volume, it appears unlikely to be any more accurate than the number of houses built.

Employment statistics were also mentioned as a measure of size. Many of the comments already made about turnover can be applied here – only post-1970 disclosure in accounts, and disaggregation problems, where disclosure practice is even less forthcoming than for turnover. There have also been substantial changes in the ratio between labour and output over time, not just because of increased productivity but because of the switch from the direct employment of all the trades to indirect employment via subcontractors. It is suggested, therefore, that for all its weaknesses (and there are many), the number of units still provides the most readily appreciated measure for comparison between companies, over time and for calculating market share. Nevertheless, for all that unit completions of houses are the preferred measure, they still need to be interpreted with care. Two particular problems are discussed below: the homogeneity of the volume statistics and the treatment of social housing.

---

[26]   Unlike car dealers, the sale of stock taken in part-exchange is normally excluded from turnover, although included in profit.

Table 1.2 Quoted housebuilders: average selling prices, 2004.

Company	Average Selling price £	Deviation %
Barratt	170,000	4
Bellway	161,400	8
Berkeley	282,000	60
Bovis	197,900	12
Crest	210,000	19
McCarthy & Stone	154,300	12
Persimmon	172,400	2
Redrow	154,700	12
Taylor Woodrow	197,300	12
Westbury	194,000	10
Wilson Bowden	206,000	17
Wimpey	193,000	9
Average	**176,400**	

Source: Figures derived from the Appendix of the *PHA 2005*.

Houses are not homogeneous

The crude measure of the number of houses is not perfectly homogeneous; certainly less than, say, tons of coal or steel. Like cars, which are also analysed by reference to physical measures, some housing units are small, some large, and some better equipped; the quantity of the internal fittings has improved significantly over time – fitted kitchens, bathrooms and central heating. Unlike the motoring analogy, there can also be a significant difference in the selling price (although not necessarily the product) according to its location. However, in practice, the difference in product mix between companies, particularly the larger ones, is not excessive. Table 1.2 shows the thirteen quoted housebuilders in 2004 with their average selling prices and the striking feature, with the exception of Berkeley which has a high exposure to expensive London properties, is just how close together are the companies. None of the other companies deviate from the average by more than 20% and an examination of earlier years suggests that there is no reason to suppose that the dispersion of selling prices shown in Table 1.2 is atypical.

Social housing is included in the more recent unit numbers

Since the virtual demise of local authority contract housebuilding in the 1980s, 'social' or 'partnership' housing has been undertaken almost entirely by housing associations. Although old-style local authority housing and modern partnership housing both serve the same social purpose, from the supplier's side they are quite different economic entities. Local authority housing was always a contracting operation; it bore no economic relationship to the development process and numbers have been excluded from the private housebuilding figures wherever possible. In contrast, the modern housing associations often operate in 'partnership' with private housebuilders; the two parties are normally interlinked in their economic relationship but the extent of the partnership can vary considerably. It may be that the housebuilder finds and owns the land and takes the development proposition to the housing association; in that respect, it is acting more as a speculative developer than a contractor. Or, it may be providing social housing as an integral part of the development under the requirements of the planning permission. Further along the economic spectrum, the developer (for example Countryside Properties in the early 1990s) may be providing design and build packages to a housing association to keep staff occupied during a private housing downturn; in that respect, it is acting more as a contractor than a speculative developer.

No clear dividing line can be drawn, either between companies or over time, and it has been found most practical to include this partnership housing output in any unit figures quoted for companies over the last two decades (in any case, this figure is not always disclosed and, therefore, could not be excluded). It follows that the inclusion of social housing will slightly distort market share statistics when company output is compared with national statistics for private housing. However, as can be seen from Table 1.3, the average social housing contribution for the top ten is estimated at only 8% and the true market share is therefore overstated by no more than 3%.

Table 1.3   Top ten housebuilders: proportion of social housing, 2004.

Company	Total units	Social units	Social %
Barratt	14,021	1306	9.3
Berkeley	4839	est.350	7.2
Persimmon	12,360	839	6.8
Bellway	6610	566	8.6
Bovis	2700	303	11.2
Westbury	4400	183	4.2
Redrow	4284	*c.*200	4.7
Bryant	9053	815	9.0
David Wilson	5588	*c.*430	8.1
Wimpey	12,232	958	7.8
Total	**76,087**	**5970**	**7.8**

Source: Appendix of the *PHA 2005*.

Unit numbers are used extensively in this book. They cannot be qualified every time they are used but it is hoped that readers will remember that their continued repetition does not make them any less approximate. The same applies to categories: when grouping companies, a line has to be drawn, and it may be by only an insignificant margin that a company is put on one side of the line or another.

2

The Pre-war Housebuilders

Introduction

The inter-war period, and particularly the 1930s, witnessed the start of the move towards mass owner-occupation, taking the levels of private house-building to heights not seen before nor since. The creation of this new market facilitated the parallel creation of speculative housebuilding firms which not only served this new demand, but many of whom also built houses for rent. Although individual housing sites were large, and the total size of the private housing market greater than at any time in the twentieth century, the housebuilders themselves remained local firms, rarely build-ing far from their home base. The geographical structure of these firms is found to be heavily influenced by the booming south-east market, so strong that it induced some northern firms to move to London. Few firms did more than build in their own local areas, but the embryonic geographic diversification in the late 1930s is noted.

It is a period for which almost no quantitative data have been published on the individual companies, and the challenge of this chapter has been to identify, and then to quantify, at least the largest ten housebuilders. It is believed that all those firms that reached an annual output of 1000 units have been identified and probably most over 500; possible omissions are discussed. The first ever construction of an inter-war housebuilders' league table need not be regarded as an end in itself, for the quantitative data can be combined with the background information available on the individual firms to address several interesting questions relating to the supply side of the housebuilding industry. The market share of the leading firms can now be estimated and this is put at 6–7% for the top ten housebuilders in the late 1930s. The proposition that local authority housing played an import-ant role in the development of speculative housing firms is discussed, but it is not found to have substance.

The private housing market

A pre-World War I background

Before starting the description of the inter-war housebuilding market, a brief comment on the period before World War I provides a perspective: it is not, however, a period overflowing with data. Richardson and Aldcroft refer in general to the difficulty of obtaining 'hard facts' about the pre-1914 building industry, while Dyos regards it as 'strange' that we know so little about how the Victorian cities were actually made.[1] Prior to World War I, most people lived in rented accommodation, a figure generally estimated at around 90% although, as the 1977 Housing Green Paper noted, there is no direct evidence for this figure.[2] Although many individual developers became well known names in their locality, where sales numbers are quoted they tend to be small. Dyos noted that between the 1840s and 1870s hardly any London firms built more than 50 houses a year; those numbers rose in the succeeding decades but it was not until the end of the 1890s that 'the really big firm' moved in. Dyos put the largest firm as Watts of Catford and in 1899 it built over 400 houses.[3] Jackson had described Ilford-based Cameron Corbett as probably the most prolific of London's suburban developers in the 1890s and 1900s and in a period of a little more than 20 years he built over 3000 houses, yet this was no more than 300 a year.[4] Edward Yates in south-east London reached around 150 houses a year at his peak in 1888–90; even when his output fell to an average of only 32 at the end of the century, he was still in the top 10% of London builders.[5] At the other end of the country in Glasgow, Andrew Mickel's property business was described as 'an extensive operation between 1889 and 1898' yet the average annual sales were no more than 150.[6] Of these four, only the Mickel business survives today, indirectly as Mactaggart & Mickel, and with an almost identical output.

Several of the leading inter-war housebuilders appeared to have their roots in the nineteenth century but their early history had little, if anything, to do with speculative housebuilding. Henry Boot and Costain were solely contractors until after the First War. Laing had built a few houses but it, too, was in essence a contractor until the mid-1920s. George Wimpey was

---

[1] Richardson, *Building in the British Economy between the Wars*, p. 22; Dyos, 'The Speculative Builders and Developers of Victorian London', p. 641.
[2] HMSO, *Housing Policy Technical Volume Part I*, p. 37.
[3] Dyos, 'The Speculative Builders and Developers of Victorian London', pp. 659–60.
[4] Jackson, *Semi-detached London*, p. 61.
[5] Jeremy, *Dictionary of Business Biography*, pp. 924–5.
[6] Jeremy, *Dictionary of Business Biography*, p. 154.

a Hammersmith road surfacing firm before it was bought by Godfrey Mitchell in 1919 and it was the late 1920s before Wimpey began speculative housing. The reality is that the creation of a nation of owner-occupiers served by national housebuilders did not have its roots in the nineteenth century, nor even the opening decades of the twentieth. Its origins lay in the inter-war period, in particular the owner-occupation boom of the 1930s.

Industry context

The early post-war stimulus to the housebuilding industry came from Government subsidies, but it was the 1923 Housing Act, described by Merrett as 'the most important legislative measure specifically concerned with home-ownership before the Second World War', that principally benefited the speculative housebuilders.[7] The 1923 Act provided cash subsidies to promote the construction of small working-class houses, although the reality was that it subsidised the sale of houses to the middle classes: between 1924 and 1929 some 363,000 private houses were built under the provisions of the Act, but reductions in the subsidies meant that the private output of subsidised housing all but ceased by 1930. In its place came the boom in unsubsidised speculative housing that reached its peak in the mid-1930s when annual private housing completions as high as 250,000 were consistently achieved. Figure 2.1 shows the magnitude of private housebuilding between the wars, in particular the growth and then collapse of subsidised private housing in the 1920s, and the acceleration in unsubsidised building after 1932. To place the industry's achievements in perspective, no post-war year ever saw annual private housing completions as high as in the mid-1930s; indeed, by the end of the century, the private housebuilding industry was fortunate to reach half that level.

Although this book is concerned with the supply side of the speculative housing industry, a brief summary of factors underlying the growth in demand provides a context, for this was the era that created the modern speculative builder. The driving forces, particularly in the 1930s, included demographic trends, differential movement in population as new industries rose and old ones declined, rising real incomes for those in continuing employment, lower building costs and falling interest rates. These contributory factors were interlinked, although there is no unanimity as to which were the most important. The rise in the number of households during the inter-war period was substantial and was driven less by total population

---

[7] Merrett, *Owner Occupation in Britain*, p. 5.

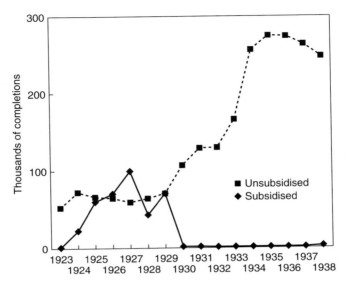

Figure 2.1 Private housing completions, 1923–1938.

Source: *Private Enterprise Housing. Report of the Private Enterprise Sub-committee of the Central Housing Advisory Committee of the Ministry of Health 1944.*[8]

growth, and more by the fall in household size. In the four decades to 1921 the average increase in the number of households was around 700,000. In the decade to 1931 this doubled to 1.4 m. with a further 1.5 m. households being created in the period 1931–1939. That population growth was not evenly distributed.

Internal migration from the depressed north to the south-east of England had a marked impact on the distribution of new housing demand and ulti-mately the location of the larger housebuilders. Between 1921 and 1936, the south-east benefited from net immigration of 689,000 in contrast to the population loss of 610,000 suffered by the northern region.[9] Elsas described London and the Home Counties as having 25% of the total population of Great Britain, but gaining 55% of the population growth between 1921 and 1937; adding the Midlands meant that 35% of the population gained nearly 70% of the increase.[10] The London housebuilders benefited not only from national migration patterns but also from movement within the region as

[8] Figures for unsubsidised housing were not collected prior to 1923 and, although approximations are available, the graph starts in 1923.
[9] Richardson, *Building in the British Economy between the Wars*, p. 87.
[10] Elsas, *Housing before the War and After*, p. 20.

new transport links opened up the surrounding areas.[11] Moreover, there were radical changes in the provision of housing finance. Thorns contrasted the 1920s, a period when only the middle class was likely to possess the necessary 20–25% deposit, with the 1930s, when improved credit allowed owner-occupation to 'spread to the lower middle classes'.[12] One of the most striking changes was the reduction in the deposit required from 25% to around 5% in the early 1930s, facilitated by the increasing adoption of the 'builders' pool' whereby the housebuilders themselves provided guarantees for the additional sum. In addition, under the Housing (Financial Provisions) Act 1933, the central government took powers to share with building societies and local authorities the risk in advances up to 90% of valuation, rather than 70%, while building societies were encouraged to lend for 30 years (compared with a more normal 20) at rates of 1% below the normal borrowing rate.[13]

Regional housing statistics were not published before the war but Marshall analysed unpublished statistics held within the Ministry of Housing. Table 2.1 confirms the importance of the south-east, primarily London and the Home Counties, accounting for around 45% of the houses built in England and Wales between the wars. If anything, the importance of the Home Counties increased during the 1930s.[14] What that meant for individual areas can be seen from local population statistics: between 1931 and 1938 five outer London suburbs (Ruislip, Bexley, Chislehurst and Sidcup,

Table 2.1   Regional analysis of private housebuilding, 1919–1939.

Region	Private enterprise units (000s)	% of total houses built in region	% of national private enterprise
South-east	1334	82	44.5
Northern	812	59	27.1
Midlands	521	66	17.4
East	103	64	3.4
South-west	135	74	4.5
Wales	96	66	3.2
Total	**3001**	**72**	**100**

Source: Marshall, J.L. 'The Pattern of Housebuilding in the Inter-war Period in England and Wales', *Scottish Journal of Political Economy*, XV, 1968, p. 184.

---

[11] Bowley, 'Some Regional Aspects of the Building Boom 1924–36', p. 177.
[12] Thorns, *Suburbia*, p. 42.
[13] HMSO, *Fourteenth Annual Report of the Ministry of Health 1932–3*, Cmd. 4272, p. 90.
[14] See Johnson, 'The Suburban Expansion of Housing in London 1918–1939', for more background.

Potters Bar and Carshalton) more than doubled their population.[15] The significant area of concentration outside the south-east reflected the population centres, namely Cheshire and Lancashire with 419,000 houses, the West Riding of Yorkshire with 198,000 and the Midlands with 521,000. Of these provincial areas, only the Midlands appeared to contain housebuilders that built in excess of 500 houses a year: like London, the Midlands was a beneficiary of the growth of newer industries. Scotland was not included in Marshall's research but it is clear that, despite the much greater preponderance of local authority housebuilding, there was also a substantial concentration of private housebuilding in the Scottish lowlands. As in the Home Counties, contemporary evidence indicated that the production of housing changed during the 1920s 'from a relatively small-scale operation to an important speculative enterprise.'[16] Even so, the peak year of 1934 saw fewer than 10,000 private houses built (unlike in the case of England, a figure destined to be far exceeded in the post-war period) and it supported only two significant speculative housebuilders based respectively in Glasgow (Mactaggart & Mickel) and Edinburgh (James Miller).

Building to rent

The speculative housebuilder was not, of course, confined to supplying the owner occupier and it should be noted that the inter-war period saw a significant level of building for rental, albeit primarily in the 1930s rather than the 1920s. In contrast with the position that pertained before the First War, Marshall maintained that, 'It is generally accepted that in the 1920s private enterprise built very few houses for letting.'[17] He quoted the Marley Committee on the Rent Restriction Acts, which reported in 1931, as concluding that local authority houses formed practically the only supply of houses to let for the less well paid.[18] This was a point made again in 1933 in the Annual Report of the Ministry of Health, which argued that 'private enterprise . . . should be encouraged to enter the field of houses for the better paid members of the working classes'.[19] The economics of private rental had improved in 1932: Britain came off the gold standard in 1931 and bank rate had fallen from 6% to only 2% by April 1933, at a time also when building costs were falling. The Housing (Financial Provisions) Act 1933 was intended to encourage the private sector to take account of those

[15] Ashworth, *The Genesis of British Town Planning*, p. 13.
[16] O'Carroll, 'The Reshaping of Scottish Housing 1914–39', p. 211
[17] Marshall, 'The Pattern of Housebuilding in Inter-war Period', p. 189.
[18] HMSO, *Report of the Inter-Departmental Committee on the Rent Restriction Acts*, p. 19.
[19] HMSO, *Fourteenth Annual Report of the Ministry of Health 1932–3*, p. 89.

changed conditions and the local authority subsidies available under the 1924 Act were removed to allow private enterprise letting to compete on equal terms. In 1924, the economic rent had been some 80% higher than the subsidised rent: by 1933 they were the same.[20]

It was not until the passing of the 1933 Act that the housing statistics distinguished between private housing built for sale and built for rent. In the five and a half years between October 1933 and March 1939, some 1,256,000 houses with a rateable value of less than £26 were built in England and Wales by the private sector; of these, 351,000 houses, or 28% of the total, were built to let.[21] For the speculative housebuilding firm itself, there was no financial difference between selling a house to an owner-occupier or to a private landlord, albeit a new source of demand had been created and needed to be served. H.C. Janes, for instance, found that the percentage of houses bought by investors became so large in 1933 that the firm had to open a property department.[22]

In addition to the private investors, there were also some housebuilders that chose to retain a part of their output to let out themselves, either corporately or as individuals. The archival records are not sufficient to make broadbrush generalisations about how widespread this practice was although the fact that no references were found in, for instance, the Laing or Wimpey archives suggests that it was not universal. Henry Boot was probably the most committed developer-landlord: it formed a new subsidiary company, First National Housing Trust, to take advantage of the 1933 Act and the Trust built around 9000 houses in some eight estates between 1933 and the War. In a unique piece of building society history, post-war sales to sitting tenants were funded by mortgages granted by Boot, which then formed the Banner Building Society to assume ownership of those mortgages. North of the border, the combination of Mctaggart & Mickel and the associated Western Heritable Investment Company were substantial builders and investors in rental housing, perhaps several hundred a year. Ideal was a later entrant into rented housing: in its Annual Report of April 1938 the directors considered that the 'present scale of housing development cannot be continued indefinitely and have therefore decided to erect blocks of property to be let to tenants and to be held as an investment'. Ideal went on to purchase more houses during the Second War and its immediate aftermath, buying estates of several hundred a time.

---

[20] Calculated from table in Connor, 'Urban Housing in England and Wales', p. 39.
[21] Marshall, 'The Pattern of Housebuilding in Inter-war Period', p. 189.
[22] Kennett, 'A Provincial Builder', p. 135.

Arthur Davis was another that retained properties with at least 700 houses, while Leech had as many as 2000 houses, primarily by default (it had failed to sell them).[23] There would also have been some inadvertent retention of houses by most developers on the outbreak of war. For instance, Janes had 400 houses under construction at September 1939; although a few individual purchasers completed, Herbert Janes himself bought 200 and the company rented out the remaining 172 houses.

Which firms built the houses?

Having outlined the background which allowed the growth in home ownership, the central question of Part I can now be posed: who were the housebuilders that supplied this booming market? Table 2.2 indicates that there were about ten housebuilders that achieved an annual output of 1000 units at some point in the 1930s. Ideal stood out, with sales at least twice those of its nearest competitor, although Henry Boot, which started building for sale in the early 1920s, may have built more houses in total in the inter-war years. The top ten in the industry were building of the order of 16,000–18,000 a year at the height of the inter-war housebuilding boom, perhaps some 6–7% of the market.

As was explained in Chapter 1, where pre-war housebuilders are mentioned by the economic historian, they tend to be brief lists of what are believed to be the larger builders, with occasional numbers thrown in for the largest estates. Nowhere does there exist a record of the number of houses built by individual developers. Who built these 250,000 houses a year? Were there any national housebuilders? To what extent was the demand for private houses met by local firms? One of the reasons that such questions have not been answered is that there has been no published documentation on the structure of the housebuilding companies. The NHBC and the industry's own trade body were both in an embryonic stage before the war and perhaps such analysis was of little interest to anyone else. Albeit with caveats, a rough and ready league table (Table 2.2) has been constructed, derived from the sources outlined in the previous chapter. Whereas reasonably accurate data are available for at least the last 20 years, the further back the data retrieval is taken, the less reliable the numbers become: for the 1930s, the data should be taken more as indications of magnitude although from time to time accurate figures are available.

---

[23] *Investors' Review*, Dec. 1937; interview with Richard Adamson, Dec. 2001.

Table 2.2   A league table of housebuilders in the 1930s: firms building 500 units or more p.a.

Date formed[a]	Company	Region	Early 1930s	Late 1930s
1929	Ideal Homes[b]	London suburbs	4000–5000	5000–7000
*c.*1886	Henry Boot[b]	London suburbs	1000	1500–2000
1901	Wates	London suburbs	1500–2000	1500–2000
1921	Taylor Woodrow[b]	London suburbs	450	1200–1500
*c.*1929	Davis Estates[b]	London suburbs	1000?	1200
1880	Wimpey[b]	London suburbs	1000	1200
1901	Mactaggart & Mickel	Scottish lowlands	1000	1000
1865	Costain[b]	London suburbs	500–600?	1000+
1928	G.T. Crouch	London suburbs	?	1000
1848	Laing	London suburbs	1000	800
	Top ten			**16,000–18,000**
*c.*1925	T.F. Nash	London suburbs	750–1000	750–1000
1864	Dares Estates	Midlands	—	800
1906	R.T. Warren	London suburbs	—	750
1904	Comben & Wakeling	London suburbs	500	600
1884	Janes	Midlands	600	600
1929	Morrell Estates[b]	London suburbs	—	500?
1933	Mucklow	Midlands	—	500
1932	William Leech	North-east	?	500
1927	Miller	Scottish lowlands	500–600	250
Late 1890s	N. Moss	Oxford	500?	500?
	Top twenty			**21,000–24,000**

[a] The dates refer to the formation of these businesses not their incorporation, but for those firms that started as general contractors, the dates do not represent the point in time that the firms started to become meaningful as housebuilders, or even as housebuilders at all. Wimpey, for example, was a Hammersmith road builder which was acquired by Godfrey Mitchell in 1919 and did not begin speculative housebuilding until 1928.
[b] Quoted companies at some point during the 1930s.

The source material used in compiling the data has already been discussed in general terms, but additional comment is provided here to give readers an understanding of the degree of reliability that can be attached to the numbers. There are no apologies for reminding readers yet again that the numbers are approximations. Even where there is access to specific numbers for each individual year, the number in the table remains no more than an average. John Laing, for instance, sold 1010 houses in 1930, 680 in 1932 and 1450 in 1934 and the 1000 given in the table is just about the average of the first five years of the 1930s. The quality of the information available varies considerably and some approximations are more approximate than others.

Seven of the companies were quoted on the London Stock Exchange: Henry Boot floated as early as 1919 and a flurry of activity between 1933 and 1935 saw the flotation of Costain, Ideal, Wimpey, Taylor Woodrow, Davis and Morrell. (This excludes companies with a quotation before World War II that became housebuilders after the war, for example Bovis and Cala.) However, despite their public status, the accounts of these companies were sparse and none clearly indicated the number of houses sold each year; but, their status as public companies did lead to a little more information being available, sometimes in the original prospectus, sometimes after the event. Thus, the Costain prospectus referred to its having built 4000 houses to 1933 (an implied period of eight to nine years); Ideal built more than 7000 from its 1929 formation to 1932 and more than 4000 in 1933; and the Taylor Woodrow prospectus stated that 612 houses had been sold in 1934 and it forecast more than 1000 for the following year. Fortuitously, the Leech prospectus of 1976 referred back to the Company building 500 houses a year before the war. Morrell Estates' prospectus of 1935 was the most frustrating, for it described itself, without any further supporting evidence, as one of the largest businesses of housebuilders in Great Britain. However, as it built almost entirely in what is now the London Borough of Bromley, it is difficult to accept that statement at face value. Some 16 estates were listed but these included ones that had been finished and ones not yet started; a debenture prospectus the following year gave only six estates in the course of construction. An estimate of 500 houses a year has been made but that may well be on the high side. Morrell survived only 18 months before its only operating subsidiary was put into liquidation; the company's name is best remembered in building society circles for its part in the celebrated Borders case.

Minute books were made available to the author for some companies and these were particularly helpful for Laing, Taylor Woodrow and Wimpey; for a limited number of years, the monthly board meetings listed every house sale. Sales for Wimpey, for example, totalled 1294 in 1933 and 1370 in 1934. Details of Miller's annual housing completions throughout the 1930s had been retained by the family and provided to me. Company histories and brochures were also an occasional source: Furnell gave 5500 for Ideal in 1935; the history of Wimpey recorded an average of 1200 houses in the 1930s, and Comben's history recorded it building 500 in 1931, a figure that had risen to 600 a year by the outbreak of war. Henry Boot managed a couple of official sources for 50,000 and 60,000 houses respectively between the wars, although most were local authority housing and company assistance was needed to approximate the number of private houses. Diane Watters has many numerical references to unit numbers in her history of Mactaggart & Mickel that allow approximations to be made.

The trade press, particularly the *Housebuilder*, was invaluable for estimating the housing volume of some of the middle-sized companies that had otherwise left little in the way of records: Crouch (around 1000 a year in

1936), Dares (800 average pre-war), Janes (600 a year pre-war), Wates (2000 a year pre-war).[24] For Moss the figure was a more general 3000 houses built in total before the war.[25] The only contemporary evidence for Moss was an August 1932 article in *Oxford Monthly* which reported four estates in the Oxford area with 900 houses under development, and a register of mortgages has survived for 1933–1935 on the Oxford Moss' Companies House file which showed over 600 transactions in 1934.[26] A much later entry in *Building* on Wood Hall Trust, by the then owner of Davis Estates, reported that Davis was building over 1200 houses a year by the outbreak of war.[27] Tommy Nash was described in Morgan's NHBC history as 'possibly the largest builder in north-west London', but without reference to the number of houses built. However, a 1933 sales brochure deposited at Harrow library included a one-page history suggesting that the company was building almost 1000 houses a year.

Interviews, primarily with people remembering what they had been told many years earlier, sometimes provided corroboration or additional information. Wates, for instance, has four separate interviewees referring to 2000 house a year or thereabouts, although one person thought the number might have risen close to 3000 in one year. The Mucklow family memories were the only source for that company's approximate level of house sales in the late 1930s.[28] Bundock's interview notes from *c*.1970, generously made available to me, draw on earlier memories, often from those who worked in the businesses during the 1930s. The figure for Wates was again confirmed as 2000 a year; Wimpey had reached 500–600 houses a year by 1930 and over 1000 a year by the outbreak of war; Warren built 10,000 houses before the war; and Davis Estates 1000 a year.

The preceding paragraphs indicate that although there are far more data available on housebuilders' volumes than have ever been used in the literature, the material is by no means perfect. Figures are not available for all companies for the same year and sometimes the period may be approximated as 'before the war' or 'in the 1930s'; where there is a run of figures, they have been averaged to give an indication of typical output in the early and late 1930s. Sometimes the sources do not agree and memories are notoriously fickle. Nevertheless, it is believed that, subject to the comments below on inclusivity, the company magnitudes are of the correct order both

---

[24] *Housebuilder*, Oct. 1952, p. 215; Jan. 1950, p. 299; Jan. 1947; June 1946.
[25] *Housebuilder*, Nov. 1949.
[26] N. Moss & Son Ltd 00256285.
[27] *Building*, 10th Oct. 1975, p. 79.
[28] Interview with Albert Mucklow, Dec. 2001.

in relation to each other and to the industry as a whole, and can reliably be used to indicate broad trends.

Inclusivity of the data

The important question that remains to be asked in this chapter is whether there could be other housebuilders not identified which should be included in Table 2.2. It may be that future research will identify other companies that could have been listed among the top ten or fifteen. However, I would be surprised if there were any building above 1000 a year that have not been identified; housebuilders do not reach that size, particularly when they are confined to one region, without leaving some record of their significance in the trade press if nowhere else. Housebuilders that were known to be large after the war have been checked to see if they had a sizeable pre-war existence. Thus, any omission from Table 2.2 would need to be a housebuilder that was significant before the war yet leaving little trace in the post-war period – perhaps never even resuming activity. The Home Counties were well trawled by Alan Jackson who, although not mentioning annual output, usually detailed the number of estates under development at any one time and he referred to over 30 individual builders. One omission by Jackson was R. Lancaster which Bundock had building some 400 houses a year in London, with a residual building operation in its home town of Blackpool;[29] it may have reached 500 a year in total. Both Jackson and Bundock refer to well known names in particular suburbs of London including Berg, Ball, Blade and Gleeson, but they tended to have only two or three estates under development at a time, with annual sales no more than 200–300 houses a year. Gleeson did actually have a brochure in the 1930s which referred to it building around 500 houses in the year, but that is regarded as probably a marketing exaggeration; nevertheless, like Lancaster, it is a firm that might well have featured at the bottom of Table 2.2 if a different subjective view had been taken of the evidence. Unit Construction, owned in the inter-war period by the Liverpool merchant house of Alfred Booth, should be mentioned as a sizeable housebuilder, possibly responsible for 20,000 houses between 1925 and 1939 in London and Liverpool. These were mainly contract houses for local authorities but Unit did build two speculative estates of around 700 houses each in Liverpool during the 1930s.

There remain two other 'developers' that, with different answers to the question, 'what is a firm?' or 'what is a developer?' might have been large

---

[29] Bundock interview notes, 1970.

enough to be included in Table 2.2: Hilbery Chaplin and Metropolitan Railway Country Estates. Hilbery Chaplin was a firm of surveyors and estate agents that switched to selling new houses in 1927; it progressed in 1928 to buying land through a separate company and employed Thomas Blade to build the houses. It also provided services and marketed the houses of other housebuilders under the name of Hilbery Chaplin Estates; in 1934 it was selling around 60–70 houses a week on commission of £25 a house, for four different housebuilders.[30] Bundock has the firm building more than 1000 units a year in London by 1938 off some 15 estates to the north and north-east of the capital but 'For the general public, there was . . . no way in which the advertisements of such firms could be distinguished from those placed by builders.'[31] It has, therefore, been treated as an agent rather than a housebuilder.

Metropolitan Railway Country Estates (MRCE) was, as the name suggests, an entirely different type of company, being the only railway company allowed to develop its own land. In 1919, the directors of the Metropolitan Railway approved the formation of MRCE but on legal advice it was decided that the railway company would take no direct financial interest in the Estates Company, but would enter into an agreement which would allow the use of the Railway's name by the new company and provide assistance in the development of the estates.[32] One guide to the level of activity is the number of estates it controlled and Rose states that although it sold off some of its land, MRCE went on to develop some ten estates.[33] The Annual Reports list the number of acres of land sold; by 1939, MRCE had sold 536 acres leaving 795 acres undeveloped. These estates were individually very large and suggest that MRCE was on a par with the larger traditional developers. Indeed, at ten to twelve houses to the acre, MRCE would have provided land for some 6000 houses between the wars. However, MRCE does not seem to have been particularly active as a housebuilder rather than just a developer of land; a Bundock interview (1969) elicited a figure of between 50 and 100 houses a year and it looks as though MRCE was more a developer along North American lines, that is, acquiring large tracts of land and processing them to a state where they could be sub-divided amongst other builders. Post-war, MRCE did become a more conventional and substantial housebuilder.

Outside the London area, with the exception of the Scottish central belt, there is a paucity of regional studies that actually refer to individual housing

---

[30] Anon, *One Hundred Not Out*, p. 23.
[31] Horsey, 'London Speculative Housebuilders of the 1930s', p. 150.
[32] Jackson, *Semi-detached London*, p. 225.
[33] Rose, *Dynamics of Urban Property Development*, pp. 120–21.

numbers. Even in Scotland, it has not been possible to determine the scale of John Lawrence's pre-war housebuilding. Lawrence was described as the primary competitor to Mactaggart & Mickel from the mid-1930s,[34] but no reference to volumes has yet been unearthed; a 1969 profile on the Company indicated that it increased its private housebuilding output between 1931 and 1936 but the tenor of the comment did not suggest that it was substantial.[35] Perhaps there is a London bias that blinds researchers to the existence of substantial corporate life in the provinces. However, when there is evidence of a large regional housebuilder such as Janes or Dares in the Midlands or Leech in the north-east, they turn out to be selling less than 1000 units a year. Other regional housebuilders that survived to become substantial housebuilders in the modern era invariably prove to have been of very modest size before the war. Bryant and McLean in the west Midlands were very localised; Wilson Connolly in the east Midlands built around 150 houses a year; the West Country Bradley Estates some 300 a year; and the Manchester-based Maunders around 200 a year – all numbers which come from interviews and company brochures.

It is unlikely, therefore, that any significant housebuilders have been missed and although accurate numbers for specific years can be provided only infrequently, it is submitted that Table 2.2 represents a broadly accurate picture of the top end of the industry in the 1930s, certainly sufficient to provide a basis for describing and analysing the characteristics of the larger housebuilder. One crosscheck is available. In a talk given by Norman Walls, a director of the NHBC, at the Housing Centre as the war ended, he asked, 'What size of firms built the houses?' He did not believe that the answer could be stated definitely but 'knowledgeable sources of information' agreed that various sizes of firms were as shown in Table 2.3.[36]

No year was given but the data were presumably taken from the mid- to late-1930s. The mathematically inclined will note that the number of units totalled 325,000 which suggests that he was working back from some rough and ready numbers or that the total included local authority housing. This book is predominantly concerned with the larger housebuilders and therefore the interest lies in the bottom line, which showed 50 firms built some 25,000 houses. The final column is deceptive in that it is an average; it does not mean that there were 50 companies building 500 houses a year. To the extent that some firms were building well over 1000 houses a year, there must have been a considerably smaller number of firms than 50 that actually reached 500 a year. If the houses identified in

[34] Watters, *Mactaggart & Mickel and the Scottish Housebuilding Industry*, p. 14.
[35] *Housebuilder*, Dec. 1969, p. 657.
[36] Quoted in the *Housebuilder*, Sep. 1945.

Table 2.3   Estimated size distribution of housebuilders, late 1930s.

No. of firms	Total houses built	Annual average
1400 firms built	8400 houses	6 houses per annum
2400 firms built	60,000 houses	25 houses per annum
1100 firms built	62,000 houses	56 houses per annum approx.
350 firms built	30,000 houses	85 houses per annum approx.
800 firms built	140,000 houses	175 houses per annum approx.
50 firms built	25,000 houses	500 houses per annum approx.

Table 2.2 are deducted, it leaves at most a few thousand houses to be spread amongst the remaining 30 firms, which does not suggest a profusion of missing large firms.

A local business

The housebuilders of the 1930s were almost entirely local businesses, although not always operating from their original base. Four of the large London developers were originally northern firms. Richard Costain was a Liverpool-based firm of builders that had begun speculative development after World War I, but Albert Costain attributed the move to London to a scarcity of suitable sites in Liverpool.[37] One of the second generation family members was sent to the London suburbs in 1922 and the first estate was started in 1923. John Laing had already moved his family from Scotland to Carlisle and in World War I was employing as many as 4000 men helping to build the Gretna armaments factory and even an aerodrome. After the war, Laing expanded as a national contractor; it was as such that the firm moved its head office to London in 1925. It was not until 1927 that Laing began speculative housing in the London suburbs, although it continued to build houses in the Carlisle area.

The 16-year-old Frank Taylor had built a house for his father in Blackpool and developed a local housebuilding business. In 1930, an engine fitter in AEC (who had seen Taylor Woodrow houses when on holiday) wrote to Frank Taylor out of the blue to tell him the whole factory was moving across London to Southall and they would be needing hundreds of houses for their employees. Taylor Woodrow immediately bought a site for 1200 houses and persuaded most of his building team to move south. Another Blackpool firm that moved to London was Lancaster, originally a contracting firm but after the First War it became predominantly a speculative

---

[37] Costain, *Reflections*, p. 26.

developer. In 1929, by then a second generation firm, it moved to London, although it retained its Blackpool office and continued to build in the north-west. Lancaster himself continued to live in Blackpool but travelled down to London once a week to oversee operations. (It is not known what happened to the firm after the Second World War and there are no records at Companies House or Blackpool Reference library.)

The opportunities available in the London market dwarfed the possibilities in such places as Blackpool, Carlisle and Liverpool and, with the exception of Boot, which operated its construction business out of offices in London, Sheffield and Birmingham, these northern firms virtually abandoned their home territory. Henry Boot appears to be something of an exception among the generality of inter-war housebuilders. Although originally a Sheffield firm, when it incorporated in 1910 it already had both a Sheffield and London address; when it floated on the Stock Exchange in 1919 it did so as Henry Boot (London). Boot became probably the largest builder of local authority houses around the country (perhaps 40,000–50,000 over the 20-year period) and it built private estates to rent in many of its operating areas, particularly centred on its three regional offices. However, its development for sale was largely confined to the London area, with one site each in Glasgow and Liverpool.

Apart from the special case of Henry Boot, there is little evidence that firms spread their speculative housing business much beyond the immediate reaches of their head office. When they did move out of their home area the 'foreign' locations did not look to be the result of a cohesive expansion strategy in the way in which the current generation of national housebuilders established their regional subsidiaries. Moreover, the purchase of the more distant sites did not start until the late 1930s. The sites in Ideal Homes' 1934 prospectus were all in London and Kent and it was 1936 before it bought sites in the Midlands, and even later when it acquired individual sites in Gloucester, Southampton and Crewe; its 1938 AGM referred to the company operating on 34 estates in and around London but with extensive operations in Birmingham and Southampton.[38] Taylor Woodrow had a few sites in the West Country in 1936.[39] Davis Estates' 1935 prospectus only contained one site (Gosport) outside its home area; however, a post-war profile indicated that, by the outbreak of war, Davis Estates had extended as far north as Birmingham and as far west

[38] *Stock Exchange Gazette*, 14th May 1938, p. 955.
[39] Jenkins, *On Site*, p. 27.

as Plymouth, but it is not known how many sites were involved.[40] Both Ideal and Davis probably overstated their geographical diversification for public consumption. Other housebuilders made only a token foray out of their home area: Wimpey, which was predominantly operating in west London, bought a site in Yeovil in 1934 but it was not until close to the outbreak of war that it purchased another, outside Glasgow; Wates bought one site in Coventry and a couple in Oxford in the late 1930s.

Most housebuilders remained firmly local: Costain, Crouch and Laing were all London-oriented and Mactaggart & Mickel remained close to Glasgow. Dropping down a little in the size range, the companies became even more identified with a particular locality. Comben & Wakeling, for instance, confined itself to north-west London and by the early 1930s claimed to have built a total of 6000 houses in the Wembley area alone. George Ball built a quarter of all dwellings constructed in Ruislip between 1935 and 1939; Warren built in north-west London and Middlesex; E. & L. Berg built in south-west London. Nash was active in the Harrow area; in 1937 he spread out, buying large acreages at Romford, Hayes (Middlesex), Sevenoaks, Northolt and St Albans, but the outbreak of war prevented any substantial building away from his original area. Some of these companies would typically have two, three or four large estates in production at any one time. N. Moss built in Oxford (although there were untraced Moss companies in Gloucester and Cardiff), but insufficient is known about this firm. In Scotland, Miller confined itself to the Edinburgh region. With the exception of Boot, which was organised to serve its construction business, there is no evidence of any housebuilder operating with a formal regional structure.

Was there any theme or underlying determinant behind what little geographical expansion that did occur during the inter-war period? Boot's regional housebuilding can probably be explained by the linkage with its construction organisation but, in contrast, Wimpey, which also had construction sites around the country, did not choose to expand its private housebuilding in that way until after the war; neither did Laing follow its construction business. An alternative explanation for the limited expansion that was undertaken by the London developers might be that the London market was running out of steam in the late 1930s. While the move of provincial firms into the London area was understandable in the early years of the boom, there is some evidence that London itself was becoming a more difficult market in the late 1930s, perhaps because of the reduced

---

[40] Profile of Wood Hall Trust, *Building*, 10th Oct. 1975, p. 79.

availability of large sites. Bundock's interview material *c*.1970 suggested that Wates was finding that the type of sites it required was becoming more difficult to obtain and the Company was prepared to look further afield. Johnson, too, referred to convenient sites near railway stations becoming harder to find by the late 1930s although his source was also Wates.[41] A Godfrey Mitchell memo said that after 1935 Wimpey's sales started to decline: 'This was due in my opinion to dearth of land purchased on which artisan houses could be erected. We were forced into a higher price market with a more restricted demand.'[42] However, Ideal suggested that its expansion was driven by the realisation that the demand potential of places like Birmingham was as great as London.

Although remaining at very high absolute levels, the rate of private housebuilding nationally started to dip in 1938 and output in Greater London had begun to decline a year or two earlier. One might ask why, against that background, there was not a greater attempt to develop a wider housebuilding base. The answer might be that by 1936, the volume of defence work was starting to increase and companies like Laing and Taylor Woodrow were switching management time in that direction. Sir Maurice Laing conceded that the decline in Laing's housing sales in the late 1930s was probably due to the Company increasing its defence work for the Air Ministry where they received a number of airfield contracts in 1935.[43] This is discussed further in Chapter 3.

The influence of local authority housebuilding

This book opened by stressing the economic distinction between contract building for local authorities and speculative housebuilding. Nevertheless, there is a recognisable similarity in the construction process, and the labour force could be utilised to produce either the public or the private product. Kemp argued that one important stimulant to the emergence of large firms undertaking the mass production of houses was the increasing importance of local authority housing contracts in the 1920s. Is this contention valid: did building for the public sector assist in the development of the speculative housebuilder, either directly or indirectly? The passage of time means that first-hand evidence of motivation, or otherwise, is hard to find, but it is possible to look at the way in which firms first came into speculative housing: in practice, only a minority of firms in Table 2.2 had

---

41 Johnson, 'The Suburban Expansion of Housing in London 1918–1939', p. 159.
42 Godfrey Mitchell memo, May 1945.
43 Interview with Sir Maurice Laing, April 2000.

engaged in substantial public sector housing projects prior to building for the private sector.

Working through the top ten, Ideal Homes was founded in 1929 by Leo Meyer, a one-time borough surveyor, specifically for the purpose of developing private housing estates. Within four years its annual building rate was up to 4000 and it was not until the approach of war that Ideal began to diversify – and then into general construction, not local authority housing. The Wates family had been building in a modest way in the Streatham area before the First World War and it was when second generation Norman Wates joined in 1923 that the rapid expansion of the business began. There is no evidence of any local authority housebuilding before the war, nor was there for Taylor Woodrow. Arthur Davis, the son of an unsuccessful flat developer, began his speculative housing in 1929 and not even war encouraged him to deviate from this. Geoffrey Crouch started a year later in 1928 and, similarly, no references to local authority housebuilding have been found. That makes five of the top ten firms which not only started as speculative housebuilders but appeared to have no involvement in local authority housing throughout the inter-war period. What of the other five?

Henry Boot has already been mentioned as a national contractor. During the First World War it had built army camps (Catterick), Manston Aerodrome, Tees Naval Base and the American hospital at Southampton; in one year alone, a thousand military buildings were completed. Raising public capital in 1919 was specifically intended to take the Group into housing, particularly in the public sector. The prospectus stated that:

> 'It is now imperative in the national interests that the erection of very large numbers of houses and the development of public works generally should be carried out . . . Provisional arrangements have been made to proceed at once with several large housing contracts involving the building of some thousands of houses under the Ministry of Health scheme and . . . the Directors propose to employ a large part of the new working capital upon this important national work.'

Speculative housing began in 1924, but because it followed chronologically from an involvement in public housing this does not imply causation. Boot had perhaps the most wide-ranging construction portfolio of the inter-war period: apart from the activities already mentioned it had been working in Greece, France and Spain since 1920 and had a substantial holding in the brick firm, Flettons. It is probable that it was Boot's national perspective, born out of both local authority housing and general contracting, that encouraged it to develop a more widely based speculative business.

Wimpey, Costain and Laing all had their roots in general contracting and evidence does survive of their reasons for beginning speculative housing. With the help of his war gratuity, Godfrey Mitchell had bought the small Hammersmith road-building firm of George Wimpey in 1919. This business was expanded during the 1920s benefiting in particular from the development of a successful asphalting process. Among the routine work was the construction of roads on other firms' housing estates. Godfrey Mitchell began to realise the money that could be made on these developments and invested personally in a small site to test his belief. When that worked, he took Wimpey into private housing in 1928. Despite a wide range of construction activity, there is no record of any significant involvement in public housing in the inter-war period. Costain is one of the few firms whose entry into speculative housing can be seen to have resulted from its prior involvement in local authority housing, but not for positive reasons. It started as a means of counterbalancing fluctuations in the Liverpool Council workload:

> 'Progressive firms were anxious to offer continuity of employment . . . but when engaged to work for a local authority continuity . . . had to depend on successful tendering . . . To overcome this problem, Costain decided to purchase land and to develop their own estates'.[44]

Laing, as mentioned above, had been a successful wartime contractor and within a few years was constructing local authority housing around the country, but it was 1927 before John Laing started speculative housing. When interviewed by Betham in the early 1930s he offered the apparently altruistic reason that he did not approve of the specifications on work he was asked to do: 'We therefore decided to carry out developments ourselves, on the principle of giving the purchaser the highest value for money.' However, local authority housing did decline from its 1926/27 peak and his son later suggested that limited opportunities for making money in contracting influenced the start of private housebuilding.[45]

Finally, John Mactaggart had been a general contractor before the First World War but he also built tenements, largely for middle-class tenants, totalling 2330 houses between 1901 and 1914 (c.180 p.a.). After the war, the firm 'plunged head first into the new world of local authority contracting' including Glasgow's Mosspark scheme, the largest in Scotland with 1510 houses.[46] There were limited opportunities for private development in

---

[44] Costain, *Reflections*, pp. 24–5.
[45] Interview with Sir Maurice Laing, April 2000.
[46] Watters, *Mactaggart & Mickel and the Scottish Housebuilding Industry*, p. 21.

those early years but Mactaggart acquired a substantial land bank for future developments. In Mactaggart's case it would seem that the local authority housing was facilitated by the earlier experience of tenement building and was undertaken as they considered that it represented the best commercial opportunity available.

On the evidence of the top ten, the proposition that local authority housing played an important role in the development of speculative housing firms does not, therefore, appear to have substance. Half of the top ten firms started as speculative housebuilders and had no involvement with local authority housing until after the Second World War; Mactaggart was a substantial local authority housebuilder but had previously been a private housebuilder. Of the others, there was more of a general construction background than a marked dependency on local authority housing. However, succeeding chapters will show that in the post-1945 period, far more of these speculative housebuilders found themselves drawn into public sector housing and into general construction. Rather than helping them, this tended to blur the essential distinction between speculative and contract work and hindered their growth as private housebuilders. These are issues that will be discussed in more detail in Part II.

3

War and Building Controls

Introduction

For a period of some 15 years, between the outbreak of war in September 1939 to the final removal of building controls in October 1954, the speculative housebuilding industry was severely constrained. There is, therefore, no housebuilders' matrix for this period and it might be thought no requirement for a separate chapter. However, the cessation of housebuilding activity and the transfer of resources to wartime construction led to profound changes in the corporate structure of the industry, the effects of which could still be seen almost half a century later. This chapter discusses the wartime activities of the housebuilders, which ranged from the passive husbanding of rental stock, through bomb damage repair, to major civil engineering: it transformed some housebuilders into major contractors; others simply vanished. The period of post-war housing controls gave further impetus to the diversification away from private housebuilding as firms developed their construction operations. It will be left to succeeding chapters to show that the dynamics that created such international firms as Costain, Taylor Woodrow and Wimpey were paradoxically to weaken their speculative housebuilding.

The collapse of speculative housebuilding

The approach of war began to impact on housebuilders' sales during 1939, but perhaps not as severely as might be imagined. Figure 2.1 showed that private housing completions remained at a high level although sales were increasingly affected as 1939 progressed. John Laing's minutes record 50 houses sold during the first seven weeks of 1939 compared with 119 for the same period in 1938, whereas Wimpey appeared more resilient with 444 units sold in the first six months against 549 in the first half of 1938. When war was declared on 3rd September, the housebuilders were quick to halt their building programmes and finish houses under construction. Henry Boot's minute book of 7th September recorded a motion 'to discontinue all housebuilding by subsidiaries as soon as the houses now in the course of erection are now completed [and] to tender for and to carry out any government contracts which offer a satisfactory margin of profit'. Ideal stopped construction of new houses almost immediately and Frank Taylor instructed that all houses that were near the roofing stage could be completed but not the others.[1] Within two months, Wimpey's minute book recorded that the building programme had been completed and sites were being tidied up.

The year to March 1940 still showed 31,000 houses completed for private owners before the figure fell to nominal levels for the duration of the war. The inevitable collapse in demand was reinforced in October 1940 by Defence Regulation 56A which stated that it was:

> 'unlawful to carry out, except under license from the Minister of Works, any work of construction . . . or maintenance on a building . . . where the cost of the work exceeded the financial limits prescribed from time to time by an order made by the Minister'.[2]

The units that were completed in 1940/41 must have represented a tidying up of estates in progress and there is no evidence that these were sold in any quantities to individual buyers. Instead, the housebuilders found themselves in the involuntary position of residential landlords. Not only did they have to let out houses that were in stock and under construction but they also found that guarantees provided on mortgaged sales were requiring them to take properties back. In December 1939, Laing's minute book discussed 'Repayments on houses'. Some borrowers were pleading that war conditions had affected their finances and the minutes showed that there were approximately 4000 guarantees over all estates, practically 50% of the total sales. The largest housebuilder, New Ideal Homesteads, took an active stance with its rental portfolio; the minute books record small purchases of blocks of houses in the early years of the war and from 1943 these increased in size to several hundred at a time, some of which were sold on.

Wartime construction

Shorn of their traditional market, the housebuilders turned inevitably to wartime construction. Of course, some had started as general contractors

---

[1]   Furnell, *The Diamond Jubilee of Ideal Homes*, p. 16; Jenkins, *On Site*, p. 31.
[2]   Merrett, *Owner Occupation in Britain*, p. 17.

(for example Boot, Costain, Laing and Wimpey), but others moved into construction as war approached (for example Taylor Woodrow). Military construction had begun to accelerate from 1936 and the Taylor Woodrow and Laing company histories record them building military camps, airfields and barrage stations. In the earlier years of the war, airfield construction featured prominently. 'Between the end of 1939 and the end of 1944, 465 flying fields were constructed for the two air forces. This was ... the twentieth century equivalent to the construction of the first generation of mainline railways between 1830 and 1851.[3] Costain was described by Catherwood as 'engaged primarily in the construction of airfields'[4] and Taylor Woodrow built 'dozens';[5] specific numbers are available for Costain (26), Laing (54) and Wimpey claimed 93 aerodromes. Ideal built aerodromes, factories and naval bases, although not on the same scale. Some had a regional emphasis like Comben with 12 airfields in East Anglia. The work ranged widely and included coastal defences, artillery sites, munitions factories and Miller was asked by the government to start opencast coal mining in Yorkshire in 1941. Of the top ten pre-war housebuilders (Table 2.2) only Davis Estates and G.T. Crouch seem to have eschewed significant construction work.

The project that more than any turned some firms into substantial civil engineering businesses was the Mulberry Harbour constructed for the Normandy invasion of 1944; it was succinctly described as 'a floating harbour twice the size of Dover'.[6] The largest task facing the construction industry was to build the caissons which would be sunk to form part of the breakwater. A team of 24 contractors led by Sir Robert McAlpine built over one million tons of these structures in only 26 weeks; Henry Boot, Costain, John Laing and Taylor Woodrow were among the 24.[7] With the breakwaters came the floating piers and roadways for the invasion force and it was Wates that was responsible for these.[8]

The records tend to be more extensive for the larger companies, but the smaller housebuilders also turned to wartime construction. A miscellaneous collection of prospectuses, company histories and press articles describe, *inter alia*, Bunting Estates building military camps, gun sites and prefabricated houses; Hubert Leach building military camps; Wilson

---

[3] Stratton, *Twentieth Century Industrial Archaeology*, p. 112.
[4] Catherwood, 'Development and Organisation of Richard Costain Ltd', p. 274.
[5] Jenkins, *On Site*, p. 38.
[6] Anon, *Teamwork*, 1950, p. 49.
[7] Hodge, 'The Mulberry Invasion Harbours', p. 192.
[8] Wellings, *The History of Marley*, p. 69.

Connolly involved in aerodrome maintenance contracts, particularly at the USAAF bases; Bryant building munitions factories and military installations; Unit Construction building military camps; Mactaggart & Mickel undertaking defence work for local authorities and the principal ministries, and so on. In contrast, some firms virtually gave up any form of trade other than repair work during the war, while others closed or kept the business going on a minimal scale. This was particularly true of the very small organisations but there were some larger firms that suffered from the exodus of staff to the armed forces; John Lawrence of Glasgow was a firm that lost most of its staff,[9] and the 685th Artisan Works Company, Royal Engineers, was largely formed from men of the Unit Construction Company – seven officers, 42 NCOs and 240 men.[10] Sometimes the lack of substantial construction activity was a matter of personal attitude. 'Unfortunately, rather than expand, [Arthur Prowting] went back into his shell'; at the end of the war Prowting had no more than half a dozen staff.[11] On other occasions, it was the proprietor who served in the forces: Ben Bailey was called up and his wife ran the war damage business in his absence;[12] George Ward enlisted as a lieutenant in the Royal Engineers and the firm switched to war damage clearance, building radar stations and lifeboats.[13]

The experience of wartime construction work, particularly on the Mulberry Harbour, gave a select band of what had been predominantly housebuilding concerns an unrivalled entrée into large-scale contracting. Catherwood said that there was no doubt that the war set Costain on its feet as a contractor and had given it a strong position in the latest contracting plant. Taylor Woodrow was raised from 'a prosperous building firm specialising in housing estates to a place among the giant names in the contracting and civil engineering world.'[14] And although not one of the Mulberry contractors, Wimpey was so successful at winning contracts that there were even suggestions that Churchill had a stake in the company (exonerated by the Clyde enquiry in 1942).

For all that construction came to dominate the operations of the 'housebuilders' for six years, there is evidence of planning during the war for the eventual resumption of speculative housebuilding, optimism that was to be misplaced. The evidence of the minute books is instructive in this

[9] From profile in *Housebuilder*, Dec. 1969, p. 657.
[10] John, *A Liverpool Merchant House*, pp. 153–4.
[11] Interview with Peter Prowting, Dec. 2000.
[12] Interview with Richard Bailey, Jan. 2002.
[13] Anon, *Work is Fun*, p. 4.
[14] Jenkins, *On Site*, p. 32.

context. In October 1943, the Laing directors discussed all their estates to determine how development would continue when war ended: 'our first two objects would be town buildings for ourselves and housebuilding for ourselves and local authorities. General buildings for architects would probably come next and civil engineering work after that.' Wimpey was naturally cautious in February 1942:

> 'directors were of the opinion that it was undesirable to purchase more land before the end of the war, but the regional offices should take any favourable opportunity of securing contracts for building houses for the Government or Municipal Authorities, thus getting a small staff . . . could be available if and when conditions render speculative house building a remunerative proposition.'

During 1943 a more positive attitude emerged in a series of personal memos sent by managing director Godfrey Mitchell:

> 'The sites cleared by blitz are not likely to be rebuilt by speculative builders; it is much more likely that Local Authorities . . . will clear them . . . It is likely, therefore, that we shall start up one or two estates in a very small way and see what results we get. If results are good, then speculative building is likely to blaze up much more quickly after this war than after the last.'[15]

However, there was no evidence of housebuilders actually buying new sites.

Peacetime controls

On 7th May 1945, war in Europe ended and on 21st July the Labour Party was elected to govern for the first time with an absolute majority. For six years there had been almost no new housebuilding while the existing stock had been reduced by bomb damage: 200,000 homes were destroyed and more than three and a half million damaged.[16] The political decision taken by the new government was that the public and not the private sector would be responsible for the rebuilding of Britain's housing. The strict private sector controls of Defence Regulation 56A were renewed; there were also controls on the supply of timber and steel. Nevertheless, some housebuilders did try to resume their pre-war activities but the licences were tightly constrained by maximum limits for price and area and by occupier requirements.

---

[15] Godfrey Mitchell memo 23rd Sep. 1943.
[16] Merrett, *Owner Occupation in Britain*, p. 18.

Alan Cherry, a founder of Countryside Properties, remembered the licensing process:

> 'When I was a kid in the estate agency I use to handle applications for building licences for one or two builders in the Ilford area, every new house you wanted to build, you had to have a licence for, you had to put all the sob stories in on behalf of the applicants. Find the buyers and then get a building licence.'

Indeed, I can remember living in a 'half a house' when a child, as my father could only get the licence for one side of what ultimately became a pair of semi-detached houses. It was only when researching this project that my father related his repeated visits to the council, the promises that all labour would be voluntary and the final granting of a licence 'so that you will stop pestering us'.[17]

By 1947, it was agreed that the speculative housing sector's contribution to the total new housing programme could be one fifth, but the reality was that speculative development became even more difficult. Contributory factors included the Town and Country Planning Act 1947 which imposed a 100% tax on the increase in the value of land that derived from the granting of planning permission, and the economic crisis which resulted in the suspension of the short-lived convertibility of sterling; this latter event led to the suspension of building licences from August 1947. In June 1948, local authorities were again allowed to issue licences but only under very strict terms and to all intents and purposes the speculative housebuilding industry was allowed only a token existence. Taylor Woodrow said that when the war ended, the company had prepared itself to meet the needs of thousands of would be owner-occupiers and was soon staffed to produce 4000 houses a year. However, in the three years from 1946 the company had been allowed to build only 205 houses for private sale.[18]

By 1951, private housing completions were no more than 23,000, substantially less than the 41,000 of 1947 and insignificant besides the 172,000 produced for the public sector. In October 1951, a Conservative Government was elected: Harold Macmillan was Minister of Housing with a target of 300,000 houses a year. Despite the promise of 'a bonfire of controls' it was some time before the speculative housebuilding industry was free of its restraints. The Wimpey archive contains file notes from December 1951

---

[17] For the curious, my father did build a few houses before he decided to become a builders' merchant; but for that, I might have become a housebuilder rather than writing about it.
[18] *Housebuilder*, Nov. 1949, p. 254.

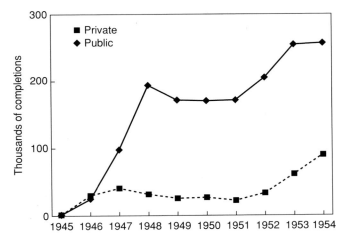

Figure 3.1 Housing completions, 1945–54.

Source: *Housing and Construction Statistics.*

of a conversation between Godfrey Mitchell and Norman Wates, reporting Mitchell's conversation with Macmillan on removing housing licences; the housebuilders were trying to convince Macmillan that the system of issuing licences to individual people would not work. Licensing was gradually relaxed and private housing output began a rapid recovery (Figure 3.1). However, it was not until 1953 that controls on timber and steel were removed and the tax on development value ended, and November 1954 before Defence Regulation 56A was revoked. By that year, housing completions had recovered to 91,000.

The response of the 1930s housebuilders to post-war controls

In effect, the speculative housing industry was constrained, to a greater or lesser degree, in its ability to function for a period of 15 years. The question becomes, what did the 1930s housebuilders do in this period, and how did their actions and strategic decisions affect the subsequent structure of the corporate sector of the housebuilding industry? Their wartime activity has already been covered and the responses ranged from shutting up shop, through war damage work to becoming major building and civil engineering contractors. After the war, it is probable that some of the more local housebuilders never returned to business; there are a number of pre-war housebuilders that do not appear to have left any significant post-war trace. F.E. Moss was President of the House Builders Federation in 1946, but in that year he and his wife resigned as directors from N. Moss & Sons and under new directors it changed its business; in 1949 the Board of Trade was enquiring of Moss' Gloucester company whether it was still carrying on a trade.[19] In 1948, Moss had joined Leo Meyer in the formation of New Ideal Homesteads South Africa and one presumes that he emigrated. Neither have any post-war references to Tommy Nash's business been located, while George Ball appears to have turned itself into an investment company.

Some housebuilders, such as Ideal Homes, Davis Estates and Janes, did try to concentrate on what was left of their pre-war housebuilding business, managing their stock of rented properties, and waiting for better times to come; for example, Ideal continued to buy properties for investment, purchasing hundreds of houses at a time, often with the intent of reselling to sitting tenants. However, for the most part, the housebuilders' strategy was to participate in the rapidly expanding local authority housebuilding programme and to develop their wartime construction business. The widespread option, as it required little in the way of new production techniques (at least for low-rise housing), was to service the expansion in public housing. Local authority housebuilding had accelerated after the war, reaching 193,000 completions in 1948; the numbers dropped a little over the next three years but by 1953 local authority housing completions had reached 241,000 (housing associations contributed another 15,000). This was a massive programme, more than double the pre-war public housing peak.

Wimpey became the largest builder of council houses and its strategy had been planned well in advance. It was minuted in 1943 that:

> 'after the war there would be large contract housebuilding programmes all over the country . . . and we should now set aside certain men who were considered the best for the purpose, and who would concentrate entirely on the technique and the organisation in advance of any future building development.'

Most of the housebuilders' contribution to the local authority building programme was as the contractor, but occasionally there was cooperation on land already owned. For example, 'Ideal became associated with Aneurin Bevan's plan for cooperation between private enterprise builders and local authorities, to construct houses to rent.'[20] One of its first schemes was at Sidcup where work began on 500 homes in October 1945, helped by 50 ex-prisoners of war, all former builders.

The post-war shortage of both materials and labour, combined with the size of the building programme, pushed the industry towards industrialised

[19] N. Moss & Son Ltd 00256285; Moss Estates (Gloucester) 00349276.
[20] Furnell, *The Diamond Jubilee of Ideal Homes*, p. 16.

construction methods. Bowley pointed out that in contrast to the inter-war period, non-traditional housing was not required to be cheaper than traditional methods, just an alternative. 'In practice as well as in policy they were rather unpopular expedients to tide over temporary scarcities.'[21] Perhaps, for this reason, what was seen as new technology had little impact on the speculative part of the housebuilding industry, which was to remain traditional in both construction and demand. Nevertheless, the local authority housing programme presented substantial opportunities for those who wished to partake. By the end of 1950, Laing had built more than 14,000 Easiform houses and the annual rate was up to 5000. Costain built 10,000 prefabricated concrete houses, 7500 steel prefabs and about 10,000 aluminium houses. Miller in Edinburgh designed its own non-traditional house, the Miller 'no-fines' house, in 1950 with factories employing around 1000 people; nearly 7000 had been built by 1955. Taylor Woodrow developed the Arcon steel house; the first contract was for 43,000 units and they employed 6000 staff. Wates developed a prefabricated housing system which was used on 40,000 houses by Wates and by licensees. Large and small, the housebuilders turned to the local authority market. By the early 1950s, Wimpey was building 18,000 local authority houses a year around the country; Maunders built 5000 council houses for north-west local authorities in eight years; Wilson Connolly built 200 houses a year for the Northampton Corporation. However, a few treated the local authority market with disdain. According to Herbert Janes, speaking at the Housebuilders' Federation AGM in 1947, 'the man who built council houses was not a housebuilder but a contractor. Contracting required a different mentality, a different technique and a different staff from housebuilding.'[22] This is a critical comment, in both senses of the word, and will be explored in Part II.

Although the larger concerns had tried to re-enter the speculative housing market immediately after the war, their enthusiasm waned as restrictions tightened and they then developed other parts of their business. It is assumed that local authority housing was a profitable operation for the participants and the cash flow may have provided some companies with the capital for later land purchases. The evidence is limited, for even today companies would be loath to provide such commercially sensitive information. However, it is noticeable that there were none of the complaints about contract losses that became common in the late 1960s and early 1970s, suggesting that there was 'good money' being made; there is also the occasional corporate reference to support that implication. The Scottish

---

[21] Bowley, *The British Building Industry*, pp. 199, 205.
[22] *Housebuilder*, Jan. 1947.

Bett Brothers built substantial numbers of council houses on margins well over 5%, 'unheard of in recent times', and that provided the finance for the land purchases.[23] More remarkable was a November 1954 minute by Wimpey that its 'no-fines' system had earned margins of 14%, an exceptionally high figure for a contracting business.

Opportunities also existed to capitalise on the new-found wartime construction expertise which enabled companies like Taylor Woodrow and Wimpey to become leading national and even international contractors. Within a year of the war, Wimpey was working in Egypt, Kuwait, Iraq, Singapore and Portugal, and over the next decade built oil refineries, power stations, dams, mines, dry docks, roads, airfields and harbours. Taylor Woodrow's minute book noted in October 1947 that the priority was to, 'carry on with existing contracts and seek new work which will be granted the highest priorities such as power stations, and factories likely to be interested in the export trade, opencast coal sites'. Laing obtained contracts in Syria for Iraq Petroleum in 1946. Costain had been drawn overseas before the war when the Air Ministry was looking for tenders for an airfield near Baghdad; although that tender was lost, Costain decided to seek other Middle East work and around 1935 was awarded a section of the Trans-Iranian Railway. Undaunted by the losses on that project, Costain went on to work for BP in Abadan in 1938 and after the war decided that its main effort should be overseas.

Occasionally, investments were made overseas in housebuilding itself. The preferred country was South Africa and housebuilders who went there included Laing and Taylor Woodrow in 1946 and Gough Cooper and Ideal Homes in 1948. No doubt the winter weather was an attraction: the founders of Gough Cooper and New Ideal emigrated for some years; Leo Meyer resigned as managing director of Ideal for health reasons and did not return until 1953. Political fears also played a part and, after failing to make any money for three years, Laing admitted that 'we should bear in mind we went forward . . . with the scare of our Socialist Government as a background.'[24] Despite the flirtation with housing, the substantial overseas commitment was made in construction and, with the development of a domestic business ranging from local authority housing to power stations, a small group of the pre-war housebuilders had transformed themselves into profitable construction groups within which the original speculative housing activity had become almost an irrelevance. By 1954, the boards of these companies were peopled by directors who may never have built

---

[23] Interview with Iain Bett, Jan. 2002.
[24] John Laing Board Minutes, 15th Dec. 1949.

houses; who had been contractors all their working lives and, moreover, who looked down on housebuilders as 'cottage bashers'. When John Laing reformed its private housing division in 1953 it did so under the name of John and David Martin to avoid tainting the image of the Laing brand name in the construction market. 'Everybody thought we were housebuilders and everybody looked down on housebuilders as the bottom end of the market'.[25]

In assessing the influence of the period between 1939 and 1954 on the private housebuilders, it is clear that those firms that were driven by dynamic entrepreneurs, unwilling to sit back and wait for their traditional market to return, were undoubtedly the stronger as firms for their pursuit of local authority housebuilding, national and international contracting. However, although they may have been stronger as firms, they were not necessarily stronger as speculative housebuilders. Those companies that had created an alternative spread of business did not readily want to divert key personnel to private housebuilding. Even as late as 1952, Wimpey's managing director, Godfrey Mitchell, was hesitating about committing too many resources to private housing saying:

> 'we should for the moment not bother about entering this market. We could use all the staff we have got at present on building remunerative "no-fines" work for Councils . . . to enter this market would mean taking men away from known remunerative work. We . . . must all watch what was happening while the smaller firms were trying it out and be prepared to switch into it when there was real money in the proposition.'[26]

The attitude of the managements had also changed in other ways. The men now at the top were more interested in the glamorous construction projects. The Wimpey history referred to wartime contracts bringing to the Company 'so many of the Scottish civil engineers who were to make their mark in the years to come'; the irony that went unnoticed by its author was that these engineers had other priorities than private housebuilding.[27] The implications of the diversification away from speculative housing will be apparent in the chronological chapters that follow and will be discussed in Part II.

---

[25] Interview with Sir Maurice Laing, April 2000.
[26] Management Board Minutes, Jan. 1952.
[27] White, *Wimpey*, p. 16.

4

The Post-war Housing Boom 1955–1973

Introduction

The period from the ending of controls in 1954 through to 1973 was a period of unrestrained growth for the speculative housebuilder, first in volume terms, as demand responded to the post-war shortage of houses, and then in profits as house price inflation accelerated in the early 1970s. By the beginning of the 1960s, the top ten housebuilders were producing some 14,000–16,000 houses a year, not far short of the level in the late 1930s and, at around 8–9%, a higher share of the market. However, with the exception of Wimpey, which stood head and shoulders above its competitors, the larger pre-war housebuilders had not been overly successful in restoring their earlier volumes; a newer generation of housebuilders was emerging. By the end of the post-war boom, there were some half-dozen companies building more than 2000 houses a year and as many as 26 building at least 1000 a year. Despite the smaller size of the industry, the top ten were responsible for 32,000–33,000 houses a year, and their market share had risen to around 17–18%.

The 1960s and early 1970s saw the development of a number of semi-national housebuilders and one undisputed national. Before the war, there was no doubting that housebuilders were purely localised concerns, with no more than a handful building outside their home area, and that little more than on a sporadic basis. By the end of the post-war boom Wimpey was operating nationally through a regional structure that had been defined at the end of the war; on a smaller scale, Bovis Homes also claimed a national organisation. More common was the medium-sized firm that covered a significant area of the country, Northern Developments and Barratt, for instance, building across the north of England. By 1973, the regional housebuilder had arrived, helped in part by Stock Exchange financed acquisitions.

The private housing market

Chapter 3 referred to the recovery in private housing completions from 23,000 in 1951 to 91,000 in 1954, as controls were progressively removed. From then on, there was almost uninterrupted growth up to 1964 with completions of 218,000. Merrett put it succinctly: 'With respect to private housing, it was essentially a matter of unleashing the industry'.[1] There can be no doubt that a substantial shortfall in housing stock existed at the time when building controls were removed. Parry Lewis estimated that the increase in households between 1940 and 1947 exceeded the increase in housing stock by 1.3 m. and that the first post-war census (1951) showed that the number of households in England and Wales exceeded the number of houses 'by rather more than a million'.[2] *Housing Policy* used the period 1938–51 to compare an increase in dwellings of 1.13 m. with an increase in households of 1.96 m., a shortfall of 830,000.[3] What increase there had been in housing supply in this period was almost all provided by local authorities; there had been minimal supply of new housing to satisfy the latent demand for owner-occupation. Demand, of course, is only effective if supported by income and the period from 1951 to the mid-1960s saw strong growth in real incomes and support from the building societies that granted mortgages on the strength of those incomes (Figure 4.1).

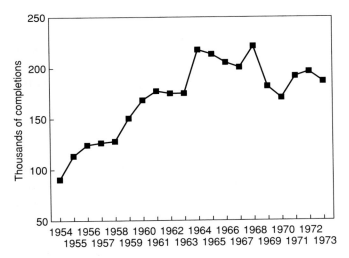

Figure 4.1   Private housing completions, 1954–1973.

Source: *Housing and Construction Statistics.*

---

1 Merrett, *Owner Occupation in Britain*, p. 26.
2 Parry Lewis, *Building Cycles and Britain's Growth*, p. 239.
3 HMSO, *Housing Policy Technical Volume Part I*, p. 22.

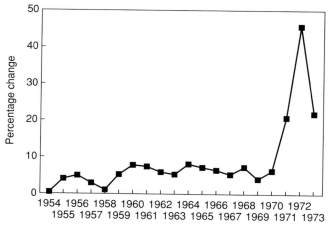

Figure 4.2   Change in house prices, 1954–1973.

Source: *Nationwide Building Society House Price Index.*

The period from 1964 to 1973 remained favourable for the private house-builders (in marked contrast to the public sector where housing completion almost halved between 1967 and 1973) but the statistical pattern was differ-ent. Private housing output no longer grew rapidly and although it remained on a high plateau, annual completions became more erratic; a post-war record of 222,000 was achieved in 1968 but the years to 1973 all saw annual comple-tions a little under 200,000. What changed was house price inflation, not a new phenomenon in the post-war period, but it had never been anything like the magnitude experienced between 1971 and 1973 (see Figure 4.2). Bank rate had fallen from the 8% ruling in early 1970 to 5% by September 1971. Competition and Credit Control came into operation in September 1971 and by the end of the year limits on bank lending had been removed; building society new lending doubled between the beginning of 1971 and the end of 1972. By the latter part of 1972, house prices were increasing at an annual rate of 40% and they more than doubled between the beginning of 1971 and the end of 1973. House price inflation had consistently averaged between 5% and 10% throughout the 1960s, encouraging housebuilders to own sub-stantial stocks of development land. The ownership of this land in a period of sharply rising house prices provided a period of exceptional profitability to conclude a two-decade bull market for housebuilders. Some 70 individual firms took advantage of this to float their businesses on the Stock Exchange. It is hard to overestimate the effect this exceptional house price inflation had on the corporate structure of the housebuilding industry. Many devel-opers had known nothing but rising house prices and incorrectly assumed their continuance, the effect of which will be seen in Chapter 5. In the meantime, the sun shone and the housebuilders reaped the benefit.

Which firms built the houses?

There are few individual unit output figures available immediately following the abolition of building controls. There was only a handful of quoted companies and little trade reference to volumes. The outbreak of war left many unfinished sites and it is assumed that builders returned first to their old sites, many of which would have had the infrastructure in place, and resumed building as quickly as they could. New land purchases followed as building controls were removed. Ideal's first significant land purchases were minuted in March 1953, seven sites for 511 units in the London suburbs, and it claimed to have sold 20,000 houses from the end of the war to 1959.[4] Taylor Woodrow built 500 houses in 1953 and 1150 in 1955, and Davis Estates was reported in *Housebuilder* as having estates in London, the southern counties and the Midlands in 1954. Newer firms, not in existence before the war, were also emerging and the south coast firm of Hallmark Homes was one of the first to build in sizeable numbers, with around 500 completions in 1955. Others were perhaps more cautious: even in June 1954 Wimpey's minutes described the speculative housing market as 'an unknown and probably a sticky one'.

It is not until the end of the 1950s that the changes in the post-war corporate structure became more visible: the individual company volumes are both larger and the numbers more reliable as a data base. This chapter tracks the changes in corporate size, showing the decline in the relative position of most of the pre-war leaders and the gradual emergence of a new generation of speculative housebuilders. The pace of change was such that it is necessary to use three separate dates; these have been taken as the periods around 1960, 1965 and 1973 (Table 4.1). Between 1960 and 1973 the market share of the top ten housebuilders doubled from around 8–9% to 18% and the number of individual housebuilders selling more than 1000 units a year rose from an estimated four or five to around twenty-six.

Table 4.1 Change in industry concentration, 1960–1973.

Year	Top ten output	Top ten market share %	Firms building more p.a. than	
			1000	**2000**
1960	14,000–16,000	8–9	4–5	2
1965	17,000–18,000	8–9	10–12	1
1973	32,000–33,000	17–18	26	6

---

[4] Furnell, *The Diamond Jubilee of Ideal Homes*, inset p. 29.

The period around 1960

By the beginning of the 1960s, the top ten housebuilders were producing some 14,000–16,000 houses a year; given the approximate nature of the company figures, this can be regarded as broadly similar to the 16,000–18,000 a year estimated for the top ten in the late 1930s. That it was a higher percentage of the industry total reflected the fact that the industry, although recovering strongly with private housing completions of around 170,000 a year, was only building at half the rate achieved in the mid-1930s.

Table 4.2 shows the picture around 1960, that is almost a decade after the re-election of the Conservatives and five years after the removal of the last of the building controls. Before the war, Ideal was producing over 5000 houses a year with a couple more firms building around 2000, and it was possible to identify another six or seven companies building 1000 houses or more a year. By 1961, Wimpey was selling 6000 houses a year in the private sector; these numbers were substantially in excess of its pre-war output and on a par with the record levels achieved by Ideal in the 1930s. Ideal itself had recovered to around 2000–3000 a year by 1960.

Table 4.2   A league table of housebuilders *c.*1960: firms building 500 units or more p.a.

Date formed	Housebuilder	Annual output
1880	Wimpey	6000 (1961)
1929	New Ideal	2000–3000
1919	MRCE[a]	1200
1884	Janes	*c.*1000 (900 in 1958)
Early 1920s	John Lawrence	500–1000?
1920	McLean	800 (1963)
1933	Gough Cooper	800 (1962)
1946	Bellway	700
1921	Taylor Woodrow	*c.*750 (660 in 1958)
1929	Davis Estates	est. 500–1000
	Top ten	**14,000–16,000**
1864	Dares	500–600?
1932	Leech	Not known, est. *c.*500
1904	Wilcon	500?
1952	Fell	*c.*500
1935	E. Fletcher	500?
1901	Mactaggart & Mickel	*c.*500
1957	Hallmark	500

[a] Includes Whelmar's 1000.

However, leaving aside Wimpey and Ideal, what is noticeable from Table 4.2 is that no other housebuilder that had been building 1000 houses a year before the war had regained those levels, although Davis Estates may have been close. After its excellent start, Taylor Woodrow was actually producing less than in 1954. Such prolific pre-war housebuilders as Wates were building only 100 or 200 a year; Costain and Laing 300; and Henry Boot, responsible for the largest number of private sector houses in total before the war, perhaps 200.

One of the explanations for the decline in numbers has been covered in Chapter 3: some of these companies had created substantial alternative streams of income derived from their wartime construction and post-war local authority housing. After a gap of 15 years there was little incentive to rebuild the speculative housing business. Moreover, the passage of time meant that most of the senior management now had their roots in construction, not development. Despite its slow start, the exception was Wimpey, which had as diversified a business as any, but the determination and foresight of Godfrey Mitchell, arguably the most important individual in the twentieth-century history of the British construction and housebuilding industry, supported by F.W. McLeod who ran the speculative building programme, created a private housebuilding business that dominated the industry. Others that had the post-war financial strength to have been in that position could not always come to terms with the more inflationary conditions in the land market: 'That is why [Taylor Woodrow] never got back to building 1000 units a year, as Frank Taylor would not buy the sites when they were going up in price.'[5]

Even where there had been no substantial diversification, the 15-year gap had changed attitudes; the driving force was now half a generation older and succession planning had been rudely interrupted. Charles Boot, the dominant individual in Henry Boot, had died in 1945; Geoffrey Crouch is believed to have died during the war; Jack Mactaggart had moved to the Bahamas for health reasons and sold out to the Mickel family in 1947; Tom Warren was nearly 70 in 1954 when controls were finally removed and he had no sons. Nash appeared to have done a little building after the war and then vanished without trace, and Moss emigrated to South Africa. Thus, it can be seen that the firms that experienced substantial decline compared with their pre-war housebuilding levels had either created other streams of income that appeared more rewarding, or the driving force of the business before the war was no longer in the same position.

---

[5] Interview with Stan Tribe, June 2000.

The corollary of pre-war names no longer being the housebuilding force that they had been was the emergence of unfamiliar names. New house-building companies were being started from the beginning of the 1950s. Hallmark Securities, for instance, which came to the stock market in 1957 through a reverse takeover, was controlled by a banker and a solicitor and had started housebuilding a few years earlier in partnership with Alan Draycott, a south coast estate agent; the 1958 accounts claimed that volumes had been around 500 a year since 1955. Fell Construction was incorporated in 1952 as a building and civil engineering contractor by Ronald Fell, then a 32-year-old Wakefield builder. Fell was born in Dewsbury and after time as a land surveyor with the Dewsbury Corporation and service with a Wakefield building firm he started his company with half a dozen employ-ees; by 1962 over 2500 houses and bungalows had been built in Lancashire, Yorkshire and Cheshire.

Some of the 'new' housebuilders did have pre-war roots but they were really post-war creations, being little more than sons following in their fathers' footsteps. The Midlands firm of E. Fletcher was started in 1935 but Edward's son, Geoffrey, joined the firm in 1952 and became managing director in 1960. John T. Bell Ltd (later Bellway) was formed in 1946 by John T.'s sons who brought in their father, a pre-war builder whose business had failed: by 1960 the firm was building 700 houses a year in the north-east, making it one of the largest housebuilders in the region. John McLean had founded his business in 1920 and remained a small Wolverhampton con-tractor and housebuilder. At the end of the war he 'was reaching an age when, to many men, retirement becomes a major aim in life. By then his eldest son Geoffrey was ready to take over the reins, and asked for them firmly – all the reins – and at once!'[6] Geoffrey McLean introduced manage-ment consultants into the business in 1952 and expanded the company rapidly: by the time it floated in 1963 its sales were approaching 800 houses a year.

More noticeable was the development of pre-war concerns that had viewed their wartime construction and post-war local authority building as an unnecessary distraction. Under the control of Sir Herbert Janes, one-time Mayor of Luton, H.C. Janes had managed to build some 120 houses in the first year of peace. By 1958, when the firm floated, the annual rate of sales was up to 900. Gough Cooper had been building around 100 houses a year in Kent but during the 1950s and early 1960s Harry Gough-Cooper[7]

---
[6] *House Beautiful*, June 1959, p. 32.
[7] The individual dropped the hyphen when naming the Company.

expanded the business across the south-east and was building some 800 houses a year by 1962. Dares, reported as building 800 houses a year before the war in the Midlands, had managed to build some 200 houses during the period of total building controls and under the continued leadership of Harry Dare had probably recovered to 500–600 a year by the beginning of the 1960s. In Scotland, John Lawrence was described in the 1950s as 'presiding over the largest private building organisation in Scotland'[8] and, extrapolating back from totals known in 1964, was probably selling between 500 and 1000 units.

The most difficult to categorise was Whelmar, which started as a joint venture between Metropolitan Railway Country Estates and Metropolitan Railway Surplus Lands but in reality it was the creation of Tom Baron, a Manchester chartered surveyor who progressed from buying land for his clients to developing the houses. As he succinctly put it:

> 'I realised how often they made a balls of it and I used to think "I could do better than this". By 1962 I was probably the biggest spec. builder outside Wimpey though nobody had heard of me, because I was working for seven companies. The involvement was total but I couldn't take an equity stake in any of my clients under the rules of the RICS.'[9]

Whelmar was then the dominant part of MRCE.

The changes in the ranking of leading firms varied considerably, but all stem from the 15-year period of war and post-war controls that had led some firms into more profitable alternatives and destroyed management continuity. Much depended on whether the dominant personality before the war, at this point always the founder or family member, was of an age and inclination to continue a vigorous development of the firm after the war. Men like Godfrey Mitchell, Leo Meyer, Herbert Janes, John Lawrence, Arthur Davis and Harry Gough-Cooper were such men; John Mactaggart and Tom Warren were not. The issue of succession is addressed more fully in Part II.

Mid-1960s

Within another five years, that is by the mid-1960s, the number of house-builders producing a thousand or more houses a year had risen substantially, certainly to ten and perhaps a dozen; the total number of houses

---

8 Watters, *Mactaggart & Mickel and the Scottish Housebuilding Industry*, p. 160.
9 *Housebuilder*, Aug. 1986.

Table 4.3   A league table of housebuilders in 1965: firms building 500 units or more p.a.

Date formed	Housebuilder	Annual output
1880	Wimpey	8100
1919	MRCE	c.1800 (inc Whelmar)
1929	New Ideal	1200–1300 (1150 in 1966)
1884	Janes	1000–1200
Early 1920s	John Lawrence	1000–1200
1957	Hallmark	1145 (1964)
1929	Davis Estates	<1000
1952	Fell	c.1000
1935	E. Fletcher	c.1000
1903	Page-Johnson	c.1000
	Top ten	**17,000–18,000**
1933	Gough Cooper	800–1000?
c.1958	Whelmar	1000
1932	Leech	Not known, possibly 750–1000
1920	McLean	c.750
1937	Bett	750 (1967)
1904	Wilcon	750
1946	Bellway	700+?
1934	Drury	600–800
1921	Taylor Woodrow	500–750?
1885	Bryant	500–750
1927	Miller	Not known, possibly 500–750
	Top twenty	**25,000–26,000**

built by the top ten had also risen to 17,000–18,000 houses a year, but with the industry's completions also higher at 215,000 the market share remained at around 8–9%. As can be seen from Table 4.3, Wimpey had further increased its leadership of the industry both in absolute terms, having raised volumes from 6000 to 8000 a year, and also relative to the other companies, particularly Ideal which had halved its volumes following the death of its founder. The pre-war leaders that had fallen behind by 1960 continued with low volumes: Taylor Woodrow barely makes the top 20 and, surprisingly, its annual output of 500–750 was halved in ten years. Costain, Laing and Wates were still building 500 a year or less, and Henry Boot only 200.

The interest in this period is not the confirmation of the failure of most of the pre-war leaders to recover their position; it lies in the emergence of the new group of medium-sized housebuilders, many of them post-war creations. Fell, Fletcher and Hallmark were mentioned earlier and they had doubled in size within the five years to around 1000 units a year and entered the top ten. For the first time, acquisitions were beginning to play a part in growth: Fell had bought the Northampton firm of Adkins & Shaw and Hallmark bought A.J. Wait, the first housebuilder to float after the war (1956). One other name that appears in the top ten was Page-Johnson. The firm was technically a pre-war business in that Herbert Johnson had a small jobbing business in the Birmingham area: he died in 1939 and his son, 'Johnnie' Johnson took over. Page-Johnson was probably typical of those entrepreneurial firms that prospered as controls were dismantled and by 1960 it was large enough to float: the company spread rapidly across the country in the 1960s, from Teeside down to Devon and Hampshire. Further afield, Page-Johnson built flats in Southern Rhodesia and developed in France and Australia.

Just as Page-Johnson could be described as a pre-war company but was, in effect, a post-war creation, so too could Bett, Bryant, Drury and Wilson Connolly; Bryant and Wilcon went on to become major forces in the industry. Andrew Bett and his three sons founded Bett Haulage in Dundee in 1936, gradually moving into construction work. After the war, the company was run by the second generation and it concentrated on building houses and shops for Dundee Corporation and significant housing volumes were completed. When the first building licences became available, Bett began building houses again in a small way in Dundee and after 1960, began to build outside Dundee, spreading across east and central Scotland. The prospectus issued when the Company floated in 1967 estimated that in 1966 the company was responsible for 10% of the Scottish housing starts. Thomas Drury and his brother-in-law, Ralph Grocock, started their Leicester based building business in 1934, incorporating it as Drury & Co. in 1935. After the war, the company concentrated on local authority contracts mainly in the Midlands and the London area, but from 1956 work was carried out in Lancashire, Yorkshire and the south-west. Private estate development, through Drury Estates, was not started until 1951 and a southern housing subsidiary was formed in 1957. By the time the Group was floated in 1964, estates were spread through Leicestershire and Northants, up to Lancashire and Yorkshire, across to the south Midlands and East Anglia, and on the south coast.

Bryant and Wilson Connolly were much older construction businesses. Bryant was founded in 1885, becoming a substantial building contractor in the Birmingham area in the 1930s; however, it did not start speculative housing until 1936 and the volumes were modest. It was under third generation Chris Bryant that Bryant Estates was formed in 1954: by 1958 it was building around 350 houses a year, and it was then that Roy Davies, who was not a family member, took over its management, leading its housebuilding expansion for almost 30 years. Thomas Wilson was a Northampton shoemaker who had returned to England in 1904 after an unsuccessful stay in the USA and started his own small building company. It ran as a general construction business before beginning speculative housing in 1932 and it averaged around 150 units a year in the late 1930s. There was no serious attempt to restart private housing until the end of controls in 1954 by which time the third generation of Wilsons was starting to enter the business. By 1965 output had risen to a very localised 750 units, 550 in the Northampton area and 200 in Swindon.

Pre-1974

By the end of the post-war boom, call it 1973 for convenience, the industry was building slightly fewer houses than in the mid-1960s but there had been a substantial increase in the number of larger companies. Twenty years had elapsed since the removal of building controls, providing ample opportunity for the creation of a new generation of medium-sized house-builders. Table 4.4 shows that apart from Wimpey, there were 25 companies building 1000 or more houses, five of which were building in excess of 2000. The top ten were completing around 32,000–33,000 units, or some 17–18% of the industry total; the next ten built a further 12,000–13,000 giving a market share for the top 20 of 24%. The larger volumes were symptomatic of wider geographic coverage (discussed below) and there was increased use of the takeover as a means of expansion.

Wimpey's dominance might now be expected: the Company's name has been synonymous with Godfrey Mitchell but it was actually F.W. McLeod who drove its post-war speculative housing business. He died in 1969 and although Wimpey reached a peak output of 12,500 in 1972 it was 30 years (and a large acquisition) before that figure was reached again. Of the top ten, Whelmar, Leech, Bryant and Bellway have been mentioned in previous league tables but half of the top ten, and most of the second ten, have not previously been mentioned. An increasing proportion of the firms may be regarded as post-war creations; indeed, that would apply to all five companies ranked behind Wimpey. Northern Developments had been formed as recently as 1959 by Derek Barnes, an ex-Blackburn Rovers footballer and bricklayer; it expanded rapidly throughout the north of England and the Midlands, helped by acquisitions in the early 1970s. Its registrations with the NHBC averaged 7000 in 1972 and 1973 although the 1974 recession meant that this figure was never achieved. Barratt Developments, as any reader will already know, achieved more lasting success. Formed out of a partnership in the early 1960s between Lawrie Barratt, an accountant, and Lewis Greensitt, a builder, Greensitt & Barratt floated in 1968 (the same week as Northern Developments) and used the quotation to launch a series of acquisitions, usually of long established quoted housebuilders. By 1973,

Table 4.4   A league table of housebuilders in 1973: firms building 1000 units or more p.a.

Date formed	Housebuilder	Output in 1973	Pre-recession peak output if higher
1880	Wimpey	11,500	12,500 (1972)
1956	Northern Developments	4000	
c.1958	Whelmar	3200	
1885	Bovis	2659[b]	
1958	Barratt	2500	
c.1954	Broseley	2200	
1932	Leech	1888	
1885	Bryant	1600	
1961	Bardolin/E. Fletcher	1500	
1946	Bellway	c.1500	
	Top ten	**c.32,500**	
1962	Francis Parker	1400	
1970	Orme	1357	
1904	Comben	1269	
1941	David Charles	1200	
1901	Wates	1000–1250?	
1933	Gough Cooper	c.1050	
1884	Janes	1000–1200	
1954	Greaves	c.1200	
1920	McLean	c.1000	
1959	Federated	c.1000	
	Top twenty	**c.44,000–45,000**	
1965	Costain	c.1000	
1929	Davis Estates	c.1000?	
Early 1920s	John Lawrence	c.1000?	
1950s	Galliford Estates	c.1000	
c.1930	Whittingham	<1000	
1952	Bacal[a]	c.800	1300 (1971)

[a] Previously known as Fell. [b] Rose to 3500 in 1974.

Barratt had expanded from its Newcastle base north into Scotland and south through Yorkshire into the north-west and Midlands. Broseley was started by Danny Horrocks, a joiner turned estate agent. Small housing estates in the late 1950s progressed to commercial developments with Royal Exchange as partner, substantial shareholder and then owner. Like Barratt and Northern, Broseley was well on the way to becoming a national housebuilder.

Tom Baron's Whelmar had been extricated from the MRCE network and placed within Christian Salvesen, one of the clients for whom Baron had been buying land. All Baron's housing was now concentrated on Whelmar and a series of regional acquisitions in the early 1970s took Whelmar from its Lancashire base into North Wales, Scotland and the north-east. Bovis was the only other company to build more than 2000 a year. Bovis was a long established building company, first quoted in 1928, and controlled by the Joseph family. It began speculative housing in 1962 but its place in the industry dates from 1967 when it bought Frank Sanderson's small housebuilding company. Sanderson had joined an estate agent after national service, setting up his own agency in 1951 and moving into development in 1956, building across Kent. Sanderson was chosen to increase Bovis' commitment to housing which he did through a series of acquisitions, particularly R.T. Warren and Page-Johnson in 1971. Bardolin was formed in 1961 and was a small housebuilder until 1968 when Jock Mackenzie joined as chairman with national aspirations: the 1969 prospectus advised that 'the policy has now been reformulated and we are now in the process of creating a national property investment and housebuilding group'; three small firms building in Birmingham and the West Country were bought in that year and the company achieved substance in 1969 with the purchase of E. Fletcher.

Many other companies building 1000 houses a year were post-war in origin, and the trades-founders continued to be evident, as at Greaves, Galliford and Francis Parker. Greaves was controlled by Edward Wheatley who had left grammar school in 1946 aged 16 following the death of his father and apprenticed as a plumber. After doing repair and improvement work, the firm moved into housebuilding in 1959 and through organic growth became one of the larger developers in the Midlands. Galliford Estates was formed by bricklayer and plasterer brothers who started building houses in the 1950s; flotation allowed the purchase of the A.J. Wait/Hallmark housing business which had itself reached volumes of 1250 in 1970 before passing under the control of Spey Westmoreland Properties. Less qualified was Bob Francis, who started as a clerk at Butlin's, Bognor Regis, began to do subcontracting work for Billy Butlin before moving into other specialist building trades and, in the late 1960s, housing development, before reversing his business into the quoted Daniel T. Jackson. Although the enlarged Company had been forecasting no more than 600 housing sales for the year to March 1972, the acquisition of the larger Drury and then Dean Smith gave the group a spread of sites from the south coast up to Lancashire and Yorkshire, and a target of 2500 units.

Some took hold of small family businesses and transformed them, for example David Charles and Whittingham. David Charles was formed during the war and started estate development in 1952 but its growth stemmed from the appointment of the founder's son-in-law, Robin Buckingham, in 1954 after service in the Royal Navy. A series of acquisitions not only took housebuilding output to 1200 a year but also moved the company into commercial development and building materials. When William Whittingham floated in 1964 it was still only developing housing estates within a 35-mile radius of Wolverhampton; it was when third generation Tom Whittingham took over a year later, aged 26, that housing was expanded, all organically, and a significant position built up in commercial property and photographic development. Federated Homes was in a category of its own as a 'family' business; in essence, it was created as a twenty-first birthday present for James Meyer, the eldest son of Ideal founder Leo Meyer. The first site was bought in 1959 and, with the help of Ideal staff, Federated expanded rapidly through the 1960s.

Other founders could be regarded as entrepreneurs who had chosen the housebuilding industry, and Jock MacKenzie's influence on Bardolin has already been mentioned. Purely financially driven was Orme, having been formed in 1970 by Messrs Whitfield and Tanner, well known at the time as founders of Clubman's Club. According to the 1971 prospectus, early in 1970 they had decided that 'there was scope for rationalisation and expansion in the construction industry, property development and allied activities' and, accordingly, they set about assembling a national housebuilding business. The first building block was the privately owned Bruce Fletcher of Leicester, purchased before the float; two more housebuilders were bought immediately after – Tudor Jenkins and Norman Ashton.

As one of the themes in this book is the pace of corporate change, it is instructive to finish this section by looking at what became of the pre-war top ten housebuilders in the post-war period. Table 4.5 brings to mind the expression, 'how are the mighty fallen'. It could be understood, perhaps, if not all the housebuilders had regained their pre-war output by 1960, a mere six years after the final removal of building controls. But that by 1973, at the end of a prolonged boom, only Wimpey was building more

Table 4.5   What became of the 1930s top ten?

Company	Late 1930s	1960	1973
Ideal Homes	5000–7000	2000–3000	7000–8000
Henry Boot	1500–2000	c.200	350
Wates	1500–2000	200–300?	1000–1500
Taylor Woodrow	1200–1500	c.750	500–750?
Davis Estates	1200	500–1000	c.1000
Wimpey	1200	6000	11,500
Mactaggart & Mickel	1000	c.500	200–300
Costain	1000+	c.200	c.1000
G.T. Crouch	1000	c.400	c.500
Laing	800	300	310

than its pre-war total is striking. Wimpey, of course, had more or less single-handed made up for the shortfall in the rest and it was literally in a league of its own. Of the others, Wates, Davis Estates and Costain were not far behind their pre-war outputs, although as the 1960s figures indicate, it was only after a very poor start. Others were but a shadow of their former housebuilding selves by 1973: Ideal and Boot, for instance, because of the loss of the driving entrepreneur, Laing and Taylor Woodrow because of their greater interest in construction. The reasons for decline will be explored in greater detail in Chapters 10 and 11.

The emergence of the regional housebuilder

Before the war, it was possible to find housebuilders that operated outside their home area, for example Davis Estates and Taylor Woodrow, but none operated self-contained regional businesses with their own operational structure. The first attempt was probably by Wimpey which had established a regional structure in 1943 to handle its expanding construction business, a decision later given philanthropic intent by Mitchell: 'Initially it was with no other purpose than to find work for our people who came off the aerodromes and back from France.'[10] An embryo plan, minuted in October 1943 for the resumption of speculative housebuilding, envisaged a head office staff that would handle land purchase, design and sales, leaving the construction to be carried out by the regional offices. When Wimpey did eventually return to private housing in June 1953, the regional plan was adopted, although with the regional manager given the additional task to 'initiate the first investigation as to possibilities in his region'. In this manner, Wimpey became the first national housebuilder, but integrating its housebuilding within the construction business of its regions was unusual. Bovis, which also had a construction business, was the only other housebuilder in the pre-1974 period with any claim to be a national housebuilder; it had structured its housebuilding on a more self-contained basis. Bovis Homes was described in P&O's 1974 accounts as 'the only national housebuilder to operate through regionally based, profit responsible companies, located as far as possible at the centre of the area each serves', a structure that no doubt seemed more logical to the estate agent that was running the business.

Other housebuilders were clearly developing organisational structures that could become national, and there were a few public statements of intent.

---

[10] White, *Wimpey*, p. 22.

One came in the Carlton Homes December 1969 newsletter, written prior to the reverse takeover of Comben & Wakeling, when Terry Roydon described his ambition to create a national housebuilding company: 'We strongly believe that within a few years Carlton Homes will be the second biggest housebuilder in England.' Bardolin, as mentioned above, had put a declaration of national intent in its 1969 prospectus and Orme, another financially driven housebuilder, had also publicly stated its intent to rationalise the industry. There were companies like Costain that could claim to be building houses across the country but these were little more than random sites – the product of a lack of organisation, not a national organisation. The reality is that most of the medium to large housebuilders were semi-national. In contrast to the pre-war pattern, the larger housebuilders were northern oriented; although still an active market, the London suburbs were no longer providing a profusion of large sites. Northern Developments and Barratt built across the north of England, as did Whelmar, with additional coverage of Wales and Scotland. Leech covered the north-east and Scotland while Broseley concentrated on the north-west and the south-west. Of the top ten housebuilders, only Birmingham based Bryant had no interest in regional expansion, although Bardolin had not progressed much further with its national aspirations than the Midlands.

The regional expansion of the housebuilders owed much to acquisitions, almost entirely through the use of Stock Exchange transactions. Wimpey, as so often, was an exception with all its growth coming organically; the growth of Northern Developments, too, was largely organic in its early years and by 1973 it was building from Glasgow down to Birmingham. Other industry leaders, however, were substantially helped by acquisitions primarily made in the early 1970s: Whelmar (using parent company capital) bought housing companies in North Wales, Scotland and Doncaster; Barratt bought Bracken for Yorkshire (1972), William Bruce for Scotland (1973), and Arthur Wardle for Lancashire (1972); while Bob Francis, based in Sussex, bought the Essex business of Daniel Jackson to form Francis Parker (1971) before buying the Manchester firm of Dean Smith (1973).

5

Recession and Recovery, 1973–1988

Introduction

The recession that hit the private housing industry in 1974 and the con-tinued decline through the 1970s did irreparable damage to many of the housebuilders and changed the corporate structure of the industry yet again (Table 5.1). By 1980 only 13 companies were building over 1000 units, half the pre-recession number, although with two large national firms against only one, the top ten's share of the reduced market increased from 18% to 28%. In contrast, the 1980s was another boom decade in which some 29 firms achieved an annual sales rate of 1000 in at least one year. More significant was the emergence of the national housebuilder – 14 firms were building more than 2000 a year compared with six pre-1974, and five housebuilders exceeded 5000 a year compared with two in the earl-ier period. The top ten firms were producing just over 50,000 units by the late 1980s, some 27% of the enlarged market. Six companies could now be considered national housebuilders, with a further six to eight having strong regional coverage. Consolidation was not the only trend. There continued to be extensive changes in the corporate identity of the industry's leaders: a majority of the firms in the 1988 league table (Table 5.3) had not previously appeared in the 1973 table (Table 4.4).

Table 5.1 Change in industry concentration, early 1970s–late 1980s.

Year	Top ten output	Top ten market share %	Firms building more p.a. than 1000	2000	5000
1973	32,000–33,000	17–18	26	6	1
1980	36,000	28	13	4	2
Late 1980s	51,000	27	29	14	5

The private housing market – the collapse

The collapse in private sector housing completions from 191,000 in 1972 to 140,000 in 1974, and the subsequent downwards drift to a low point of 115,000 in 1981, does not do justice to the scale of the problems faced by the speculative housebuilding industry. It has to be viewed in the context of the unprecedented fall in the stock market; the failure of the secondary banks that had provided so much of the speculative finance in the closing years of the post-war bull market; and the collapse in the land values that supposedly underpinned the housebuilders' balance sheets.

During 1972, the inflationary pressures increased: the Bank of England asked the banks to curb lending to the property sector in August; a prices freeze was introduced in November 1972. MLR was raised from $7^1/2$% to a record $11^1/2$% between June and July 1973; the Arab-Israeli war came in October (leading to the rise in oil prices) and MLR reached 13% in November. In that same month, the first secondary bank, London & County was rescued, as was Cedar Holdings in December. 1974 started with the three-day week and the financial background progressively deteriorated. During 1974, the FT Index fell 55% reaching its low of 146 a few days into 1975, some 73% below its 1972 peak.

Although private housing completions fell by 24% in 1974, a better indication of the state of demand, and housebuilders' confidence, was housing starts, which halved. According to the indices, house prices did not actually fall but the annual rate of increase dropped from 40–50% to 4–5% by the end of 1974 and the reality was that some builders were reducing prices against a background of a fast rise in the general rise in inflation. Continued house price inflation had been built in to many housebuilders' land purchasing decisions and the combination of falling demand, weak pricing and rising construction costs had a devastating effect on land values. The weighted index of land prices fell by 32% between 1973 and 1975, and by 39% in the south-east;[1] this would have understated the real fall in values as sites without planning permission were virtually unsaleable. On top of this, work in progress rose and high interest charges pushed up the cost of finance. The secondary banks that had provided much of the housebuilders' finance were also collapsing and were not best placed to provide long-term support to their clients. A parallel impact on the commercial property sector is described in Scott's *Property Masters*.

---

[1] HMSO, *Housing and Construction Statistics 1971–81.*

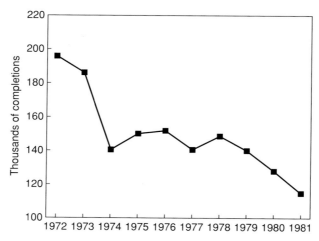

Figure 5.1   Private housing completions, 1972–1981.

Source: *Housing and Construction Statistics.*

The stock market staged a dramatic recovery in 1975, which was accompanied by a modest increase in housing completions. However, in October 1976 the mortgage rate was actually raised to a record $12^{1}/_{4}\%$ and private housing drifted lower for the rest of the decade. After a rally in 1978 and 1979, a period that saw house prices once again rising by 25–30% per annum, the decade finished with another sharp setback. Bank rate was raised to 17% in November 1979 and stayed there for eight months: private housing completions fell by 18% between 1979 and 1981. In 1980 alone, housing starts fell 31% to under 100,000, lower even than in 1974 and the lowest figure since 1953 (Figure 5.1). The financial background for the housebuilders in the period 1974–1981 could not have provided a greater contrast to the post-war boom.

Which firms built the houses?

The recession produced many immediate casualties and for others a lingering death. The contrasting financial strength of the individual housebuilders and, where relevant, the attitude of their parent companies, created significant changes to the relative standing of the companies. By the end of the 1970s, there were only 13 companies building more than 1000 units a year compared with 26 before the 1974 recession. However, thanks to the presence of two very large housebuilders, Barratt and Wimpey, as against only Wimpey before, the top ten accounted for around 36,000 units, slightly more than in 1973; moreover, the industry's volume was smaller, which gave the top ten a market share of around 28% as against 18% in 1973.

The first of the quoted company failures came in September 1974 with the relatively small Budge Brothers, a mixed construction and housing business which had only refloated in July 1973. However, the failure that sent shock waves through the industry was of Bovis, the fourth largest housebuilder and a long established contractor. It was brought down by the secondary bank crisis when there was a run on deposits at Twentieth Century Banking, a subsidiary Bovis had bought in 1971. In December 1973 Natwest advised Bovis that it could no longer provide financial support; in the following month Bovis was forced to accept a rescue by P&O. Amongst the unquoted companies, Marc Gregory had a high profile: it was aiming for 1000 units and had recently brushed with the Takeover Panel which had forced it to bid for the quoted Greencoat Properties. In January 1974, Marc Gregory found it could not pay its interest and called a moratorium on its main lenders; a winding-up order was made the following month. Mike Ratcliffe, one of the directors, contrasted the debt of some £40 m. against a £2 m. asset base.

The first half of 1975 saw the collapse of two small quoted companies, Greensquare and Lewston and the larger Bacal, previously known as Fell (1300 units). However, by now the recession was digging even deeper. Northern Developments, led by ex-footballer Derek Barnes, had expanded rapidly to become the country's second largest housebuilder; it was building at an annual rate of around 4000, with plans to raise this to 6000–7000. The growth was largely financed on borrowed money and by the middle of 1974 debt had risen to £41 m. against reduced equity of £6 m. Northern Developments made arrangements with its banks whereby interest was 'rolled up'; this lasted until June 1975 when the receivers were appointed. Northern Developments may have been the largest housebuilding failure but it was not the last. Further quoted company failures in 1976 were Joviel Properties (500) in February, Lawdon (c.150) in March and two of the large Midlands companies, Greaves (1200) in December and David Charles (1200) in January 1977. Other companies gradually withdrew from the industry, some like Francis Parker because they were financially crippled; others, like Mucklow, which had been building a steady 500 a year, because they saw safer ways of investing their capital. Orme was acquired by Comben in 1978; well known names like Sunley and Dares made their exit from the industry. By 1980, there were substantial differences in the industry leadership compared with pre-1974.

Those still building over 1000 units a year by the end of the decade can rightly be considered the survivors of the volume builders, in contrast to names mentioned in earlier paragraphs (Table 5.2). However, their performance had by no measure been uniform, nor were their strategies always

Table 5.2   A league table of housebuilders in 1980: firms building 1000 units or more p.a.

Housebuilder	1979–81 average volume
Barratt	10,833
Wimpey	9300
McLean/Tarmac	3806
Broseley	2496
Bovis	1860
Leech	1768
Bryant	1667
Comben	1657
Ideal	1367
Whelmar	1229
Top ten	**36,000**
Wilcon	1076
Bellway	1103
Fairview	1069

Note: some of the housebuilders experienced substantial annual variation in volumes around 1980 and it was considered more representative of the underlying position to show an annual average.

entirely of their own choosing. Wimpey's volumes had declined and it was no longer the market leader. Cliff Chetwood, later chief executive, ascribed the decline to people: 'You had two exceptional men and McLeod [who ran post-war private housing] died and Sir Godfrey [founder] began to get frail.'[2] At the same time, Wimpey was benefiting substantially from the Middle East contracting boom and was able to generate profits growth without relying on private housing: group turnover more than doubled between 1973 and 1978 and profits rose from £32 m. to £57 m. entirely due to overseas construction. The new industry leader was a dedicated housebuilder, Barratt Developments, whose founder was determined to create a national organisation. The public face of Barratt was its high profile advertising and marketing; the oak tree, the helicopter and Patrick Allan became so familiar on television that they would even feature in comedians' jokes. Sales were predominantly targeted at the first-time buyer and everything was done to make the transaction as easy as possible. Tom Baron commented that 'I'm always amazed at the way Lawrie Barratt has persuaded the rest of us that we are in a marketing business rather than a building business. He alone convinced the industry that it had to be market orientated'.[3] Geographical expansion in the 1970s was achieved through a series of acquisitions, the largest being Wardle in Lancashire and Janes in the northern Home Counties.

---

[2] Interview with Sir Cliff Chetwood, April 2000.
[3] Tom Baron interviewed in *Housebuilder*, Aug. 1986.

McLean, which had been acquired by the construction and quarrying group Tarmac at the beginning of 1974 to improve the performance of the latter's own housing operation, was now a comfortable third with around 4000 units a year; like Lawrie Barratt, McLean's Eric Pountain had also wanted to develop the firm as a national housebuilder since it became part of Tarmac, although the greatest volume gains were to come in the following decade. Although some of the pre-1974 leaders (Broseley, Leech, Bryant and Comben) had managed to sustain their volumes, others had experienced significant falls – Bovis and, in particular, Whelmar. Both Bovis Homes and Whelmar had come under the control of larger diversified groups (P&O and Salvesen, respectively) that were more concerned with restoring profitability than volume growth. In contrast, other companies were now coming into greater prominence. Wilson Connolly had built 1000 units for the first time in 1978, as had Westbury in 1980; both were being run by professional managers, Mike Robinson and Geoff Hester respectively, on behalf of the Wilson and Joiner founding families, and both firms had no other means of generating profit growth than via speculative housing. Fairview had been started by estate agents in the early 1960s concentrating entirely on the north London area; its strategy was unusual in that it responded to the recession by trebling its output to 1600 units between 1973 and 1975, selling its houses for what it could to liquidate the high cost land, and subsequently letting the volumes drift back as profit margins increased.

The private housing market – recovery

The collapse in demand in 1980 was short-lived and, although completions continued to fall in 1981, housing starts rose by 20%. Despite the rapid rise in unemployment in the early 1980s, the decade as a whole was one of substantial recovery for the private housebuilders both in volumes and pricing and, hence, profitability. Private completions rose from their 1981 low of 115,000 to a peak of 200,000 in 1988, with only a small fall in 1989 (Figure 5.2).

Once demand began to recover, house price inflation followed at a fairly steady 12% per annum between 1983 and 1987. In 1988, house prices rose around 30%, a rate that continued through the first half of 1989 (Figure 5.3). The volume and price growth created a boom in housebuilders' profits at the end of the 1980s that rivalled that of the early 1970s: between 1986 and 1988 the trading profits of the top five housebuilders trebled; as will be seen in Chapter 6, there were similar consequences.

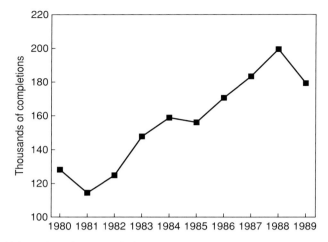

Figure 5.2   Private housing completions, 1979–1989.

Source: *Housing and Construction Statistics.*

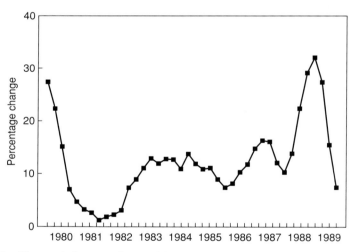

Figure 5.3   Change in house prices, 1979–1989.

Source: *Nationwide Building Society House Price Index.*

Which firms built the houses?

The increase in the size of the private housing market allowed the emergence of a greater number of medium and large housebuilders. Some 29 companies built over 1000 units in at least one year in the late 1980s; some 14 had built more than 2000 compared with six before 1974; and five companies had built more than 5000 against two. Managements that wanted to grow their business could do so in the context of rising housing demand and a stock market background that facilitated fundraising and acquisitions. The peak year for completions was slightly different from company to company but, in round figures, the top ten were producing 51,000 units a year at the end of the 1980s. With industry volumes substantially higher than a decade earlier, the market share was little changed at 27%. Despite the strength of the market, four of the top ten at the beginning of the decade did not survive. The founders of both Broseley and Whelmar were approaching retirement and their parents, an insurance company and food distribution company respectively, sold them. Comben, too, had found itself within an alien grouping (Hawker Siddeley) and was sold. Leech's profit performance had been poor and it fell to a takeover bid from Beazer.

Looking at Table 5.3 it can be seen that yet another new number one had emerged – Tarmac's McLean. Barratt had actually reached a peak of 16,500 units in 1983, over 10% of the total market, before two devastating television programmes nearly forced it out of business; Wimpey was no more than drifting. In contrast, some familiar names were being revived under new management teams – Ideal, now part of Trafalgar House, Laing Homes and, to a lesser extent, Costain; all three were part of wider groupings that had decided to give a new impetus to their private housing operations. The most striking new entry into the list was Beazer which, having built under 300 units a year at the end of the 1970s, had become the fourth largest housebuilder, as well as having significant interests in construction and building materials. The Beazer group was largely the creation of aggressive stock market acquisitions, including Monsell Youell, Second City Properties and William Leech as housebuilders, but also a range of building material and construction companies in the UK and USA. In contrast, Persimmon, formed by Duncan Davidson in 1974, reached its 2000 level predominantly through organic growth. Other 'new' companies to reach 1000 completions, primarily through organic growth, were the eponymous David Wilson and Bryan Skinner's Crest, dating from the early 1960s, and Steve Morgan's Redrow, which had been building houses for no more than ten years.

Two companies that have not previously been mentioned occupied specialist niches in the industry. McCarthy & Stone built its first sheltered housing for sale in 1976 and came to dominate its sector of the market. Lovell was a construction company that dated back to the eighteenth century but an acquisition in 1978 brought with it the small business of Rendell which had just completed a pioneering scheme for low cost housing for sale to council nominees in Swindon. Lovell built that business into a national operation and, with some conventional private housing as well, entered the top ten by unit volume.

Table 5.3 A league table of housebuilders *c.*1988: firms building 1000 units or more p.a.

Housebuilder	1987–89 average volume	Peak pre-recession volume
McLean/Tarmac	11,809	12,165
Wimpey	8589	9581
Barratt	6800	7000
Beazer	5968	6276
Ideal	4568	5153
Laing	3019	3436
Lovell	2991	3060
Bovis	2473	3000
Westbury	2305	2415
Wilcon	2194	2600
Top ten	**51,000**	
McCarthy & Stone	2116	2596
Bryant	2013	2150
Persimmon	1851	2043
Bellway	1687	1720
Costain	1593	2212
Fairclough	1474	1942
Raine	1379	1913
David Wilson	1372	1592
Crest	1364	1429
Clarke Homes	1317	1610
Top twenty	**67,000**	
Alfred McAlpine	1209	1350
Redrow	1113	1208
Galliford Estates	1061	1121
English China Clays	1041	1289
Walter Lawrence	1029	1176
Mowlem	967	1200
Croudace	958	1100
Wates	917	1100
Abbey	875	1027

General contractors without a significant presence in the private housing sector observed its rising profitability, contrasted it with the low margins available on construction, and bought their way into housing, often at a late stage in the housing cycle. Thus, Balfour Beatty created a housing company in 1986 and bought Clarke Homes in 1987; Alfred McAlpine, which had some small housing interests since the 1970s, bought the entrepreneurial business of Finlas in 1982 and the larger Canberra in 1988; and in 1986, Mowlem bought Unit Construction, Amec bought Hammerfine and Higgs & Hill bought Southend Estates. The contractors were back.

As in Chapter 4, this section concludes by looking at the fate of the top ten housebuilders from the previous chronological period. This time Table 5.4 shows a slightly different pattern. Whereas it had been the effect of war and

Table 5.4 What became of the early 1970s top ten?

Housebuilder	1973	1987–89 average
Wimpey	11,500	8590
Northern Developments	4000	Liquidated
Whelmar	3200	Sold
Bovis	2659	2470
Barratt	2500	6800
Broseley	2200	Sold
Leech	1888	Taken over
Bryant	1600	2010
Bardolin/E. Fletcher	1500	Sold
Bellway	c.1500	1690

planning controls that had impacted on the corporate structure of the industry, this time it was the 1974 recession and its aftermath that so substantially changed the fortunes of the top ten. Half of the companies were no longer: Whelmar, Broseley and Bardolin had been sold by their parents, the quoted Leech had been acquired by Beazer, and Northern Developments had gone into liquidation. Of the survivors, Barratt had become the new Wimpey, being the only housebuilder to achieve a substantial increase in volumes. In broad terms, Bovis, Bryant and Bellway were of a similar size while Wimpey, although still the industry leader, had entered a period of stagnation that was to last decades.

The emergence of the national housebuilder

Chapter 4 concluded with the observation that there was only one national housebuilder but several regional builders, particularly those covering the north of England. The second housebuilder to develop a national coverage was Barratt, first through acquisition and then through organic growth. With its concentration on marketing, Barratt led the change in the industry away from the production-driven attitudes that had characterised the post-war boom and by the early 1980s it was planning a national output of around 20,000 houses through a network of over 30 regional subsidiaries. Indeed, it was Barratt's national prominence that probably led to it being singled out for the television attacks that crippled its business.

It was not until the 1980s that another truly national housebuilder could be said to have arrived, in the shape of Tarmac's McLean; its regional offices had been increased to 16 by the end of the 1970s and they duly delivered their capacity of 8000 by the mid-1980s. McLean passed Wimpey and Barratt in 1987 to become the largest housebuilder, reached 12,000 units by

1988 and was planning for 15,000. Although its volumes were smaller, Beazer could also be regarded as a national builder. Starting from a small base (around 250 units in the late 1970s) in the West Country, a string of acquisitions took it through the Midlands and into the north; the acquisition of Leech gave it a structure, building just short of 5000 houses by 1986, and a stated strategy (in the 1985 rights issue document) to be a national: 'Your Board intends to consolidate the Company's position as a national housebuilder'. Ideal's volumes had been rebuilt under its Trafalgar House parent; the acquisitions of Comben and Broseley extended Ideal's coverage through the west, Midlands and north-west. Although there were gaps, it could more properly be regarded as a national rather than a regional housebuilder. There was also McCarthy & Stone which, although its volumes were much lower, had a national organisation for its specialised sheltered housing product. In all, that gave six companies that could be classed, at one stage or another, as national or near-national housebuilders.

Outside that grouping, there were another six to eight housebuilders that had strong regional coverage. Some had what looked like national coverage but it was thinly spread and required substantial infilling. Newcastle based Bellway had seven regions with a strong presence in the north-east and the London area; however, it was hardly present in the Midlands. Persimmon listed eleven regional offices in its 1989 accounts, ranging from Glasgow down to Crawley and across from Taunton to Lowestoft. The map suggested a national structure but the south-east was barely covered (5% of sales in 1988). Others with similar levels of output had extended more gradually from their home base, with a higher degree of concentration in the areas that were covered. For instance, Wilson Connolly, based in Northampton, had four regions, Midlands, Northern, Anglia and Southern but there was a heavy concentration around the original Midlands base whereas London and the southern Home Counties were barely covered. Westbury (Cheltenham) had a historically strong position in Gloucestershire and had expanded into South Wales (where it was one of the larger builders), the south-west and the Midlands.

6

Recession and Recovery Again, 1989–2004

Introduction

The house price boom at the close of the 1980s ended, as it did in the early 1970s, with a collapse in the housing market and a weakening of the corporate balance sheet. Key differences were that the fall in real house prices was translated into nominal prices so house buyers as well as house suppliers suffered losses. However, in contrast with the mid-1970s, the banks were more supportive of the corporate sector and immediate bankruptcies among the biggest companies were largely absent. Nevertheless, the financial shock, and land write-offs totalling around £2.5 billion, once again produced extensive change within the corporate sector: the 1990s saw the weak, particularly housebuilders owned by contractors, depart the industry; the financially stronger housebuilders consolidated their position. In a market which saw little overall change in demand, some of the more successful housebuilders substantially increased their volumes. By the end of the decade, there were fewer companies building over 1000 units but the top ten had increased their share of the market from 27% to 44%; the age of the national housebuilder had arrived (Table 6.1). Further consolidation took place in the opening years of the new millennium as companies used debt, with its low cost of finance, to buy housebuilders on high earnings yields, and the peak of 47% was reached in 2002. (Readers are referred back

Table 6.1 Change in industry concentration, late 1980s–2004.

Year	Top ten output	Top ten market share %	Firms building more p.a. than			
			1000	2000	5000	10,000
Late 1980s	51,000	27	29	14	5	1
1995	48,400	32	28	14	4	0
2000	63,300	44	25	14	5	2
2004	76,100	46	24	14	6	3

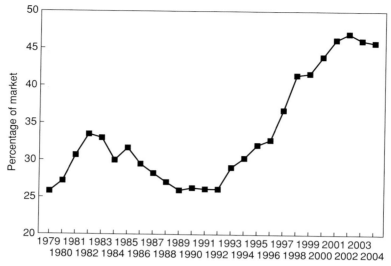

Figure 6.1   Top ten market share, 1979–2004.

to the social housing text in Chapter 1 for comments on the accuracy of the crude market share estimates, which probably now overstate the true position by around 3%.)

Without wishing to anticipate too much of the text, Figure 6.1 vividly illustrates the rise and fall in market share of the top ten in the 1980s and its rapid growth in the next decade, rising to a peak of 47% in 2002, or 44% if adjustment is made for social housing.

The private housing market – the collapse

The housing recession of the early 1990s mirrored that of 1974. The 30% fall in housing completions, from 200,000 in 1988 to 141,000 in 1992 was almost identical to the collapse between 1972 and 1974 (from 196,000 to 141,000). Housing completions had risen by some 60% between 1982 and 1988 and there was a final period of frenetic activity in 1988 as the Chancellor gave six months' notice of his intention to abolish double mortgage relief. House price inflation in 1988 and the first half of 1989 increased to an annual rate of 29%. Base rate had fallen to 7.5% in May 1988, its lowest for exactly ten years, but was progressively increased to 15% in October 1989, where it remained for a year; the mortgage rate peaked at 15.4% in March 1990. The exit from the exchange rate mechanism in September 1992 (when interest rates rose 5% in a day) marked the industry's low point. Private sector completions fell 30% from 200,000 in 1988 to a low of 141,000 in both 1992 and 1993. The fall in starts, a better indication of housebuilders' attitude to corporate life, almost halved, from 222,000 to 120,000.

A crucial distinction between the two recessions, which will be well known to all house-owners, is that house prices fell, for the first time in living memory, introducing the expression 'negative equity'. Real house prices had fallen in 1974 but the high rate of underlying inflation had not caused nominal house prices to fall. Between the third quarter of 1989 and the first quarter of 1995, the Nationwide house price index fell by 19%. The fall in the south-east started earlier and went deeper: 31% between the end of 1988 and the beginning of 1993. The impact on the value of unsold stock was considerable but even more so was the effect on land holdings. The value of land is a residual, being the difference between anticipated selling price and building cost. Like 1974, there were extensive write-offs and provisions. The 1994 *PHA* took the 29 companies that had built more than 700 units in their last pre-recession year and the results are summarised in Table 6.2. These companies made total provisions against their land and work in progress of £1 billion over a four-year period; on a pro rata basis that would have implied write-offs of £2.5 billion for the industry as a whole. Four housebuilders suffered write-offs of over £100 m. each with another seven exceeding £50 m.

Which firms built the houses?

As in the 1974 recession, 1990 and its aftermath produced a wave of corporate failures but this time the banking system stood behind their house-building clients to a greater degree, believing that their best chance of repayment lay in the management building out the assets in a controlled manner. Not one of the housebuilders that had been building over 1000 units a year in the late 1980s was forced into receivership. In total, some 28 housebuilders were building 1000 houses or more by 1995. Although there were no longer any companies building more than 10,000 units a year, there was roughly the same number building over 2000 and over 5000 as before the recession. The top ten accounted for a slightly lower number of completions than before, at around 48,000, but this represented a higher market share at 32%.

The forced bankruptcies may have been fewer than in the 1970s but the recession just as quickly changed the corporate order in the housebuilding industry. There were relatively few failures or acquisitions amongst the

Table 6.2   Housing provisions 1989–1994, £m.: companies building at least 700 units in 1988/89.

		1989–94 Total provisions	1989/90 No. of plots	Write-off per plot £	1989/90 No. of units
Tarmac/McLean	Dec.	132.1	26,000	5081	12,020
Wimpey	Dec.	71.3	24,500	2910	7100
Barratt	June	65.1	17,000	3829	6600
Beazer	June	118.5	18,000	6583	6070
Trafalgar House/Ideal	Sep.	54.0	13,500	4000	3400
Lovell	Sep.	55.3	5900	9373	2960
Laing	Dec.	66.7	7000	9529	2550
Westbury	Feb.	36.7	7500	4893	2300
Wilcon	Dec.	10.4	15,300	680	1800
Persimmon	Dec.	5.5	9700	567	1796
Bellway	July	9.3	4000	2325	1700
Bryant	May	23.0	7200	3194	1690
Bovis	Dec.	5.4	6000	900	1600
McCarthy & Stone	Aug.	13.6	2400	5667	1570
Amec	Dec.	107.0	5000	21,400	1480
Raine	June	3.5	4400	795	1400
Crest	Oct.	29.5	3000	9833	1320
Wilson Bowden	Dec.	—	6500	—	1220
Redrow	June	—	3800	—	1208
Bloor	Mar.	—	3500	—	1200
McAlpine, Alfred	Oct.	11.6	4500	2578	1100
Cala	June	6.5	1400	4643	900
Lawrence, Walter	Dec.	9.5	2400	3958	860
Mowlem	Dec.	16.3	2200	7409	850
Abbey	Apr.	15.3	1600	9563	800
Tay	June	—	4600	—	800
Heron	Mar.	58.3	10,000	5830	765
Church	Aug.	59.8	2050	29,171	740
Costain	Dec.	113.3	3000	37,767	700
Total		**1098**	**221,950**	**4945**	**68,499**

Source: *PHA* 1994.

medium-sized and larger housebuilders. Federated Homes (run successively by Leo Meyer's sons) went into receivership when its bankers discovered the extent of its commitments to buy land at pre-recession prices. Fairbriar, another smallish south-east housebuilder, initially went into administration, from which it emerged in 1991 after a £64 m. loss. Walter Lawrence was crippled by its American diversification and sold out to Raine Industries. Other disposals tended to be driven by wider groupings selling their house-building operations, sometimes from necessity, others from disillusion-ment. Thus, Costain Homes, having reduced volumes from 2200 to only 410, was sold to Redrow in 1993; the major part of the assets of Heron Homes (950 units before the recession) was sold by Gerald Ronson's Heron

Corporation to Taylor Woodrow in 1994; Sears sold Galliford to its management, who promptly sold it on to Prowting. The early years of the 1990s was the period when housebuilding share prices were at the most depressed. Yet of the top twenty housebuilders at the end of the 1980s, only Raine went on to make an acquisition (and that provided its downfall). That there were few quoted company takeovers reflects the fact that the potential buyers were more concerned with their own survival, and that they had the alternative of buying land at equally depressed prices without the administrative hassle that comes with corporate acquisitions.

Although there were few unequivocal exits from the industry, there was no lack of corporate downsizing. Those that survived, but only in straitened financial circumstances, tended to reduce volumes. Amongst the larger companies, McLean (part of Tarmac) and Ideal (within Trafalgar House) both halved their unit volumes compared with their pre-recession record. Examples from further down the list include McCarthy & Stone, supported by its banks, which saw volumes fall from 2600 to 900; Clarke Homes, by then part of BICC, down from 1600 to 400; and Wates, building little more than 200. ECC, having failed in its earlier bid to win Bryant, gradually ran down its housing and sold the rump to Higgs & Hill.

In complete contrast were a group of medium-sized housebuilders that had come through the recession with lowered profits but with their finances secure. Realising that there was little possibility of profit margins returning to the unsustainably high levels of the late 1980s, they saw that the only method of restoring, or even increasing, the absolute level of profits was to increase volumes substantially. In this, they were supported by shareholders, and funds were raised to buy land at low prices – often the land that the less successful companies were forced to sell. These include a group of housebuilders that could be described as 'two thousand going on four', in that they increased their volumes from around 2000 before the recession to around 4000 by the mid-1990s, all of which was achieved through organic growth. Bellway produced the fastest growth (120%), followed by Persimmon (76%), Bryant (74%) and Wilcon (49%).

There were even more dramatic increases further down the order. Fairview repeated the strategy it adopted in the previous recession and increased its volumes from 650 to 1950. Countryside, having seen its volumes halve in 1990 to 320, drove them up to 2200 in 1995 albeit largely through an increase in social housing. Newer companies were also emerging. Berkeley Homes, formed in 1976 to specialise in upmarket housing in the Home Counties, had increased its volumes from 600 in 1988 to 1400; Tay Homes, another 1976 creation, almost doubled its pre-recession output of 800; and

Table 6.3   Fundraising by quoted housebuilders 1990–1994.

Housebuilder	Year	Fundraising	Amount £m.
Bellway	1991	5 for 11 rights	25
	1993	2 for 7 rights	34
Berkeley	1991	3 for 7 rights	44
	1993	1 for 4 rights	44
Bryant	1990	1 for 4 rights	40
	1993	share placing	18
Cala	1994	1 for 5 rights	8
Countryside	1991	2 for 3 rights	20
	1993	3 for 11 rights	17
Crest	1994	1 for 4 rights	19
McCarthy & Stone	1991	3 for 8 rights	13
	1994	2 for 5 rights	16
Persimmon	1991	2 for 11 rights	33
	1993	share placing	11
	1994	2 for 11 rights	49
Westbury	1991	2 for 11 rights	33
	1993	share placing	11
	1994	2 for 11 rights	49
Wilcon	1992	share placing	17
Wilson Bowden	1991	1 for 7 rights	34
	1993	1 for 5 rights	57

Source: *PHAs*.

J.S. Bloor, formed in 1969, steadily increased its volumes through the recession to become the largest privately owned housebuilder in the country. None of these companies had owed much to acquisition.

The extent to which the stronger, in relative terms, were able to restore their balance sheets and take advantage of the land buying opportunities was considerably enhanced by their ability to raise funds via the stock market. Table 6.3 shows the fundraising that took place between 1990 and 1994.

And finally, we come to the product of that corporate change: Table 6.4 shows the list of housebuilders with output in excess of 1000 units in 1995; the right-hand column indicating the companies' relative positions in the period before the recession demonstrates the full extent of the changes that took place.

The private housing market – recovery

If the statistics for housing completions are examined for the 1990s, 'recovery' would not be the obvious descriptive word; there was virtually no change in volumes for ten years. Private sector housing completions in

Table 6.4 A league table of housebuilders in 1995: firms building 1000 units or more p.a.

Housebuilder	Annual output	Ranking 1988
Wimpey	7609	2
Beazer	6679	4
Barratt	6601	3
McLean/Tarmac	6140	1
Wilcon	3873	11
Bellway	3813	16
Bryant	3733	13
Persimmon	3593	12
Raine	3458	19
Lovell	2943	7
Top ten	**48,400**	
Westbury	2678	10
Ideal	2644	5
Redrow	2258	25
Countryside	2201	48
Bovis	1995	8
Fairview	1951	40
David Wilson	1916	18
Fairclough	1811	14
Crest	1717	20
Alfred McAlpine	1715	24
Top twenty	**69,000**	
Laing	1675	6
Tay	1559	39
Berkeley	1411	50
Bloor	1300	30
Wain	1300	33
Prowting	1154	38
Maunders	1089	37
Taylor Woodrow	1063	29

Note: The ranking is based on actual figures for 1988; the positions may therefore differ slightly from Table 5.2, which was based on the 1987–89 average.

Great Britain averaged 141,000 in the two years 1992–1993, the post-recession low point; after a period of modest growth, completions in the three years to 2003 averaged no more than 144,000. What did happen to the industry was financial rather than physical. By the mid-1990s, the land write-offs had all been made, house prices had stabilised and confidence was returning to the corporate sector. House buyers returned in greater numbers and, with planning restrictions restraining volumes, house prices and, hence, profits began to accelerate. The statement that housebuilding volumes were held back by planning restrictions rather than by a deliberate attempt by the companies to force up house prices might not be accepted by all, but it is the most rational explanation; for the purpose of this book, it is sufficient to note that volumes were static. With the rise in corporate profitability came the confidence to make acquisitions and the closing years of the millennium saw strong housebuilders acquiring the weak – the companies that had been supported by the banks during the recession but were not necessarily strong enough to retain shareholder confidence. Then followed a further period of consolidation in the industry as some of the stronger housebuilders used cheap medium term finance to purchase competitors.

Which firms built the houses?

The year 2000 is a natural point at which to close the analysis of the twentieth century, and it has so been recorded. However, further significant corporate activity took place in the succeeding years so, without wishing to replicate the annual function of the *PHA*, Table 6.5 also includes the

Table 6.5   A league table of housebuilders in 2000 and 2004: firms building 1000 units or more p.a.

Housebuilder	2000	Housebuilder	2004
Wimpey	11,437	Barratt	14,021
Barratt	10,636	Persimmon	12,360
Beazer	8223	Wimpey	12,232
Persimmon	7035	Taylor Woodrow	9053
Bellway	5714	Bellway	6610
Westbury	4435	David Wilson	5588
Wilcon	4215	Berkeley	4839
McAlpine	4007	Westbury	4400
Bryant	3961	Redrow	4284
David Wilson	3604	Bovis	2700
Top ten	**63,267**		**76,087**
Redrow	3330	Crest	2524
Berkeley	3210	Miller	2505
Bovis	2360	McCarthy & Stone	2055
Countryside	2122	Lovell	2051
Taylor Woodrow	1919	Fairview	1990
Miller	1844	Bloor	1916
Lovell	1815	Countryside	1911
Crest	1731	Gladedale	1874
Fairclough	1707	Fairclough	1547
Bloor	1700	Cala	1505
Top twenty	**85,005**		**95,965**
Prowting	1579	Cruden	1200
McCarthy & Stone	1539	Kier	1158
Fairview	1459	Morris	1100
Wain	1371	Linden	1018
Laing	1235		

position in 2004 to provide a fuller picture of the new industry structure. The number of companies building more than 1000 a year reduced a little through the period, but this reflects acquisitions within that group. The top ten increased their combined volumes to 63,000 in the year 2000, representing a crude market share of 44%; by the year 2002 market share had peaked at 47%. The number of companies building more than 2000 a year stayed constant at 14, but there was an increase in the over 5000 housebuilders and by 2004 there were three firms building over 10,000 a year. The average size of a top ten housebuilder was 7600 a year against around 5000 a year at the end of the 1980s boom.

The league table for 2000 reflected some striking departures from the 1995 list. McLean, the industry's largest housebuilder in 1988, and still number four in 1995, was absorbed within Wimpey the following year in exchange for Wimpey's construction and quarrying divisions; Raine was acquired in 1997 by Alfred McAlpine (later to fall to Wimpey); and Y.J. Lovell's housing was bought by Morgan Sindall in 1999 (although continuing to operate under its own name). Further down the scale, Ideal, the pre-war number one, had been bought by Persimmon in 1996, Maunders by Westbury (1998), and Fairclough by the American Centex (1999), only for Centex to sell it on to Miller in 2005. Of these acquisitions, all but one reflected weakness on the part of the seller – Maunders being the exception where the controlling shareholder sold ahead of fears that the incoming Labour Government would change the capital gains legislation. Raine, Lovell, Ideal (as part of Trafalgar House) and Fairclough had all been fundamentally weakened by the recession; Tarmac, also weakened, had wanted to focus on its traditional quarrying business.

By the end of the century, it looked as though the consolidation process may have run its course, but the opening year of the next decade saw yet more large acquisitions. Beazer and Bryant had announced their own merger plans in 2000, in what was described as a merger of equals. They were third and ninth respectively in the league table and their combined unit sales would have put them at the head of the industry. However, they had both suffered from managerial problems towards the end of the decade and were perceived to be 'in play'; instead of merging they fell respectively to Persimmon (briefly making it the number one by volume) and Taylor Woodrow. Subsequently, Taylor Woodrow rebranded its own housing under the Bryant name, but to avoid confusion this book continues to refer to Taylor Woodrow's housing under the parent company name. Having absorbed Bryant, Taylor Woodrow went on in 2003 to buy the industry's number seven, Wilson Connolly, yet another housebuilder forced to issue a profits warning at the top of the boom.

Wimpey went on to make two more acquisitions after its purchase of McLean: McAlpine Homes, again a product of a contractor wishing to focus its business, and Laing Homes, whose parent had been nearly crippled by the losses in its construction business. Despite these two acquisitions, Wimpey scarcely increased its UK volumes. Further down the scale both Wainhomes and Tay (which dropped below 1000 a year after 1995) experienced sharp profit falls from localised difficulties and fell victim to Wilson Connolly and Redrow in 2001. Finally, Prowting had to issue a profit warning in 2002 and it was only months before the controlling family sold to Westbury. In total, six of the 1995 top ten had lost their independence within a ten-year period.

The progress of those housebuilders that increased their volumes was, in part, the corollary of the failures above. Persimmon briefly headed the league table in 2001, by virtue of its acquisitions of Ideal and Beazer, and it remained the largest company by size of UK housebuilding profits in 2004.[1] To complete the circle, Wimpey was the volume leader in 2002; however, despite absorbing McLean, McAlpine Homes and Laing Homes, the enlarged entity built no more than Wimpey had on its own 20 years previously, and less than the pre-recession figure for McLean. Taylor Woodrow resumed its pre-war housing ranking with the purchase of Bryant, while Westbury had bought Clarke Homes and Maunders. But other companies within the top ten owed their growth to the organic development of the business. Barratt continued the steady rebuilding of its national position which had restarted with the return from retirement of Lawrie Barratt in 1991; at the time of writing it was once again the industry leader by number of completions and is almost back to the levels of 1983. Bellway had achieved another 50% growth in its volumes by 2000 and had trebled its pre-recession size; and in the same period, David Wilson had just about doubled with the help of only one small acquisition. Berkeley, which before the recession had been building only a few hundred houses a year in the stockbroker towns of the south-east, had turned itself into an urban regenerator in London and the provinces, was just outside the top ten by units in 2000 and by 2004 stood as the fifth largest housebuilder by turnover.

There are also names in Table 6.5 that have not been encountered so far in this book. Those with a long memory might recall Miller from the pre-war list, now revived under Keith Miller and one of the few remaining examples of a reasonably successful contractor/developer hybrid. Apart from

---

[1] The acquisition of Westbury in January 2006 is expected to make Persimmon once again number one by volume. In December 2005, Persimmon became the first housebuilder to enter the FTSE 100.

Miller, there are some seven new names in the table. Kier is another that has opted for the contracting/developer hybrid structure. As French Kier, it had been acquired by Beazer in 1985 but was then demerged in 1993, solely as a contractor. It almost immediately began to rebuild its housebuilding through a series of small acquisitions, including Twigden and Bellwinch, which took it through the 1000 mark in 2004. Of the new names, Kier is the only one with quoted status, although Cala and Linden had both been quoted before their MBOs in the late 1990s. The contrast in history between these two could not be more stark. Cala dates back to 1875 as the City of Aberdeen Land Company, although it took another 100 years before speculative housebuilding started. Linden was only formed in 1991, by Philip Davies, one-time head of McAlpine Homes, backed by venture capital funds. The north-west Morris Homes had a tangled history since its formation in 1964 but, under the leadership of Mike Gaskell since 1993, it has steadily expanded, and the purchase of Allen Homes in 2000 virtually doubled its size.

We then have two housebuilders that produced just short of 2000 units each in 2004, Bloor and Gladedale, with entirely different histories. John Bloor was a plasterer by trade who began housebuilding in the late 1960s. All the company's growth has been organic and, although one of the consistently profitable housebuilders of the late twentieth century, John Bloor is best known for his rescue of the Triumph motorcycle brand. Gladedale, in contrast, has expanded substantially by acquisition, financed on bank borrowings. It was formed by Remo Dipre, one-time owner of Fairbriar, and at the end of the 1990s was only building around 60 units a year. The acquisition of the London-based Furlong was the first step but it was the acquisition of Bett Group (920 units) in 2003 that took Gladedale to well over 1000 units a year, and the acquisition of Country & Metropolitan (760 units) early in 2005 may be just enough to take Gladedale into the industry's top ten – a remarkable achievement in just a few years. The last company to be mentioned is the Scottish Cruden, a substantial builder of industrialised council housing in the post-war period. Private housebuilding was not started until the late 1960s and still only amounts to around 2000–3000 a year; however, there is a substantial social housing operation and it is that which has taken Cruden to over 1000 units a year.

As in the earlier chapters, this section finishes with a retrospective look at the previous period's top ten. The earlier text has covered most of the events, but Table 6.6 does highlight, as did its equivalents in earlier chapters, just how quickly the industry leaders can fall. There were six straight takeovers, including five of the top seven, and each one was a product of financial weakness, albeit more often at a group rather than an operating

Table 6.6   What became of the late 1980s top ten?

Housebuilder	1987–89 average	2004
McLean	11,809	Taken over by Wimpey
Wimpey	8589	12,232
Barratt	6800	14,021
Beazer	5968	Taken over by Persimmon
Ideal	4568	Taken over by Persimmon
Laing	3019	Taken over by Wimpey
Lovell[a]	2991	2051
Bovis[b]	2473	2700
Westbury[c]	2305	4400
Wilcon	2194	Taken over by Taylor Woodrow

[a] Bought by Morgan Sindall but still trading separately   [b] Demerged from P&O   [c] A takeover by Persimmon was announced in November 2005.

level. Lovell did continue as an entity in its own name, and Bovis likewise changed ownership, having been demerged in 1997 from P&O into the quoted arena. Thus, there were only three of the top ten that had not changed ownership and, of those, only Barratt achieved significant organic growth.

The era of the national housebuilder

It has already been stated that the top ten housebuilders had reached around 44% of national output by the end of the century. All of the top ten can be said to operate nationally or near nationally, with clearly defined regional structures. The larger companies would typically have a tiered structure with a number of local companies reporting to a regional managing director or chairman who in turn reports to the group managing director. In 2004, Barratt, for instance, had four regions each with six or seven companies, plus Kingsoak comprising two divisions of five companies each. Persimmon had two entirely independent north and south regions, comprising 12 and 14 operating companies respectively with its separately branded division (Charles Church) having a further nine. Most of the remaining companies building in excess of 1000 units a year have varying degrees of semi-national coverage and it is only Fairview that has taken the policy decision to remain in its home (London) area.

7

Market Share Through the Century: a Summary

The chronological chapters in Part I have charted the progression of the industry's leading companies. The source material becomes more accurate as the century progresses but the corporate data are sufficiently robust to present a meaningful picture of change and consolidation within the housebuilding industry from the 1930s onwards, summarised in Table 7.1. Ball's assertion, made over 20 years ago, that 'It is very difficult to give a broad outline of the speculative housebuilding industry as . . . the number of volume builders . . . cannot be discovered',[1] is no longer valid. For the first time, it is possible to show the absolute volumes and the market share of the top ten housebuilders from the inter-war period through to the end of the twentieth century. In addition, the table shows the number of house-builders within the size ranges 1000, 2000, 5000 and 10,000 units.

Table 7.1 Market share summary, 1930s–2004.

	Top ten volume units	Top ten %	Number of firms building more than			
			1000	2000	5000	10,000
1930s	16,000–18,000	6–7	c.10	c.3	1	0
1960	14,000–16,000	8–9	4–5	2	1	0
1965	17,000–18,000	8–9	10–12	1	1	0
1973	32,000–33,000	17–18	26	6	1	1
1980	36,000	28	13	4	2	1
1988	51,000	27	29	14	5	1
1995	48,400	32	28	14	4	0
2000	63,500	44	25	14	5	2
2004	76,100	46	24	14	6	3

---

[1] Ball, 'The Speculative Housebuilding Industry', p. 31.

Within an industry that saw its volumes halve between the 1930s and the end of the century, the top ten housebuilders (an ever changing list) had quadrupled their collective volumes and increased their market share from 6% or 7% to 44%. Although there remained an abundance of local firms, from the 1960s the industry saw the emergence of first regional and then national housebuilders. Whereas no housebuilder had achieved volumes of 10,000 a year before the 1970s, there are now three in excess of that number; there were six companies building over 5000 a year against one before the war; and from the late 1980s, a steady 14 companies building over 2000 a year compared with three in the 1930s.

It is not surprising that the pre-war housebuilders were smaller in size than housebuilders of the last 20 or 30 years. The 1930s housebuilding market was still a local market: 'the builders of British towns were, by 1939, for the most part, still experiencing only the early stages of competition from non-local firms. And most of that competition was from nearby towns.'[2] However, local operation did not mean small scale; the housebuilders did not need to be large enterprises to support large-scale production units. The pre-war housebuilders all operated off very large sites, often with only a few in full flow. Many of the London sites ran into thousands of houses, for example Costain's Elm Park of 5000 houses. In the mid-1930s Wimpey was operating off nine sites for its 1300 units, averaging around 150 a site per year, while Ideal was producing 5700 houses in 1934 on its 16 sites, an average of 350 per site per year. In reality, as some of those sites would be finishing and some starting, the active sites would have an even higher annual throughput. In comparison, a housebuilder producing, say, 5000 units a year today could well be operating off more than 200 individual sites. Although large sites do still exist, they are few and far between and with around 70% of the industry's output accounted for by 'brownfield' land there are probably little more than 50,000 units a year now being built on 'greenfield' land. The industry has changed from mass building on large open spaces on the edge of conurbations to a process that relies more heavily on infilling and reusing sites. The irony is that the post-war corporate consolidation of the industry has been accompanied by a significant reduction in the average size of the 'production unit' or site.

World War II and the controls that followed had a profound influence on the structure of the speculative housing industry. Housebuilding stopped for the duration and the requirements of a wartime economy meant an increase in specialist construction, especially airfields and the Mulberry

---

[2] Whitehand, 'Makers of British Towns', p. 435.

Harbour. The more dynamic firms of housebuilders became successful contractors, sometimes even international in scope. By the early 1950s, when the post-war speculative housebuilding boom started, these firms were dominated by contractors who looked down on housebuilding; death and old age had killed off other firms: the pre-war leaders were not necessarily the people to lead the post-war revival. Although Taylor Woodrow and Ideal tried to resume where they had left off, by the end of the 1960s only Wimpey remained in the top ten. Table 7.1 shows that by the mid-1960s, the output of the top ten was little more than it had been in the 1930s although with lower industry output the market share was two or three points higher.

It was not until the late 1960s and early 1970s that the volumes of the top ten significantly increased as firms created in the post-war era, such as Barratt, Whelmar (both of which relied on acquisitions) and Broseley, rapidly increased their volumes into the 2000–4000 unit range; indeed, five of the top six housebuilders were firms that had not built before the war. The market share of the top ten had doubled to 18% and as a measure of the abundance of medium-sized firms there were 26 housebuilders building more than 1000 units a year compared with ten before the war. It was the post-war boom that also marked the arrival of the regional housebuilder, and by 1973 most of the medium to large housebuilders were semi-national; Barratt, for example, built widely across the north of England. One or two housebuilders, for example Bovis, claimed national status, while others, such as Carlton and Bardolin, aspired to it; however, only Wimpey had the coverage to claim legitimately to be a national housebuilder.

Since 1973 the housebuilding industry has suffered two devastating recessions (for convenience, noted as 1974 and 1990) and the concomitant company failures accelerated the process of corporate change as the culling of established firms enabled others to take their place at the top table. The recessions and their aftermath also provided the opportunity for the strong to acquire the weak: those managements that had the ambition to expand regionally could use their Stock Exchange status to feed in the corporate pond. In the 1970s, industry output collapsed, but the top ten managed to hold their volumes (largely a result of Barratt's growth) and, in consequence, they increased their share of the reduced market to 28%. When the strong recovery in the housing market occurred in the 1980s, the top ten's volumes rose in line with the industry; Tarmac and Beazer led the unit growth and by then all the top ten housebuilders exceeded 2000 units a year. Moreover, during this period two more firms, Tarmac and Barratt, had developed national coverage and exceeded 10,000 units a year, albeit Barratt was subsequently damaged by adverse television coverage. Although their volumes were smaller, at around 5000–6000 units a year, both Ideal and Beazer also built across the country, while below them were a number of sizeable regional businesses planning on national status. The national housebuilder had started to arrive.

After the 1990 recession, as happened in the 1970s, the top ten held their volumes and therefore increased market share, which rose to 32% by 1995. Although the second half of the 1990s saw a housing boom in the sense that house prices rose, industry volumes showed little change. However, the increased profitability of the corporate sector, and the low cost of finance, facilitated a wave of mergers, for example Persimmon's acquisition of Ideal and then Beazer propelled it into industry leadership, while Wimpey's acquisition of Tarmac's McLean allowed it to restore volumes to earlier levels. By the end of the century, all the top ten could claim to be national housebuilders.

As well as illustrating the rise in concentration, the chronological league tables have also recorded the considerable change in the composition of the leading housebuilders. Table 7.2 lists the top ten housebuilders in each time period with their respective positions and, with the exception of Wimpey, the table demonstrates the lack of continuity at the top. Of the 1930s top ten companies, only four (Davis, Ideal, Taylor Woodrow and Wimpey) were in the 1960 top ten, and only Wimpey consistently remained in these league tables. The same pattern can be observed at each chronological stage. Thus, of the 1960 list, only Bellway, Whelmar and Wimpey remained in the 1974 top ten. From the pre-1974 top ten, again only three were in the late-1980s list (Bovis, Barratt and Wimpey); and of that late-1980s top ten, only four were still represented in 2004 (Barratt, Bovis, Westbury and Wimpey). In all, 38 housebuilders appeared in one or more of the top ten listings. Of those 38, only 13 were extant at the time of writing – and two of those were under different ownership; while another couple build less than 200 units a year. Corporate change has been extensive and leadership has often proved transient. The reasons underlying this corporate change, both growth and decline, provides the subject of Part II.

A note on the NHBC data

Since 1979, the aggregate company data contained in this book can be cross-checked with NHBC data. There are occasional references in the literature to data from earlier periods but these are not supported by the NHBC archives. The NHBC gives the number of builders in different size categories, the two largest being 501–2000 units a year and over 2000, and the share of total starts taken by each category. There is no NHBC category

Table 7.2 Top ten housebuilders: a chronological record, 1930s–2004.

Housebuilder	1930s	1960	1965	Pre-74	1980	1987–89	1995	2000	2004
Ideal	1	2	3		9	5			
Boot	2								
Wates	3								
Taylor Woodrow	4	9							4
Davis	5	10	7						
Wimpey	6	1	1	1	2	2	1	1	3
Mactaggart & Mickel	7								
Costain	8								
Crouch	9								
Laing	10						6		
MRCE/Whelmar		3	2	3	10				
Janes		4	4						
John Lawrence		5	5						
McLean		6			3	1	4		
Gough Cooper		7							
Bellway		8		10			6	5	5
Hallmark			6						
Fell			8						
Fletcher			9						
Page-Johnson			10						
Northern Developments				2					
Bovis				4	5	8			10
Barratt				5	1	3	3	2	1
Broseley				6	4				
Leech				7	6				
Bryant				8	7		7	9	
Bardolin				9					
Comben					8				
Beazer						4	2	3	
Lovell						7	10		
Westbury						9		6	8
Wilcon						10	5	7	
Persimmon							8	4	2
Raine							9		
David Wilson								10	6
McAlpine								8	
Berkeley									7
Redrow									9

that matches the 1000 and above used in this book, their most relevant being builders over 2000; that shows a rise from 24% in 1979 to a peak of 50% in 2003, falling to 48% in 2004.

As can be seen from Figure 7.1, the number of housebuilders identified as building more than 2000 units in any one year is similar for both sources, often being the same and rarely more than two apart. Any discrepancy can

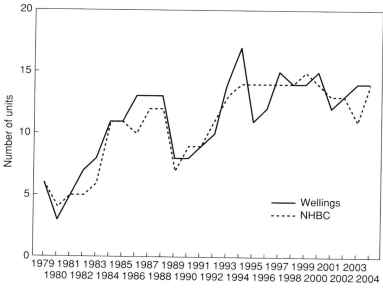

Figure 7.1   A comparison of NHBC and Wellings data (number of firms building more than 2000 units).

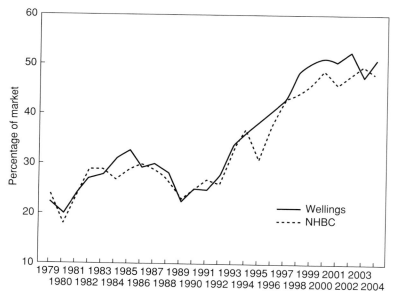

Figure 7.2   A comparison of NHBC and Wellings data (market share of firms building more than 2000 units).

be explained by reference to Chapter 1, in particular, differences between starts and sales, and year ends. In some years the Wellings data contain companies building only 50 units above or below the 2000 limit and it is easy to see how a marginally different definition would change the ranking. Further small differences may arise from the inclusion of social housing within the published sales totals by some housebuilders, while the NHBC has only 85% coverage of the industry.

The percentage market share for the two data sets is also similar (Figure 7.2). It is subject to the same differences discussed above which become more noticeable when demand changes sharply.

A note on overseas comparisons

This book covers the British speculative housing market only[3], but the author is not aware of any other developed economies where speculative housebuilders have achieved the same degree of concentration. Indeed, in many markets the structure of the housebuilding industry is quite different from that of Great Britain. Martens' survey of private housing in western Europe noted substantial variations between the individual countries but the differences were 'especially marked between Britain and the rest of Europe'.[4] It was not just that the UK had the highest proportion of owner occupiers, and was unusual in its speculative building boom of the 1930s; from the standpoint of this book, the crucial distinction is in the nature of the supply of private housing. In the Netherlands, West Germany and France, the housebuilding industry is dominated by contractors rather than by speculative housebuilders: 'the latter are, in a European context, a specific British phenomenon.'[5]

The British speculative housebuilder does find a parallel in the USA, where it is sometimes called a merchant builder. The US market still differs from the UK by virtue of its size and less restrictive planning and it is therefore more common to find some firms purchasing large tracts of land, landscaping and providing services (roads, utilities etc.) and selling off lots to other builders. Nevertheless, there remain the essential economic similarities with the UK industry – the speculative purchase of land well in advance of sales, the wholesaling and development function and the range of independent and (often) quoted companies. US concentration levels are discussed

---

[3] The industry statistics used are for Great Britain, not the UK; there has been almost no involvement in the Northern Ireland housebuilding by the mainland firms.
[4] Martens, 'Owner Occupied housing in Europe', p. 605.
[5] Ibid., p. 608.

by Grebler (1973) and Buzzelli (2001) and contemporary data can be found in *Professional Builder*. The top ten housebuilders had only around a 5–6% market share in the early 1980s, a figure that changed little until the late 1990s. By 2001, the top ten market share had risen to 10% and even the top 50 produced no more than 17%.

Part II   Analysis

8

Who Were the Builders?

Introduction

This is a book about entrepreneurs, successful and otherwise, and Chapter 8 provides the background to the builders themselves. The concept of the dominant individual is developed to describe the creator of growth: it can be the founder, a later generation, or in some cases a paid manager. This avoids the more familiar taxonomy of family and non-family firms which sometimes equates entrepreneurial drive with the former. Finally, the chapter charts the routes by which the dominant individual in housebuilding firms arrive, be they founders, inheritor generations, acquired entrepreneurs or managers.

The entrepreneurial character of the housebuilding industry is epitomised by the continued success, at the end as at the beginning of the twentieth century, of first generation firms and trade- and skill-based management. Jeremy's chapter on entrepreneurs and management concluded that for most of the twentieth century, UK business leaders came from the middle and professional classes; that in the first half of the century the public schools were disproportionately responsible for educating business leaders; and that in the largest companies the chairmen and managing directors were two or three times more likely to have been to university than managers.[1] This is far removed from the profile of the dominant individual in the housebuilding industry. Jeremy also referred to apprenticeship as the traditional form of training, which had reached its peak by the mid-1960s, after which it fell into disfavour and 'precipitate decline'. However, if there was one single route by which the twentieth-century housing developers entered the industry it was as tradesmen.

---

[1] Jeremy, *A Business History of Britain 1900–1990s*, pp. 378–408.

Given the large number of very small businesses in the housebuilding industry, it is not surprising that founders tend to be trade-related, although as firms grew in size, and further education extended its reach, those running housebuilding firms were more likely to be educated to a higher standard. However, the professional manager, with general rather than industry-specific skills, remained a small minority throughout the period under study. Surprisingly, there is more evidence of the generalist being at the helm of the larger pre-war housebuilders than tradesmen, possibly because there was not then a pool of tradesmen who had been accustomed to working with large housebuilders.

The post-war period saw the larger housebuilders predominantly run by tradesmen, building-related professionals and a sprinkling of accountants. From the 1960s, surveyors and estate agents (qualified or not) feature more prominently as the skills involved in land assembly and acquisition became more important. There were also lawyers and accountants, but these tended to be entrepreneurs who provided either the finance or the professional management, rather than starting a business themselves. Surprisingly, by the end of the century there was an increase in the number of first generation founders running the larger companies, and the founders continue to include people with no post-school qualifications.

The dominant individual within the housebuilding firm

This section examines the characteristics of the people that both founded and developed the housebuilding businesses, typically the entrepreneur who has been accorded an increasingly central role in the theory of the firm. Nomenclature can confuse: entrepreneurs may be equated with the founder, but they may be later generations or even managerial. Nor is the distinction between family and non-family firms the proxy for entrepreneurship that some of the literature implicitly suggests. Indeed, Casson admitted that 'although the family firm has long been an important feature of business enterprise, the concept is rarely defined in a rigorous . . . way.'[2] However, his own definition, which centred around the proportion of shares held by family members, does not fully capture the dynamics of control which is more often determined by the personality of the leader.

What is often forgotten when defining individual (or family) control by reference to the percentage holding in the business, is that the shareholding

---

[2] Casson, *Enterprise and Leadership*, p. 197.

may be substantially reduced without the individual ever losing his dominating influence. No better example could be provided than Frank Taylor, who sold most of his holding in Taylor Woodrow before the war but continued to dominate the group until the end of the 1980s – even after standing down in an executive capacity. Frank Taylor was probably unusual in the sale of so much of his personal holding so early in the development of his firm but many controlling shareholdings reduced in absolute size in the 1980s and 1990s through share sales, but especially in percentage terms as firms used their Stock Exchange quotations to raise additional capital through 'rights' issues or to make acquisitions for shares. Barratt's early success was built on acquisitions and by 1985 the directors held only 1% of the share capital; also as a result of acquisitions, Brian Beazer held less than 2% of his 'family firm' by 1989. Two companies that floated in the 1980s and went on to be among the most successful in the industry also saw substantial reductions in directors' shareholdings: in 1985, directors held 52% of Berkeley and 62% of Persimmon; by 2004, this had reduced to 2% and 7% respectively. Retirement of other directors had contributed to the reduction but in each case the dominant founder was still on the Board. Of the 13 quoted housebuilders in 2003 the average holding by directors was under 5% and in only two cases was there a holding of over 10%.[3]

The characteristics of 'the business leader' were summarised by David Jeremy, who had studied enough of them in his capacity as editor of the *Dictionary of Business Biography*. He reported that interest in leadership first centred on 'the traits of the great person' citing Barnard's study of the chief executive in the late 1930s which had argued that the individual was more important than the situation. The most common traits observed were 'intelligence, initiative, self-assurance and . . . the ability to rise above the details of a situation'.[4] Jeremy noted that the 'trait theory' fell out of favour to be replaced by 'style theories of leadership' which suggested that, 'a democratic style will show a better response from employees than an authoritarian style'. It is unlikely that such theorists ever worked on a building site.

Maude's description seemed more relevant, at least for the early stage of a housebuilding company, describing 'rough, tough leadership' as highly effective – his examples specifically include construction gangs where threats, punishment and 'energetic man-to-man influence' may be needed to sustain control.[5] Maude offered a more encompassing description of the

---

[3] *PHA* 2004.
[4] Jeremy, *A Business History of Britain 1900–1990s*, p. 381.
[5] Maude, *Leadership in Management*, p. 103.

authoritarian style, describing successful leaders in industry as intensely individualistic in ideas, tastes and lifestyles with strong opinions about their own companies, industry in general, the unions, the government, politics, society. But despite their individual ideas, a pattern emerges amongst these leaders: they work long hours with 'drive and diligence', are extremely competitive, and have 'an intense desire to succeed.'[6] For those starting in the housebuilding industry, literally and metaphorically, at grass-roots level, the ability to exercise personal authority over what is an extremely independent labour force can be paramount. Descriptions of authoritative personae abound in the individual company histories: 'a steely individual who is not easily crossed' (Brian Beazer);[7] 'a very hard-nosed man who ruled the company with a rod of iron – a very tough character' (Arthur Davis);[8] 'a rugged individualist' (Leo Meyer);[9] 'through force of character and a gift for publicity, Mactaggart became established in those years as one of the most prominent figures in Scottish housebuilding' (John Mactaggart); [10] 'tough and feisty' (Steve Morgan);[11] 'quick-thinking and decisive, he doesn't suffer fools gladly' (Jack Bradley).[12] These characteristics of a dominant individual remained evident even after retirement: 'The self-possession and charisma . . . were difficult to resist even after he had relinquished an executive role' (Frank Taylor).[13]

Over the years, the author has met literally hundreds of business leaders and it is not easy to generalise about their personality. The descriptions above fit many of them; strong personalities abound but the way in which those personalities express themselves can be very different. Lawrie Barratt, for instance, one of the industry's strongest post-war leaders, has been described as 'almost diffident at times'.[14] This book recognises the descriptions of leadership, but they are not sufficient to explain success: unfortunately for those engaged in forecasting, the analytical difficulty is that many of the failures also share the same personality traits as the successful; indeed, some of those quoted above did fail – and spectacularly. Strong and charismatic leadership may be the sine qua non of the successful entrepreneur but it is a misunderstanding to equate it with success. The crucial differences between managerial successes and failures lie in

---

[6] Ibid., Preface.
[7] *Management Today*, Oct. 1986, p. 142.
[8] Interview with Paul Bliss, May 1999.
[9] Edward Erdman, *People and Property*, p. 27.
[10] Watters, *Mactaggart & Mickel and the Scottish Housebuilding Industry*.
[11] Burland, *The Redrow Group*, p. 8.
[12] *Yorkshire Evening Press*, 27th May 1968.
[13] *Financial Times*, 16th Feb. 1995.
[14] *Building*, April 1982.

the exercise of the leader's judgement, and this is discussed more fully in the final chapter. The historian has the benefit of hindsight (although not in itself a foolproof tool); in trying to forecast which leaders would prove successful, it has always seemed more productive to assess the leader's strategic judgement than his personality.

Founders are the most recognisable dominant individuals within business but there can be a grey area between the nominal founder and the effective founder; it may actually be a later generation that takes a small existing business and grows it. Sometimes the dominant individual in an organisation arrives through the acquisition of a smaller but more dynamic and entrepreneurial company. And, although less common, there are striking examples of managerial dominant individuals. Most of the successful housebuilding firms that started in the inter-war period fell into the founder category, which is not surprising as this was the period when the modern speculative housebuilding industry came into being. Notable examples were Arthur Davis of Davis Estates; Leo Meyer, who rapidly made Ideal Homesteads the largest of the pre-war housebuilders; Frank Taylor, who created the international construction group Taylor Woodrow; the eponymous William Leech; and, of course, Godfrey Mitchell – although to be strictly accurate, he bought the existing road making firm of George Wimpey to start his construction career.

Post-war examples of the dominant founder are legion and one can instance Derek Barnes of Northern Developments, perhaps second only to Wimpey in 1974 before it crashed; Lawrie Barratt, an accountant who made Barratt Developments the largest ever housebuilder; Danny Horrocks, whose Broseley was controlled by an insurance company for most of its existence; Dennis Cope, an estate agent who built up Fairview Estates; Duncan Davidson, one-time pageboy at the Coronation, who sold his first company to Comben before founding Persimmon which he took to number one in the industry by 2001; and Steve Morgan, who took his small contracting company Redrow into housing development in the early 1980s, liquidating most of his holding in the company between 1995 and 2000. Occasionally the founders were two individuals, often of disparate temperaments or skills, who reinforced each other, for example James Comben and William Wakeling in the inter-war period and Jim Farrer and Tony Pidgley of Berkeley some 50 years later.

Sometimes the dominant individual was a second, or even later, generation in a previously small family business. Norman Wates and John Laing provide good examples from the inter-war period. Norman Wates was educated at Emmanuel School Wandsworth and received some accountancy training before turning the little family firm into one of the pre-eminent London housebuilders; John Laing actually joined his father at the end of the nineteenth century and backed his grammar school education with an apprenticeship to a bricklayer and a mason. Post-war examples are provided by Brian Beazer and David Wilson: the former entered his father's Bath-based firm as company secretary after a spell in the City, while David Wilson joined his father, having abandoned plans to become a dentist. These last two examples illustrate the difficulty in distinguishing between founder and second generation. Brian Beazer entered a long established, albeit localised, construction business and could not be regarded as any-thing other than second generation; David Wilson joined no more than a carpentry workshop where his father employed only four or five people and common sense would suggest that he should more properly be regarded as a founder. Also difficult to disentangle are businesses where the second generation has founded the business and then brought in the father; for instance, John T. Bell (later Bellway) was founded by brothers in 1946, nam-ing the company after their father.

Another entry route for the dominant individual is for his small business to be acquired by a larger concern. He may have been a founder of the acquired business but then moves to a salaried position; often with a shareholding in the larger entity, he occupies a halfway house. Frank Sanderson came into Bovis when his housebuilding company was acquired in 1967. He rapidly expanded the housebuilding operation, became group managing director in 1970 only to expand the group to the verge of bankruptcy. When Bovis was rescued by P&O in 1974, Sanderson had no more than a 5% shareholding. Eric Pountain's route to managing director of Tarmac was more tortuous. He had joined the Wolverhampton estate agents Maitland Selwyn as a sales executive, going on to become joint principal, and founding the housebuilding business of Midland & General Developments. Midland & General was acquired by McLean in 1969; McLean's profits fell that year, precipitating a boardroom coup and Eric Pountain replaced Geoffrey McLean as managing director. In 1973, McLean in turn was acquired by Tarmac specifically for its development skills. In 1977, Pountain was appointed to the main Board and when Tarmac's construction business went into deficit, yet another boardroom coup (in 1979) saw Pountain appointed group managing director; with no more than a nominal share-holding, he dominated the group until 1992 when he, in turn, was eased out of his position.

The driving force of a company is not necessarily an entrepreneur in the sense of someone who owns all or part of the business; the person respons-ible for growing the business may be managerial. Livesay pointed out that individuals do often control massive corporate bureaucracies, many prevailing without benefit of ownership position; he argued that the long run success of major corporations depended more 'on the ability to attract and hold people with the right combination of talent and personality than on any particular form of corporate organisation.' He went on to argue that, regardless of firm size, it was 'dominant individuals' that held the key to success.[15] The expression 'dominant individual' is therefore used on occasion in this book to describe the individual who has control of the business entity for a long period of time, the person who literally dominates the decision making, although not necessarily the ownership of the firm. Whereas the increasing role of managerial staff through the twentieth century is extensively discussed in the literature of the firm, there is little quantitative discussion as to the extent of the 'professionalisation' of the leader's role. It is hard, therefore, to tell whether, compared with other small to medium sized enterprises, the housebuilding industry was slow to move away from founders or family successors as business leaders.

There is little evidence of salaried directors running housebuilders before the Second War. Early post-war examples of salaried administrators taking over the management as founders aged, became incapacitated, or developed other interests included accountants John Adamson at Leech and Ernest Uren at Laing, and a buyer, John Boardman, at Gough Cooper. Other salaried directors were specifically recruited for the benefit of their already established talents. The key figure in Bryant's post-war housing history was Roy Davies, who ran Bryant Estates from 1958 until he retired in 1987, serving under Chris Bryant, himself third generation. Westbury, which was founded by the Joiner family in the late 1960s, was always run by salaried professionals, first Geoff Hester (a surveyor) then Richard Fraser (an accountant) who led the business out of family ownership in 1984.

Within the housebuilding industry, one of the best examples of a managerial dominant individual was Wilson Connolly's Mike Robinson. Lynn Wilson had become sole managing director of Wilson (Connolly) in 1970 on the death of his father and later that year Wilson, only 26 years old at the time, recruited Mike Robinson as chief executive of the construction and housing division. Robinson had a first in civil engineering from London University and was then working for Page-Johnson. Lynn Wilson said that:

'I realised that the executives my father had merely took his instructions and were not capable of running the thing without his direction.

---

[15] Livesay, 'Entrepreneurial Dominance in Business', pp. 2, 4.

I realised that if you are a public company then you have to perform. I wanted to be first division so you have to get first division management. I don't know that I ever said to myself I can't do this but what I did say was that I definitely need some help.'[16]

Robinson became group managing director and created one of the most successful housebuilding companies of the 1980s. After his sudden death in 1990, the Company proved as unsuccessful without him as it had been successful with him. (The firm was taken over by Taylor Woodrow in 2003.)

From the discussion above, it will be clear that labels are not, and cannot be, prescriptive. Categorisation becomes a matter of degree, particularly when ownership and management overlap: it has to be recognised that any classification ultimately relies on subjective judgement. There will be individuals that have played a prominent role in a company for a significant period in its history without their names necessarily being synonymous with the company. There are also housebuilding entities that have been run without the benefit of a dominant individual, as in the later histories of Costain Homes and Wates. The next section explores in more detail who were the dominant individuals in the larger housebuilding firms, and their backgrounds.

Despite the occasional claims of their leaders, no industry is unique. However, the continually moving production base, such a marked contrast with most fixed-base industries, and the capital commitment to land, which may be purchased years before it can be processed, gives the speculative housebuilding industry a distinctive character and makes it a fertile field for the observation of entrepreneurial talent and judgement. These features underpin the analysis in the later chapters of Part II, particularly Chapter 12.

The housebuilders – pre-war

Who were the new breed of estate developers? In an analysis of 57 housebuilders operating within the London area Bundock wrote that:

'Prior to 1913, it is probable that the vast majority of speculative housebuilding firms had been founded [by craftsmen] while between the wars there can be no doubt that the tradition continued, although to a lesser extent and in a more adulterated way.'

---

[16] Interview with Lynn Wilson, Sep. 2000.

He found that carpenters were the most common tradesmen starting housebuilding firms. One explanation was that they were active in all stages (floor joists, roofing timbers, and doors and windows) and therefore they had organisational experience. His second suggestion was more provocative: 'the probability that in general the woodworking trades required a higher level of intelligence than did the other trades,'[17] an opinion quickly supported by my father. In contrast, Jackson noted the entry of some 'extraordinary people' – a milkman, estate agents' clerks, a maker of silk ties, a gown manufacturer and a Liverpool iron and steel merchant, many of whom later found the going tough.[18]

Table 8.1 draws on the list of large housebuilders shown in Table 2.2 and identifies the background of the dominant individuals. Fifteen of the

Table 8.1 The origin of dominant individuals in pre-war housebuilders.

Company	Dominant individual	Founded	Background
Ideal Homes	Leo Meyer[a]	1929	building surveyor
Henry Boot	Charles Boot	c.1886	night school educated
Wates	Norman Wates	1901	secondary school; joined small family housebuilder
Taylor Woodrow	Frank Taylor[a]	1921	greengrocer and night school
Davis Estates	Arthur Davis[a]	1929	father a developer
Wimpey	Godfrey Mitchell[a]	1919[b]	army, shipping and quarrying
Mactaggart & Mickel	John Mactaggart[a]	1901	mercantile clerk
Costain	Richard Costain	1865	privately educated third generation 'builder'
G.T. Crouch	Geoffrey Crouch[a]	1928	'builder'
Laing	John Laing	1848	bricklayer and apprentice mason in small family firm
T.F. Nash	Tommy Nash[a]	c.1925	carpenter
Dares Estates	Harry Dare	1864	third generation
R.T. Warren	Tom Warren[a]	1906	plasterer
Comben & Wakeling	James Comben[a] William Wakeling[a]	1904	master mason carpenter
Janes	Herbert Janes	1884	'building manager'
Morrell Estates	Morrell brothers[a]	1929	tradesmen?
Mucklow	Albert and Jothan Mucklow[a]	1933	grammar school (no trade)
William Leech	William Leech[a]	1932	window cleaner
Miller	James Miller[a]	c.1927	architect
N. Moss & Sons	Nathaniel Moss[a]	late 1890s	'builder'

[a] Founder. [b] Date of acquiring small company.

[17] Bundock, 'Speculative Housebuilding', pp. 368, 374–5.
[18] Jackson, *Semi-detached London*, p. 105.

companies in Table 8.1 were run by the original founder; the other five were run by people whom, if they did not actually start the business, had taken over what had been no more than a very small concern and turned it into a substantial business; they could be thought of as the pseudo-founder. They appear to have less in common than Bundock's analysis suggested. Education ranged from minimal to boarding school although it is not easy to be definitive about qualifications as night school was used extensively when the school leaving age was no more than 14. (Prior to the Fisher Education Act of 1918, extensive concessions had permitted children to leave school at 12.) An excellent example of the extent of night school education is provided in Kennett's account of Herbert Janes, who had left school at the age of only 12. He was aged 17 before he resumed education at evening classes: in 1906 he took exams in advanced book-keeping and mensuration; in 1907 building quantities; in 1909 building construction; and 1910 carpentry and joinery. By 1911 he had finished at Luton Technical College and took a correspondence course on reinforced concrete technology.[19] Others had a professional background: Leo Meyer had been a building surveyor with the local authority; James Miller was an architect who had inherited his father's practice at an early age; John Mactaggart was privately educated and had risen to be the accountant of a timber merchant before starting on his own; Richard Costain had also been privately educated before being introduced into the family firm; and Godfrey Mitchell had been trained in his father's quarrying business and had risen to army captain in the First World War. At the other end of the scale William Leech was a window cleaner and Frank Taylor helped in his parents' Blackpool greengrocery shop; neither knew anything about the mechanics of the building process.

Bundock may have found an abundance of tradesmen in the smaller firms, and it will be seen that they are frequently founders of successful housebuilders after the war, but tradesmen are less evident in the list above. John Laing was apprenticed in his own family firm and it is only Messrs Comben and Wakeling, Tommy Nash and Tom Warren that could genuinely be described as rising from the ranks of the tradesmen. Two companies mentioned in Part I as possible omissions from the list of leading housebuilders do no more than add to the mix. Hilbery Chaplin was an estate agent; and Metropolitan Railway Country Estate's development activities were started by staff lent by the Railway Company. Some were described in the company records as 'builder', but without further information it is not known if this meant a recognised technical competence or a post hoc description.

---

[19]   Kennett, 'A Provincial Builder', p. 28.

The diversity of dominant individuals can be noted without necessarily having an explanation. Probably, the skills involved in running a number of very large sites required a different mix of talents to those needed for running one or two sites, for the only link between the men above is their organisational ability and intense determination. These new housebuilding entrepreneurs needed to combine traditional building skills with development and marketing skills; they needed to buy the right land, to lay out the estates and to sell the houses – not just build them. Later periods in the history of the housebuilding would see firms started by men who had drawn their experience from working in the housebuilding industry. When the private housing boom started in the 1930s, that pool of specialist experience did not exist; those that exploited the opportunities were, therefore, likely to have a more diverse background.

The housebuilders – the post-war boom

In the inter-war period, the founder (or occasionally the family successor) and the dominant individual in the business were synonymous. As firms developed over time, encompassed more than one activity and changed leadership, the dominant individual becomes less easy to identify and therefore to characterise. For the post-war boom period, there were 31 companies that attained 1000 units or more in at least one of the years, and those companies have been taken as the sample. Of these, 14 were pre-war creations (although not necessarily large enough then to qualify for Table 2.2); these 14 are listed in Table 8.2.

The dominant characters running those companies that existed before the war are harder to categorise as they include second and third generation family members who will have had on-the-job training which could have included periods on site and in technical college. It is now possible to find housebuilders where there was no dominant individual: there might be several family members, or a succession of line managers reporting to a main board that had other interests, for example Costain. The traditional trades feature less than for the post-war creations; although John Lawrence (a carpenter) remained at the helm of his Glasgow business and Godfrey Mitchell's right-hand man, F.W. McLeod, driving the largest of the country's housebuilders, had been a bricklayer. There is an estate agent in the form of Eric Pountain, whose own business was reversed into the older McLean and a surveyor, Roy Davies, developed Bryant's housing for the family. Employee management on behalf of the family can be seen at Leech, run by accountant John Adamson, and Gough Cooper, where John Boardman, originally the firm's buyer, was in charge.

Table 8.2   The origin of dominant individuals in post-war housebuilders: companies that were active before the war.

Company	Dominant individual	Position	Origin
Wimpey	Godfrey Mitchell	founder	ex-army, shipping and quarrying
	F.W. McLeod	employee	bricklayer
Leech	John Adamson	employee	accountant
Bryant	Roy Davies	employee	surveyor
Wates	Neil Wates et al.	third generation	lawyer/SAS officer
Gough Cooper	Harry Gough-Cooper	founder	architect
	John Boardman	employee	buyer
Janes	Leslie Sell	son-in-law	solicitor
	Robert Janes	second generation	presume in house building
McLean	Geoffrey McLean	second generation	civil engineer
	Eric Pountain	acquired/founder	estate agent
Costain	None		
Davis Estates	Mixed		
John Lawrence	John Lawrence	founder	carpenter/night school
Whittingham	Tom Whittingham	third generation	surveyor
Ideal	Mixed		
Taylor Woodrow	Frank Taylor	founder	greengrocer/night school
E. Fletcher	Geoffrey Fletcher	second generation	builder?

The other 17 housebuilders, out of those that had reached an annual output of 1000 units, were post-war creations and are listed in Table 8.3. Page-Johnson has been treated as a post-war creation although there had been a small family business before the war; 'Johnnie' Johnson would have worked in that briefly before wartime service. Bovis was a pre-war builder but its private housebuilding only began after the war. Comben was a pre-war housebuilder but the post-war acquisition of Carlton Homes was a reverse takeover. It does illustrate the problems of arbitrary classification. Trades-related companies predominate, including bricklayers, carpenters and a plumber at Northern Developments, Broseley, Wait, Galliford and Greaves. Working builders included Bob Francis of Francis Parker, Geoffrey Fletcher of E. Fletcher and later Bardolin, and Johnnie Johnson should also be included in this category as he had been brought up in his father's small building business. Some founders described themselves as builders, without having what today would be regarded as a recognised building qualification; they would undoubtedly have had some trade expertise, on the job experience, possibly supplemented by night school.

The site acquisition route, as opposed to construction expertise, was represented by surveyors and estate agents. Tom Baron of Whelmar had been the senior partner of a Manchester firm of surveyors, a contrast to Jimmy Meyer, who had been gifted Federated when newly qualified; Ronald Fell was a land surveyor for Dewsbury Council before gaining building experience with a local firm. The estate agents were not necessarily qualified: Danny

Table 8.3 The origin of dominant individuals in post-war housebuilders: companies that were created after the war.

Company	Dominant individual	Position	Origin
Northern Developments	Derek Barnes	founder	bricklayer
Whelmar	Tom Baron	founder	surveyor
Bovis	Frank Sanderson	acquired founder	estate agent
Barratt	Lawrie Barratt	founder	accountant
Broseley	Danny Horrocks	founder	carpenter/estate agent
Bardolin	Jock Mackenzie	shareholder	lawyer
	Geoffrey Fletcher	acquired founder	builder?
Bellway	Russell Bell	founders	surveyor/accountant[b]
	John Bell		
Francis Parker	Bob Francis	founder	clerk/working builder
Orme	Peter Whitfield	founders	financiers
	Bob Tanner		
Comben/Carlton Homes	Leon Roydon	founder	grammar school/
	Terry Roydon	second generation	entrepreneur degree in estate management
David Charles	Robin Buckingham	son-in-law	Royal Navy
Fell	Ronald Fell	founder	land surveyor
Federated	Jimmy Meyer	founder	surveyor
Greaves	Edward Wheatley	founder	plumber
Page-Johnson[a]	'Johnnie' Johnson	second generation	builder/designer
Hallmark/Wait[a]	Sidney Bloch	founder	solicitor
	Alan Draycott	acquired founder	estate agent
	Arthur Wait	acquired founder	technical school/carpenter
Galliford Estates[a]	John Galliford	founders	bricklayer
	Cecil Galliford		carpenter

[a] Companies taken over during the period. [b] These were probably not qualified positions; Russell had worked with his father in the building trade before the war.

Horrocks, who started as a carpenter, moved into estate agency; Frank Sanderson had first been a clerk in an estate agents; and Alan Draycott, who started the housing companies that went into Hallmark, was an established south coast agent. Bellway's two brothers described themselves as a surveyor and an accountant; in neither case did they appear to be qualified and their building expertise would have come from working with their father immediately before and after the war. In total, it can be seen that some 14 of the 17 companies (or 82% of the sample) had their origin in, or substantial influence from, practical building and development skills.

Beyond that, there is evidence of housebuilding being approached from a financing standpoint: Barratt was run by an accountant, although in partnership with a builder in the early days; Orme was created by Messrs Whitfield and Tanner solely as a financing exercise; and Bardolin under Jock Mackenzie became one. Carlton Homes (which reversed into Comben & Wakeling) was founded by Leon Roydon, son of a textile entrepreneur, although his son, who later took over the management of the enlarged Comben, was the first housebuilding managing director to have a degree in estate management. That left only David Charles, run by an ex-naval officer for his father-in-law, as an isolated case.

If the dominant individuals running the larger housebuilders in the pre-war and post-war periods are contrasted, the surprise is that in the later period the founders had a greater tendency to come from directly relevant backgrounds. The tradesmen, in the wider sense of the word, showed a greater propensity to build substantial housebuilding businesses than they had done before the war.

The housebuilders in the late 1980s

No specific date has been selected for Table 8.4. The intent is to capture those who dominated the industry towards the end of the 1980s, that is before the collapse of the housing market in 1990. By now, the determination of company size has become easier, but the identification of the dominant individual becomes progressively harder. The passage of time has meant that, on average, there are more mature companies than in the earlier tables; they are larger and with a more diffuse management structure. Thus, although the managing director of a housebuilding operation might accurately be named, it does not mean that he is dominant in the way defined earlier; for those categorised as employees, they may only have been there for a few years.

Compared with the earlier time periods reviewed, the housebuilding company is now frequently part of a larger group where power and control may or may not be easy to categorise (even for those working there) and such control may or may not be centred on the housebuilding business. To illustrate this, the companies have been given an 'independence ranking' to indicate the extent to which the housebuilding companies, if not their heads, could be regarded as dominant within their organisation.

1: Wholly or almost entirely private housing; most of the directors would consider themselves housebuilders.
2: Housebuilding an important part of the group but only one of a number of building industry related activities – key directors have a housebuilding origin.
3: Housebuilding only one of a number of building industry related activities – key directors do not have a housebuilding origin.
4: Housebuilding owned by unrelated parent company.

Table 8.4 The origin of the dominant individual: housebuilders building more than 1000 a year in the late 1980s.

Housebuilder	Independence rank[a]	Dominant individual	Status	Origin
McLean/Tarmac	2	Eric Pountain	acquired	estate agent
		Sam Pickstock	founder employee	conveyancer
Wimpey	3	Nelson Oliver	employee	builder FCIOB
Barratt	1	Lawrie Barratt	founder	accountant
Beazer	2	Brian Beazer	second generation	company secretary
Ideal	4	David Calverley	employee	accountant
Laing	3	David Holliday	employee	builder
Lovell	2	None		
Bovis	4	Philip Warner	employee	builder
Westbury	1	Richard Fraser	employee	accountant
Wilcon	1	Mike Robinson	employee	university/civil engineer
McCarthy & Stone	1	John McCarthy	founder	carpenter
Bryant	1	Andrew McKenzie	employee	surveyor
Persimmon	1	Duncan Davidson	founder	'aristocrat'
Bellway	1	Howard Dawe	employee	builder MIOB
Costain	3	None		
Fairclough	3	Malcolm Hawe	acquired founder	surveyor
Raine	2	Peter Parkin	acquired founder	surveyor
David Wilson	1	David Wilson	founder	building diploma
Crest	2	Roger Lewis	employee	accountant
Clarke Homes	3	Mixed		
Fairview[b]	1	Dennis Cope	founder	estate agent
Alfred McAlpine	3	Bobby McAlpine	third generation	company trained
		Philip Davies	employee	building college
Redrow	1	Steve Morgan	founder	builder
Galliford Sears	4	David Brill	employee	carpenter
English China Clays	4	John Reeve	employee	surveyor
Walter Lawrence	2?	Trevor Mawby	employee	accountant
Mowlem	3	Roger Clark	employee	surveyor
Croudace	2/3	Tony Timms	employee	civil engineer
Wates	2/3	Bill Gair	employee	articled architect
Abbey	2	Mixed		

[a] See text above. [b] Not included in Part I Table 5.2 as it last exceeded 1000 units in 1985.

The subjective element in all these categorisations must be stressed: Bryant's construction was not insubstantial and a purely statistical approach might have placed it in category 2; conversely, a more liberal approach to Crest and Lovell's peripheral interests might have deemed them to be in category 1. Nevertheless, the broad sweep of the classification is probably reasonable.

Of the 30 housebuilders that reached 1000 units a year in the late 1980s, just one third (or ten to be precise) could be regarded as substantially house-building companies. A further 16 housebuilding companies were part of much larger construction and building materials groups. Of these, perhaps half or less of the parent groups were dominated by directors that had their roots in housing; in the others, the housing managing directors were not dominant at main board level. Finally, Ideal was part of the Trafalgar House conglomerate which, although built up by a property developer (Nigel Broakes), had spread across shipping, hotels and newspapers as well as housing and construction; Bovis was part of the P&O shipping group; Galliford Sears was part of a retailer and English China Clays speaks for itself.

There is a preference for objective criteria when it comes to identifying the individuals who could fairly be described as dominant within their organisation; the obvious ones being the position held and the length of time in that position. Unfortunately, some degree of subjectivity is required when, for instance, housebuilding is part of a larger group, for example Ideal's David Calverley under Nigel Broakes' Trafalgar House. Generally speaking, those category 3 and 4 companies involve more subjective judgements than the category 1 companies. Length of time would appear to be an objective criterion but if, for instance, a term of ten years in charge was considered a minimum it would exclude Peter Parkin who arrived at Raine in 1986 when it was building 400 units a year and increased it to around 2000 within three years. Ultimately, the judgements have been based on the author's own knowledge of the companies and the individual histories prepared as background for this book.

All bar two of the category 1 firms were deemed to be run by dominant individuals; although at Bryant, Roy Davies had run Bryant Homes for 30 years and retired in 1987 to be replaced by Andrew McKenzie. At Bellway, Howard Dawe had similarly been a recent appointee to the top job. Four of the category 1 firms were still run by their founder and two by long-standing chief executives who had substantially enlarged the business for the founding family. Outside the category 1 firms, it was harder to find dominant personalities. Eric Pountain and Brian Beazer were such; one was a founder of a constituent housebuilding company and the other a second generation owner. However, in both cases they dominated the larger business rather than the housebuilding subsidiary. The only other people deemed to be 'dominant' were Philip Warner who ran Bovis Homes for a quarter of a century, and Malcolm Hawe who had a much shorter reign after he merged his Hammerfine company with Fairclough Homes.

The fact that there is so much difficulty in defining who is or is not a dominant individual in comparison with the pre-1974 position tells its own story. At the top end of the industry, the firms were becoming more managerially controlled. Only ten of the thirty companies were run by someone with entrepreneurial roots compared with a substantial majority pre-1974. Professionally, there was less evidence of the humble beginnings or tradesman route. There were five accountants (only one of whom was a founder), the rest having backgrounds related to the industry, including another five who were surveyors. Only John McCarthy, the sheltered housing pioneer, had come via the tradesman route and there were two school leavers without additional qualifications: Eric Pountain worked his way via estate agency whereas Duncan Davidson, a pageboy at the Coronation, came from the landed classes. Otherwise, there was a range of builders and surveyors, largely qualified through technical college and night school, with one university first in civil engineering.

The housebuilders in the 1990s

The analysis of the top 20 housebuilders at the end of the century shows differences from the 1980s table, not all of which would have been expected. What stands out is the preponderance of category 1 companies. It had become the age of the focused housebuilder: the construction hybrids and the conglomerates had virtually vanished from the scene. Wimpey had swapped its construction for Tarmac's housing; Beazer Homes had emerged as an independent company after Hanson had bought the larger Beazer entity; Bovis Homes had been similarly demerged from P&O; Amec had sold Fairclough Homes for it to become the UK housing arm of the American housebuilder Centex; and Ideal and Costain Homes had been sold to other housebuilders. Other pure housebuilders had appeared in the top 20 for the first time (Redrow, Berkeley, Bloor, Countryside and Fairview), each one being run by its founder. This is demonstrated in Table 8.5.

The first generation founders, although in a minority, are now a clearer grouping than in 1988, all seven being active executive heads of their companies. Although some of these have their origins pre-1974, they are primarily creations of the period after the 1974 recession; their greater prominence at the end of the 1990s reflects the additional time available to them to grow their business. The founders continue to include people with no post-school qualifications. Duncan Davidson, grandson of the 15th Duke of Norfolk and Tony Pidgley, brought up by gypsies, provide an interesting contrast. John Bloor was a plasterer. The other founders comprise a couple of estate agents, a surveyor and civil engineer, but all these

Table 8.5   The origin of the dominant individual: top 20 housebuilders in the late 1990s.

Housebuilder	Independence ranking	Dominant individual	Status	Origin
Wimpey	1	Denis Brant	employee	civil engineer
Barratt	1	Frank Eaton	employee	joiner
Beazer	1	Denis Webb	employee	civil engineer
Persimmon	1	Duncan Davidson	founder	'aristocrat'
Bellway	1	Howard Dawe	employee	builder MCIOB
Westbury	1	Martin Donohue	employee	surveyor
Alfred McAlpine	2/3	Graeme McCallum	employee	accountant
Wilcon	1	Ian Black	employee	accountant
Bryant	1	Andrew McKenzie	employee	surveyor
David Wilson	1	David Wilson	founder	surveyor
Redrow	1	Steve Morgan	founder	civil engineer
Berkeley	1	Tony Pidgley	founder	ground worker
Bovis	1	Malcolm Harris	employee	accountant
Crest	1	John Callcutt	employee	lawyer
Countryside	1	Alan Cherry	founder	estate agent
Taylor	2/3	None		
Woodrow Fairclough	1	Stewart Baseley	employee	school leaver
Lovell	2/3	None		
Bloor	1	John Bloor	founder	plasterer
Fairview	1	Dennis Cope	founder	estate agent

qualifications were earned the hard way. The more successful did not appear to regret their trade background: according to Steve Morgan, 'I do think there's far too much emphasis on higher education. I'm sure that many would be better off taking up a good old trade at 16. Many of our directors at Redrow came through the trade route.'[20]

The review of housebuilders' origins has been compartmentalised into chronological periods for ease of analysis. In the inter-war period, craftsmen predominated in the smaller companies, but there were a number of leading housebuilders founded by generalists with no particular experience of the industry; all the large firms were run by dominant individuals. Those firms that survived the war gradually matured and it became harder to identify the driving force, particularly if housebuilding became only one of a number of divisions: there emerged a broader mix of founders, successors and now employees, and their origins began to include the professions as well as the trades. By the 1970s and 1980s, the mixed businesses were more prevalent, but this reversed sharply after the 1990 recession, and housebuilders once more became focused businesses. Interestingly, the dominant individuals

---

[20] Steve Morgan, *Daily Post*, 21st Aug. 2000, p. 9.

at the end of the 1990s were either employees or founders – there were no 'successors' running any of the top twenty companies, and trades origins could still be found.

Table 8.5 is the only contemporary table from the original thesis that has not been updated. The slightly vague 'late 1990s' had been chosen because it marked the end of a long period of continuity of top management. Since then, there have been a number of phased handovers, which makes it almost impossible to determine at what point the successor actually becomes 'the dominant character', coupled with a succession of other changes at the top which makes the choice of a terminal year somewhat arbitrary. Equally important, judgements on management ideally require to be delivered from a little distance, even on something as apparently simple as who is running the business. Nevertheless, some form of postscriptial comment can be made.

The last few years have seen the phased handover of executive control by chief executives of four of the current top ten housebuilders, Persimmon, David Wilson, Redrow and Bellway; the first three being from founders, Duncan Davidson, David Wilson himself and Steve Morgan, and at Bellway the long-serving Howard Dawe. Phased handovers will be discussed later under 'relay succession' in Chapter 11 and the only point to be made here is that the office holder and successor in each company ran in tandem for several years; whatever the change in nominal titles, authority would have passed gradually. As for changes in origin, Duncan Davidson's successor, John White, had started as a bricklayer, and at Bellway a surveyor followed a builder. However, the succession at Redrow and David Wilson both went to accountants rather than the civil engineer and surveyor occupations of their founders, albeit the accountants had enjoyed long careers in the housebuilding industry.

Two other companies need mention – Taylor Woodrow and Wimpey, the only two with substantial overseas interests and both, therefore, having group chief executives with wider responsibilities than just UK housing. Taylor Woodrow had been noted in Table 8.5 as having no dominant individual running its UK housing. Since then its UK housing has seen a succession of changes including the acquisition of Bryant and the adoption of not only the latter's name but its head office; when asked for the identity of its UK housing managing director for the 2005 *PHA*, a quartet of names were provided. At Wimpey, the UK housing passed most recently to Pete Redfern, an accountant, although unlike the Redrow and David Wilson accountants above, not one with a long history in the industry. Of the remaining 2004 top ten, Berkeley, Bovis and Westbury still had the same chief executive; at Barratt, the sudden death of Frank Eaton led to the appointment of David Pretty, a one-time graduate trainee with Procter & Gamble, but with a long history of marketing and sales within Barratt.

Whatever the reader might have expected to see, the origins of the house-building industry's leaders cannot have come as a complete surprise; they nearly always have a related skill that can be applied to the business, be it a traditional trade, a building qualification or land assembly skills. Those without a specific skill base have worked their way through the trade as have most of those listed as accountants or solicitors. What is interesting is the dog that didn't bark: by the end of the 1990s, there had been no example of a managing director being brought in to run a UK housebuilder, having been a managing director in an unrelated business, in the belief that managerial skills are universal and can be applied to any industry. For the opening years of this decade, this needs a partial qualification in the light of events at three housebuilders – the departed Wilson Connolly, Taylor Woodrow and Wimpey.

In 1999, Lynn Wilson announced the appointment of Allan Leighton, chief executive of Wal-Mart Europe, as deputy chairman, with the intent of succeeding him as chairman in 2001. Leighton arrived with some challenging views for the housebuilding industry:

> 'I think this industry is about to explode; it will just get completely reinvented. I am a change agent, and I have an intuitive feeling that we can lead this change. We will develop the most efficient supply chain in the world for the housebuilding industry.'[21]

Although Leighton did not have a formal executive position, with a new chief executive in place, his role was influential. The attempt to apply retailing philosophy to the housebuilding was also leading to changes in operational methods, including rationalisation of the supply chain and the purchase of a timber-frame business. The impact on the actual business was less flattering. A profits warning in October 2001 (at the height of the boom, profits were to fall from £71 m. to £43 m.) led to the resignation of the managing director, and the architect of the change, Allan Leighton, assumed temporary executive control. In March 2002, Graeme McCallum, formerly managing director of Alfred McAlpine Homes, was appointed chief executive and began a reorganisation which he described as no more than going back to basics: 'It doesn't require rocket science to put it right.'[22]

---

[21] *Building*, 11th Feb. 2000.
[22] *Building*, March 2002.

After a recovery in profits, the Company was sold to Taylor Woodrow in September 2003.

As mentioned above, Taylor Woodrow and Wimpey had wider group structures than most of the UK housebuilders and had brought in what must be regarded as genuine outsiders to the position of group chief executive. Peter Johnson had been chief executive of Rugby Group (cement) before being appointed chief executive of Wimpey in 2000. Iain Napier, an accountant with a marketing background, was appointed Taylor Woodrow chief executive in 2002, having previously been chief executive of Bass Brewers. This is not the first time that there have been group chief executives unversed in the practicalities of the domestic housebuilding subsidiaries that lie below them; after all, housebuilders have been part of much wider groupings than Taylor Woodrow and Wimpey, and this is a topic that we will return to later. However, the dominant part of these two companies is UK housing; the experience of Wilson Connolly does not set a good precedent and it will be the performance of these companies in recessionary times that will test whether there could be a new managerial model.

9

The Rationale for Growth: the Economies that Accrue to Size

Introduction

This chapter explores the reasons behind the growth in size of individual housebuilders and the trend to consolidation by examining what the industry generally refers to as 'economies of scale', but more specifically divides into the twin economies described by Chandler as scale (the site) and scope (the firm). It is these economies that have driven concentration in other industries but, despite the claims of management, they do not appear to offer an intellectually rigorous justification of why housebuilding firms need to grow.

As a preliminary to discussing the economies of scale, this chapter first addresses the ease with which companies can enter the industry. To some extent, the same considerations apply to both entry and growth, for the more that size makes larger companies more efficient, and therefore profitable, the harder it will be for individuals to enter the industry and compete. Nevertheless, there are some distinctive points to be made about ease of entry which deserve their own distinct section. It will be argued that, although housebuilding is an industry with high working capital requirements, there is no substantial fixed capital barrier to cross and the supply of funds to the new entrant is as plentiful today as it was in the inter-war period.

Economies of scale, in their narrow sense of returns to the increasing physical size of the individual operating unit, are found to have no explanatory power. There are some limited gains to be made by developing on large rather than small housing sites but these sites do not have to be owned by large firms. Moreover, and perhaps uniquely, the housebuilders themselves have only limited control over the size of their operational units; even if there were economies of scale on site, there is little that management could do to obtain them. Allied to economies of scale is technological change, a contentious issue in the housebuilding industry, but this book argues that technological change is driven by suppliers, is therefore available to all housebuilders and does not require increased size for its exploitation.

There are stronger reasons for suggesting that there are economies of scope, economies deriving from the size of the firm rather than the individual operating unit. The housebuilder with many sites, equivalent to the multi-plant firm in manufacturing, may secure cost savings over a firm with few sites. Indeed, where acquisitions are made in the public arena and explanations to shareholders and media have to sound rational, it is economies of scope that are instanced in justification. The arguments for increased size in the key areas of land acquisition, marketing and purchasing are all addressed in this chapter but even where they do exist, the economies of scope are not overwhelming, in the sense that they do not confer such a competitive advantage that smaller firms are unable to compete; they do not *necessitate* increased size. Where there are economies that accrue to the larger firm, they are offset not just by organisational diseconomies but also by the dissipation of entrepreneurial flair, particularly in the land buying which lies at the heart of the development process. These diseconomies manifest themselves through the establishment of extensive regional structures, all replicating the original single unit firm.

The accounts of some 80 housebuilders for the year 2001 were analysed to see if there is any statistical evidence to indicate that large companies do earn superior rewards to small companies. There was no consistent evidence to support the proposition and examples are provided of smaller companies that have profit margins substantially greater than the national housebuilders.

Ease of entry

Housebuilding may thrive on the exercise of entrepreneurial character but the entrepreneurs still need to be able to enter the industry. There appears to be no shortage of small firms: there were over 16,000 housebuilders on the NHBC register in 2004 (down from 29,000 in 1990); leaving aside the interesting (and growing) group of 10,600 housebuilders that built no houses, there were as many as 4600 firms building from one to ten units a year. Although this is down from a 1988 peak of over 10,000, when these small firms can still be totalled in their thousands, the pool of entrepreneurs cannot be considered small. Neither does there appear to be a paucity of firms as the size ranges increase: in 2004 there were some 800 house-builders building from 11–30 units a year; 300 building 31–100 units, and still well over 100 firms building more than 100 units a year.

Trade and professional expertise offer a natural route into the housebuilding industry; they provide a skill base for the entrepreneur. But access to the industry also requires that there be limited barriers to entry and here there is an apparent contradiction. The housebuilding industry is relatively capital intensive. For instance, the average sales capital ratio was around one to one during the early 1990s. However, the requirement is almost entirely for working, not fixed, capital. There is no minimum fixed capital hurdle to cross; there are no factories to be built; no distribution centres to be established; no computer networks to be installed. The operation can be started on a very small scale, building in ones and twos where necessary; many a housebuilder has worked out of his own home, with his wife providing the secretarial function. (Lest this be thought politically incorrect drafting, I have not come across the reverse.)

Burnett described the small speculative builders of the late nineteenth century, relying mainly on local networks of private sources of finance, built up over the years on the basis of personal knowledge and trust. Frequently eschewed by the banking system, these men were financed by landlords, other builders and informal partnerships.[1] This did not appear to have changed in the inter-war period. Many examples of small firms financed in this way can be cited, but could the same be said of those housebuilders that eventually became the industry leaders? To gain a wider perspective, the top ten housebuilders of the 1930s (as per Table 2.2) were examined to see if there were any broad conclusions that could be drawn. Some had entered the industry from an existing small business base, presumably using surplus cash flow: Costain, Laing and Henry Boot were already contractors and the Wates family had a furniture shop. Use of personal savings features in a number of cases such as Frank Taylor and John Mactaggart, from what must have been modest incomes, and Leo Meyer (Ideal) from a professional salary. Meyer also teamed up with an older man (Philip Shephard) who was an agent for Royal Exchange and was able to introduce land. Little is known of Geoffrey Crouch's origins other than that he started in a small way, while Arthur Davis' father was a failed developer who presumably passed on more in the way of know-how than finance. Family help is documented for some: Frank Taylor's greengrocer father

---

[1] Burnett, *A Social History of Housing 1815–1985*, p. 25.

added £70 to his son's £30 savings. Only Wimpey was financed in a more substantial way: Godfrey Mitchell bought George Wimpey in 1919 for £3000, raised from his post-war gratuity and the sale of shares with a further £3000 loan from his father for working capital; however, when Mitchell did begin private housing some years later, he started by using his own money.

One could continue outside the top ten for more illustrations. In their early years, Comben & Wakeling, for instance, had the support of a wealthy private individual who bought the sites for the Company so that he could subsequently purchase the ground rents as an investment. John Lawrence started in the 1920s with money borrowed from his aunt. William Leech used the profits from his window-cleaning business to build a house for himself, then selling it and building another two. Harry Gough-Cooper, who studied building construction at night school, worked as a carpenter's labourer while saving to buy his first land, plot by plot. Edwin Bradley found one of the more pleasurable ways of fundraising; having sold a house to a local businesswoman while a site foreman, he married the lady and later added the proceeds from the sale of her business to his own somewhat smaller savings. In a different variation on the same theme, Harry Cruden worked as a timber merchant in a business owned by his wife; when the Company was incorporated in 1943, they had equal shares, and it was that timber business which subsequently developed into a housebuilder.

A similar exercise on the source of funds was carried out for the post-war period using the 1973 league table (Table 4.4), and taking the ten largest businesses that had been formed since the war, only excluding those formed by merger. Here, there was even less evidence of the need for outside capital than there had been in the pre-war cohort. Again, there were housebuilders that had developed out of existing businesses: Greaves and Galliford came out of small building firms (indeed, much smaller than Boot, Costain and Laing had been), and Broseley's origin lay in estate agency. Personal savings still featured as a source of initial capital for several firms, sometimes just to build the first house. Derek Barnes (Northern Developments) and Bob Francis (Francis Parker) had only modest employment; the Bell family had been builders before the War and put £200 of their own money in to form Bellway in 1946; and accountant Lawrie Barratt had built his own home before going into partnership with a local builder. The only housebuilders that had more substantial resources at their disposal from the beginning were Whelmar, formed with the backing of Metropolitan Railway Country Estates, and Federated, established for Jimmy Meyer by his father, Ideal's Leo Meyer, who also organised a £1 m. bank overdraft.

There is little evidence to suggest that barriers to entry have become any harder in more recent times. The concept of entry into the industry is used here not just to mean the ability to start a business but also in the wider sense of being able to freely move upwards and enter the highest ranks of the industry. Of the top ten housebuilders in 2004 (Table 6.5) there were three that had been formed as recently as the 1970s. Duncan Davidson's Persimmon was formed in 1972, albeit with the proceeds of the sale of a previous company, Ryedale, formed in 1965 with the help of a £10,000 loan, half from his mother and half from his fiancée. Steve Morgan started Redrow in 1974 with £5000 backing from his father to take over one small civil engineering subcontract, moving into housebuilding a few years later. Tony Pidgley, founder of Berkeley in 1976, was brought up by gypsies; he had no access to capital and the first lorry was purchased for £500 cash out of savings; from that developed a fleet of lorries and a ground clearance business; 25 years after being founded, Berkeley became (briefly) the largest housebuilder by market value.

In the closing years of the twentieth century, housebuilders continued to be formed by entrepreneurs using a wide variety of resources. The passage of time meant that there was a greater availability of family money and expertise made out of the same industry: Tony Pidgley junior formed Thirlstone; John McCarthy's sons formed another sheltered housing business, Emlor (now Churchill Retirement); and Percy Bilton's grandsons formed Raven. Others used their own resources, in one form or another: Colin Brooks used his share of the proceeds from the sale of Scotchbrooks estate agency in 1990 to form Bewley Homes; after 15 years with Berkeley, Peter Owen formed Grenville Homes in 1999 backed by a private individual from Philadelphia; and in 1993 Graeme Simpson 'remortgaged his house, sold his car, and squeezed loans from every available source' to form Millgate Homes.[2] The 2004 *PHA* contained yet more housebuilders that had been founded within the previous ten years: for instance, there are three AIM-quoted companies, Oakdene founded in 1996, City Lofts in 1997 and Telford as recently as 2000. Although the circumstances were not identical, in effect all three were financed from the savings of the founding shareholders, typically earned out of previous employment and business ventures.

Financial institutions, both banks and venture capitalist, have played a larger role in housebuilding start-ups, being prepared to invest substantial sums behind individual housebuilders. Remo Dipre, ex-Fairbriar, formed Gladedale at the end of 1992 as a £2 company with the Bank of Scotland

---

[2] *Housebuilder*, May 1997.

providing all the finance; it did not begin to build houses in a meaningful way until the late 1990s yet, by the time you read this book, Gladedale may well be in the top ten. David Holliday, previously managing director of Laing Homes, formed Admiral Homes in 1989 with Phildrew Ventures' capital support of £75 m. believed then to be the UK's largest start-up; two years later, Philip Davies, ex-managing director of McAlpine Homes, received venture capital backing to form Linden, now building over 1000 houses a year. The willingness of financial institutions to back what they consider to be a promising entrepreneur, and the growing number of high net worth individuals looking for investment opportunities, means that entry into the housebuilding industry appears as easy now as it was in the inter-war period. Access to capital cannot be regarded as a barrier to entry in the speculative housebuilding industry.

The most cited reason for growth in market share across the economy in the twentieth century has been technical change and innovation whereby the increasing scale of production drives down unit costs of production, typical examples being power generation and chemical plants. This view was articulated succinctly by David Jeremy: 'historically, the foremost motive for expansion has been to gain economies of scale'.[3] While low barriers to entry and a requisite skill base enabled entrepreneurs to flourish in the early history of manufacturing industry, these were conditions that did not, in general, last. Today, it is difficult to envisage a host of individual entrepreneurs creating businesses of significance from scratch in, for instance, bulk chemicals, volume car production, power generation or breweries. This book is not arguing that housebuilding is an entrepreneurial industry apart. One only had to read the *Daily Telegraph* of 10th October 2005, which produced a list of 40 entrepreneurs who had made a fortune of at least £50 m. by their fortieth birthday, these coming from a range of predominantly service businesses. As it happened, the largest number came from the construction and property sector: the essential point being made here is the extent to which entrepreneurs still start new firms on a regular basis and with considerable success in the speculative housebuilding industry.

Scale – the economies of the large site

Inter-war studies of the housebuilding industry argued for the benefits of large sites. According to Jackson, 'Conditions in the boom years of the late

---

[3] Jeremy, *A Business History of Britain 1900–1990s*, p. 197.

twenties and early thirties favoured the establishment and growth of larger
units . . . a builder could not make a reasonable profit unless he already
held land or could erect 100 or more houses in one batch.'[4] Johnson was
another to make the same point: 'The larger builder was also favoured in
the competition for business by his ability to construct a greater number of
houses at one time.'[5] And immediately after the war, a NHBRC director
commented that: 'The bulk of the houses were built by firms who had
remodelled their business along lines particularly adapted to repetitive
production.'[6] These quotations were all supportive of the contention that
large sites were more economic production centres, albeit without indicating the materiality of such advantage. Beyond that, there was an implied
assumption that large sites meant large firms. To the contrary, there is no
evidence that ownership of large sites required the creation of large firms.
Indeed, Bundock's thesis actually includes a section on the role and importance of the large single estate developer, giving George Ball (Ruislip) as an
example, building an estate of 3300 houses in Ruislip and Northwood.[7] Nor
has the passage of time changed these economic relationships: examples
will be provided later of contemporary small companies controlling large
urban developments.

In any event, the advantages of the large site need to be kept in perspective:
the bricklayer does not lay his bricks any quicker, nor the tiler his tiles; the
painter does not paint the walls more quickly nor the plumber connect
his pipes more speedily. There are organisational advantages in that work
can be progressed more efficiently across a range of standardised house
types and the costs involved in site management will be lower per unit.
These site organisational economies were applied to full advantage by the
contractor-housebuilders in the 1960s. They would 'efficiently' clear all
the site, put in all the roads and services across the whole site and then
systematically start building rows of similar looking houses. The effort
was actually counterproductive: large amounts of capital were locked up as
production ran far ahead of sales. The production-driven approach lacked
flexibility, not just when there were major cyclical changes in demand but
also when local tastes necessitated a change in product range. Ron King
described what they found when McLean Homes joined the Tarmac construction group in 1973:

---

[4] Jackson, *Semi-detached London*, p. 105.
[5] Johnson, 'The Suburban Expansion of Housing in London 1918–1939', p. 157.
[6] Talk by Norman Walls at the Housing Centre quoted in *Housebuilder*, Sep. 1945.
[7] Bundock, 'Speculative Housebuilding', p. 317.

'We were pretty good at housebuilding whereas they were construction. I can remember the day after the deal was done – Eric [Pountain] asked me to go round all the Tarmac sites . . . they were just totally construction oriented, building houses.'[8]

This attitude by construction-led housebuilders was not uncommon and the uneasy relationship between construction and speculative housing is discussed in more detail under 'Focus versus diversification' in Chapter 11.

The standard expositions on economies of scale assume, explicitly or implicitly, that, if they exist, they will be exploited to the economic benefit of the enterprise. However, the housebuilder is in an unusual position. Even if the economies of scale of the large site were to be significant, there is little the housebuilder can do to ensure that he can maximise those advantages. The size of the site is the size of the site; he may tell the planning authorities that he could build more cheaply if they gave permission for a site, say, five times as large but there is no record of such special pleading being accepted. And for urban sites and infilling, the physical limitations are insurmountable. Moreover, when housebuilders are fortunate enough to control a very large site, they will sometimes deliberately abandon the putative economies of scale and choose to divide the site, either swapping land with other housebuilders or using group companies operating under another name, preferring the increase in sales derived from diversity of housing types to potential construction economies. Even the Barker Report has suggested that: 'Local authorities . . . should discuss the build out rates for large sites, and, where appropriate, encourage developers to split up these sites.'[9] This book argues, therefore, that the production economies accruing to the large site are limited; can be offset by what is sometimes called 'the contractor mentality'; and even if the economies are advantageous, it is outside the control of individual firms to increase site size.

Technological change

There is a wider issue of technological change within the housebuilding industry and, rightly or wrongly, the industry has been criticised for its lack of innovation. Even those within the industry do not always regard housebuilding as being technologically driven: during the interview process, and in their own literature, housebuilders have variously claimed that their firm's success was driven by land purchasing, or marketing, or building efficiency, but never by technological innovation. Some developers

---

[8] Interview with Ron King, Nov. 1999.
[9] Barker, *Review of Housing Supply, Final Report*, p. 8.

took a positive pride in the simplicity of the process: Ramon Greene's 'What am I doing? It didn't seem to me that you had to be Einstein to start building houses;'[10] and Tony Pidgley's 'You don't need a degree to know that the drain has got to go in at the right level'.[11] Such honest admissions may provide ammunition for both sides of the debate. Michael Ball has been one of the most consistent critics, for instance opening his 'Chasing a Snail' with the pronouncement that 'British housebuilding has an exceptionally poor record at introducing innovation in design and production methods', although he did proceed to give a balanced defence of the housebuilding industry, pointing out the constraints of varying production locations and the conservatism of the house buyers.[12]

However, for this book it matters not whether the rate of technological change within the housebuilding industry is as slow as its critics suggest: what is relevant in the arguments over economies of scale is whether technological change offers an explanation for individual firms' growth. Is it necessary for housebuilders to increase to a particular size to profit from whatever technical change is taking place? Prais went as far as to suggest that, based on his study of giant manufacturing firms, 'on the whole one cannot ascribe to technological factors . . . any great part in the process [of concentration] we are examining'.[13] How much less likely, then, can the evidence be found within the peripatetic housebuilding industry. The point is made in Chapter 11 that, unlike manufacturing businesses, housebuilders do not appear to fail for technological reasons; it is suggested here that they do not succeed for technological reasons either.

If the expression 'builder' was removed from the term housebuilder and replaced by developer it may be that the accusation of being slow to adopt technical change would be diverted to those further down the supply chain. The Barker Report claimed that the housebuilding industry 'needs to address its weak record of innovation and remove barriers to the take-up of modern methods of construction',[14] but there is no reason why technological change should be led by the 'house developers' themselves. Their underlying economic function is to find land, procure the construction process, and market and distribute the end product to the customer; they employ groundworks contractors for site preparation, use subcontracting trades for the construction, and purchase the materials from large manufacturing

---

[10] Interview with Ramon Greene, April 2001.
[11] Interview with Tony Pidgley, May 2001.
[12] Ball, 'Chasing a Snail', pp. 9–21.
[13] Prais, *The Evolution of Giant Firms in Britain*, p. 165.
[14] Barker, *Review of Housing Supply, Final Report*, p. 103.

firms. In practice, technological innovation is led by the plant and material suppliers and, when developed, the technology is available to all. Ball himself conceded that changes in groundwork, a significant part of housebuilding, were independent of the housebuilder. Above ground, the innovations occurred through 'a piecemeal improvement of building elements, rather than through radical transformation', and he instanced plasterboard replacing wet plaster and roof trusses replacing traditional roof construction.[15] When new products become available, they are available to any housebuilder; moreover, the implementation of the technological change is, to some extent, in the hands of subcontractors who use the materials, and restrained by buyers who, financed by conservative lenders, may be resistant to change, rather than the housebuilders themselves. If a technologically advanced material or process became available, the increase in market share would go first to the supplier, and then to the subcontractors that adopted it. Moreover, the nature of the incremental process of change is such that size is not a prerequisite to its being used. This author cannot think of a material or a process that is only available to builders of, say, 5000 rather than 50 houses a year.

If the successful adoption of new technology has been incremental and, for the housebuilder, low in adoption cost, the holy grail has been prefabrication or off-site production, a matter of recent topicality as volume housebuilders such as Beazer, Westbury and Wilson Connolly all established factories to produce timber-framed houses in the late 1990s in an attempt to exploit the economies of scale. The reality is that off-site production has been increasing throughout the twentieth century. Ive and McGhie stressed that the discussion of industrialised or prefabricated buildings 'has tended to distract' from the significance of industrialised building materials and equipment.[16] Go back to the inter-war period and carpenters were making staircases, doors and windows on site; in the 1920s concrete roof tiles were made in small presses.[17] Now, when whole bathroom units can be provided in prefabricated form, the ultimate conclusion is to move to producing prefabricated buildings.

There has been considerable debate on the merit of prefabricated structures but the most recent experiments have not proved successful. One of Persimmon's first actions on acquiring Beazer in 2001 was to dispose of the latter's factories. Wilson Connolly bought a timber-framed factory in 2000

---

[15] Ball, 'Chasing a Snail', p. 13.
[16] Ive, 'The Relationship of Construction to other Industries', pp. 3, 6.
[17] Wellings, *The History of Marley*, pp. 14, 21.

but its 2001 Annual Report confessed that 'the Group embarked upon a major shift to timber-framed construction without much attention being paid to the commercial benefits of doing so'. In 2002, a new chief executive announced 'a dramatic shift back to traditional housebuilding'.[18] Westbury invested £13 m. in a factory capable of producing 5000 prefabricated housing units a year; 'Space4' was to supply a substantial part of Westbury's requirements, and generate sales to third parties. Although instrumental in Westbury winning the 'Best building efficiency initiative' in the *Building Homes* Quality Awards in 2001, Space4 incurred pre-tax losses of £4 m. and £3 m. in financial years 2003 and 2004 respectively.

Other housebuilders refused to be drawn too far down the path of prefabrication. At a press conference in December 2000, the Berkeley Group managing director was asked about the economics of prefabrication:

> 'There's no savings in costs. I don't believe you will see modular construction at, say, Imperial [a site in Hammersmith with over 1500 units planned] because you do not get the flexibility. You couldn't build that as attractively using a modular system.'

The advantages or otherwise of using prefabricated units on large sites can make for an interesting debate but, as with the earlier discussion on technological change, it is a debate that is not really germane to the economics of large sites. Prefabricated buildings can be used or not as suits the site; there is no more need for the production facilities to be owned (which would necessitate scale) than the housebuilder needs to own the brick manufacturer.

Scope – the economies of the large firm

Economies of scale do not provide an adequate explanation for the growth in size of housebuilding firms; to be fair to the housebuilders, where the term is used by them, it is in the sense of the economies which relate not to the size of the production unit but to the size of the firm. This is a distinction well recognised in the literature although the analysis tends to be manufacturing oriented and the speculative housebuilding industry does not sit neatly within the various descriptive frameworks. Chandler uses *Scale and Scope* as a title and described the 'three-pronged investment in

---

[18] *Building*, 1st March 2002, p. 22.

production, distribution and management that brought the modern industrial enterprise into being'.[19] Prais and Penrose also use manufacturing
analogies to distinguish the concepts of scale and scope: Penrose notes that
'one can distinguish the economies of size applying to plants from those
applying to firms' and Prais discusses 'the rise of large multi-plant manufacturing firms'.[20]

Although the economies that Prais identified related to manufacturing
firms, his exploration of the desire for market power as a driving force provides an interesting starting point for the examination of the housebuilding
industry.[21] Could the exercise of market power be the rationale behind the
housebuilders' drive for increased size? The 'desire for greater market
power' in the sense of an ability to control the marketplace can be dismissed
fairly quickly. No doubt housebuilders, like any other business, would use
whatever power was available but no group of companies has the requisite
control over its customer, the house purchaser. Even though the top ten
housebuilders had over 40% of the market for new houses at the end of the
1990s, their product competes, more or less equally, with second-hand
houses; new houses represent, in broad terms, around 12% of the total
number of housing transactions. The top ten new housebuilders account,
therefore, for around 5% of total housing sales: housebuilders are price-
takers, not price-setters.

The larger firm may have a number of advantages derived from its size;
land is the key to a housebuilder's success so any advantage that size brings
to its ability to find land, and finance its purchase could be an important
determinant of increased concentration in the industry. Land acquisition
and its finance are therefore discussed in detail below, followed by marketing and purchasing economies. It will be argued that, although the larger
firm can be seen to have certain advantages, they are not considered to be of
such magnitude as to *necessitate* an increased size of firm.

Land acquisition and finance

The most important raw material for any housebuilder is land, and
specifically land which either has, or can obtain, planning permission. Can
larger housebuilders exercise market power as buyers? Clearly, the top ten
housebuilders have a much larger share of the market for residential land

---

[19] Chandler, *Scale and Scope*, p. 8.
[20] Penrose, *The Theory of the Growth of the Firm*, p. 89; Prais, *The Evolution of Giant Firms in Britain*, p. 60.
[21] Prais, ibid., p. 60.

than for total housing, although with development land having alternative uses (commercial, industrial, leisure) they are also in competition for some land with those outside their immediate peer group. Moreover, it is not just the top ten that would have to exercise some form of market power as land buyers; there might be many times that number capable of bidding for any particular piece of land that came on to the market. Vendors normally retain professional advice and it is difficult to imagine scenarios in which housebuilders could systematically exercise monopsonistic power over what is their scarcest raw material.

Even if the idea that large companies can control the market for land is dismissed, does being a large company provide a competitive advantage over the small company? Does size (rather than collusion) confer an advantage? The larger firms have specialised land departments but these should not necessarily be regarded as a benefit of scale but a consequent cost and perhaps even a dilution of the entrepreneurial flair of the founder. In practice, land departments may cover a variety of functions ranging from identifying the land buying opportunity and the purchase negotiation, down to the processing of the land through the planning system. The ability to acquire suitable land rests on a whole variety of factors – knowledge of what might be for sale, expertise in assessing its development potential, negotiating skill and the financial ability to effect the purchase. The first three of these factors are typical entrepreneurial skills; they do not require large organisations for them to be effective. Indeed, many vendors appreciate the advantages inherent in dealing with the top man in a smaller organisation rather than the more bureaucratic structures of the larger firm; the necessity to acquire large quantities of land each year to service the requirements of the volume housebuilders requires many employee land buyers, and this diffuses the skills of the entrepreneur at the head of the firm.

Financial strength is a factor where size might automatically be assumed to be an advantage in facilitating the purchase and exploitation of large sites; indeed, the statement might even be deemed 'obvious'. However, some of the largest sites to have been developed in the twentieth century were those in the London suburbs before the war, and these were frequently acquired by individuals or firms that were still of modest size. In his study of Bexley, Carr argued that:

> 'The rise in the price of land since the 1920s was of comparatively little importance, for although the biggest single capital outlay for any individual builder it constituted only a relatively insignificant proportion of total development costs.'[22]

---

[22] Carr, 'The Development and Character of a Metropolitan Suburb', p. 245.

The 1953 AGM of MRCE confirmed this view: 'Before the war the supply of building land available and suitably planned greatly exceeded the demand in many areas and thus kept the pre-war price of virgin land very moderate indeed.'[23]

Funds for land purchase in the inter-war period appeared to come from a variety of sources, including the clearing banks. The 'Macmillan Gap' epitomised the problems that small and medium sized businesses faced in obtaining capital; however, it was not fixed capital that the housebuilders required, but finance for working capital and it may be that they found more favour with the clearing banks than did manufacturing industry. Bundock argued that the importance of the banks should not be underestimated as it was probably 'more significant in their land purchase considerations than many of the builders interviewed admitted'. He also noted that banks appeared willing to lend to housebuilders 'even where they were inexperienced',[24] a foretaste of lending policies to come. Capital also came from private sources and there was some direct financial support from building societies. The Coventry Building Society asked, 'How far was the Society financing builders . . . builders' finance was supplied in the Oxford area . . . but literally all over England and Wales.'[25] Henry Boot received building society support for its large rental estates at Sheffield, Corby and Croydon;[26] John Laing turned to what had been his local building society, the Cumberland, to provide mortgages for his first London estates,[27] and the history of the Haywards Heath Building Society records that 'the Society lent money to . . . developers in the 1930s, such as Summerhill Estates'.[28] There is little evidence from the limited archives, or the few histories, that access to finance for land purchases was any more of a problem for small rather than large housebuilders.

If papers can be written asking whether banks have failed British industry by insufficient lending, the banking system could more properly be criticised for over-lending to the housebuilding industry. Surveys in the *Investors Chronicle* of over 20 predominantly small quoted housebuilders showed that, in 1974, average borrowings were 82% of the cost of land holdings and, in 1975, 162% of equity capital. In the late 1960s and early 1970s, the secondary banks lent to a wide range of developers. Unquoted

23 *The Times*, 24th Feb. 1954.
24 Bundock, 'Speculative Housebuilding', pp. 634–5.
25 Davis, *Every Man his own Landlord*, p. 74.
26 Ritchie, *The Abbey National Story*, p. 85; Hobson, *A Hundred Years of the Halifax*, pp. 111–12.
27 Coad, *Laing*, pp. 112–13.
28 Ford, *The Story of the Haywards Heath Building Society 1890–1990*, p. 18.

companies could be found with even higher borrowing ratios: 20 years later Richard Fraser still marvelled at the ability of his finance director to get the secondary and tertiary banks to lend Westbury 'large sums of money on very iffy schemes. We were highly geared, never mind 50%, we were geared something like 10-1. You wonder how the banks ever lent these sums of money to the company.'[29]

Similar willingness to lend was seen in the late 1980s as, once again, the housing boom reached a peak. The borrowing ratios were not as excessive as in the early 1970s as some of the quoted companies operated a prudent borrowing policy. Nevertheless, the average gearing of 24 of the larger quoted housebuilders and housing contractors had reached close to 50% by the onset of recession in 1990; within that, companies such as Countryside and McCarthy & Stone had gearing ratios of over 150% and Beazer and Costain were close to 100%. Even these figures ignored the substantial off-balance sheet borrowing that many developers had used to finance their land purchases. (The same observation was made about commercial property developers in Scott's *The Property Masters*.) Outside the ranks of the larger quoted companies, higher debt percentages could be found: for example, when Fairbriar went into administration in 1990, £41 m. of its equity was supporting £93 m. of loans plus unquantified off-balance sheet debt.

The financial lessons of the 1990 recession appear to have been well learnt in the quoted sector and, as boom conditions emerged again in the late-1990s, the quoted companies operated with relatively modest gearing levels. However, a more relaxed attitude to debt financing could be found in the private arena, with the venture capital firms and the Scottish clearing banks playing a more prominent role. For instance, six housebuilding MBOs were financed in 1999 and 2000 (Banner, Wainhomes, Cala, Ward, Linden and Fairview) and, for the five that remained independent,[30] the gearing levels in 2001 were staggering: a combined debt of £515 m. was supported by only £66 m. of net equity – and almost all of that equity consisted of goodwill.[31] The banks were also prepared to provide substantial support to new entrants to the industry, the most striking example being Gladedale, mentioned above. It was financed by the Bank of Scotland and when Gladedale was building less than 300 units in 2000, its accounts showed debt of £83 m. supported by net tangible assets of only £8 m. Gladedale was subsequently able to use bank debt to finance the acquisitions of Furlong, Bett Homes and Country & Metropolitan.

---

[29] Interview with Richard Fraser, Sep. 2000.
[30] Wainhomes was taken over in 2001.
[31] See *PHA* 2002, pp. 12–14.

Although it does not appear that the financial sector has limited access to capital, it may be helpful to outline some of the specific means of site finance, outside the banking system, that have been available to the house-builder. Bundock wrote extensively about land acquisition in the inter-war period, and although he argued that quantitative analysis was not possible on the basis of the evidence known, he detailed a wide range of examples. He noted that the purchase of the whole of a landed estate or farm was a rarity, 'generally the speculative housebuilder appears to have purchased just one part . . . of farms, private estates, or other single ownerships for his development purposes'. Estates were subdivided, sometimes because the whole estate had failed to achieve the desired price, or it was considered too large by potential purchasers; while some of these subdivisions ran into hundreds of acres, appropriate only for the larger firms, there were also many sales of a few acres a time, permitting the smaller housebuilder to operate in the same market. For those housebuilders that could not even afford small undeveloped acreages, serviced sites were advertised for a 10% deposit and several years to pay; indeed Bundock noted that those interviewees who had experience of inter-war purchase of serviced land said that they were almost always able to defer the balance of payment for each plot until they had sold the house.[32]

Land acquisition methods have changed little over time and in the 1980s Short et al. were still able to argue that financial strength was 'a useful but not overriding factor in the acquisition of prime land – much more important is early knowledge and early securing of the resource by outright purchase, option agreement or conditional contract.'[33] Vendors may still split the sale of large sites because it suits their own financial or taxation position, or because they receive a better price by acceding to developers' cash flow requirements. The plot-by-plot sale has been adopted by public sector, often referred to as 'on the drip'. Perhaps the most common form of deferred payment today is through options or conditional contracts which are subject to satisfactory planning consent and allow the developer time to deal with all the planning issues and consents. However, there is nothing new about option arrangements and Bundock describes their extensive use in the inter-war years as a means of reducing development risk.[34]

---

[32] Bundock, 'Speculative Housebuilding', pp. 419–687.
[33] Short, *Housebuilding Planning and Community Action*, p. 45.
[34] Bundock, 'Speculative Housebuilding', pp. 639–48.

Access to brownfield land

One of the changes that has taken place in the industry is the increasing proportion of urban building on previously used sites. Before the war, and through the 1960s and 1970s, the industry was overwhelmingly developing 'greenfields'; today, some 70% of private housing units are built on 'brownfield land'. The public sector initiatives of the 1970s in urban regeneration gradually gave way in the 1980s to private sector redevelopment, London Docklands being the best known example. It might be logical to expect that urban regeneration would place a greater importance on financial strength. The sites are expensive to buy, infrastructure and decontamination costs are incurred before building starts and the flats have to be built in complete blocks (as opposed to a few houses at a time). There is less scope for physically splitting the site between builders to reduce the capital outlay; thus the capital requirements of urban regeneration would drive the industry further towards larger units and hence consolidation. If this is the theory, the empirical evidence suggests that it is seriously flawed. If financial resources necessitated scale then the industry's mergers and acquisitions would have featured urban developers. To this author's knowledge, there had been no acquisitions of predominantly urban developers until Lend Lease bought Crosby Homes from Berkeley in 2005; instead, the acquisitions have been of substantially greenfield builders. More to the point, neither would the small urban developer have prospered if the larger developer possessed overriding economies of scale.

Large companies can undoubtedly claim that their size makes it easier to facilitate the purchase of large urban sites and, more to the point, finance the subsequent work in progress. During the 1990s the Berkeley Group, for instance, purchased individual sites costing more than £30 m. with subsequent capital commitments in excess of that. As the top ten housebuilders became ever larger in the second half of the 1990s, their relative financial economies of scale were greater than they ever had been. Nevertheless, there are numerous examples of small companies buying hospitals, army barracks, and developing large sites in city centres; they manage to do so with limited, at times extremely limited, capital resources. One early example is Regalian, which had only just emerged from a period of heavy losses when (according to its chairman) it 'pioneered the whole urban regeneration movement in 1980, when it broke completely new ground with the refurbishment and launch of its Battersea Village project', following the purchase of an estate of 450 vacant flats from the local authority at Battersea.[35]

---

[35] Regalian accounts, 1988.

Moving forward to more contemporary transactions, a range of examples can be found of small housebuilders undertaking urban renewal. The privately owned Weston Homes first achieved 100 units a year in 1997 and 200 in 2001 by which time its capital base was £7 m.; it had completed such projects as the refurbishment of Highlands Hospital, Winchmore Hill, with a sales value of £7 m.; was about to start a 350 unit development in the Isle of Dogs, with a sales value of £96 m.; and to purchase the Royal Earlswood Hospital, Redhill, at a cost of £4 m. Operating off an even smaller capital base at the time, Gladedale, mentioned above, built only 58 units in 1999 but was still able to buy the 180-acre former Shoeburyness Barracks for a proposed 430 unit development: 'We won it because we did a great deal of homework and made the best presentation in the design and tender process.'[36] Entrepreneurial flair and flexibility are even more important in urban redevelopment than in greenfield building, and were epitomised by Raven Homes' redevelopment of a 46-acre asylum near Hereford in 2002:

'The site had been on the market for a while and I know of other companies that were interested but no one could get the site to work out. It would have frightened the life out of most housebuilders because there were all these conversions and there's a lot more problems with them than straight new-build housing, which is what most housebuilders want.'[37]

There are even small companies that do nothing other than urban redevelopment. Tom Bloxham, through his company Urban Splash, pioneered city centre redevelopment in Manchester and Liverpool, and by the age of 32 had redeveloped 750,000 square metres of warehouse space in the two cities.[38] Another example of the ability of small companies to handle at least medium-sized urban renewal projects can be found in City Lofts, founded in 1997; by the time it had obtained an AIM quotation in 2003, City Lofts had completed nine developments to a value of £117 m. and had a further eight developments worth £193 m. in progress.

It would be naive to suggest that financial clout does not help from time to time in facilitating the purchase of large sites; how much easier to put the corporate hand in the corporate back pocket than negotiate with financiers who always seem to want an unfair share of the profit. But negotiation and putting deals together is what development is all about, and the range of examples above, both for greenfield and the supposedly more complex brownfield land, shows that small companies can, and do, prosper. Finance

---

[36] Remo Dipre quoted in *Building*, Sep. 2000.
[37] *Housebuilder*, Aug. 2002, p. 26.
[38] *Building*, 1st Nov. 1996, p. 26.

for land acquisition is not, therefore, regarded as *necessitating* increased scale – merely making it easier.

Marketing economies

Both Prais and Chandler instanced marketing as one of the important economies. However, as it has already been argued that Chandler's first 'prong', namely production facilities which are large enough to exploit economies of scale, is scarcely relevant for the housebuilding industry, it somewhat undermines the second element, the investment in marketing and distribution necessary to sell that increased production. In the inter-war period, promotion of the product was entirely site specific, and most of the marketing tools 'invented' by the modern housebuilding industry have their precedents in the inter-war era. Apart from extensive advertising, with its claims of healthy suburban living (in Croydon of all places), fast commuting times and modern houses complete with all the latest appliances, there were fully furnished show houses, not only on the sites but also at the Ideal Home exhibition and at central London railway sites; free travel by private car to the site (redolent of modern time share selling); appearances and commendations by media stars (including, for those with long memories, Elsie and Doris Waters); *son et lumières*; stamp duty paid; £1 deposits; free furniture and season tickets. These incentives were frequently offered by firms operating on only a limited number of sites. It could be asked whether these marketing costs were born more economically by larger sites, but it may have been that it was only the very large sites that required such expenditure; in any case, it has already been indicated that large sites did not equate to large firms.

With some exceptions, housebuilders' advertising remained predominantly local throughout the post-war period, resting on point of sale site promotion, local agents and local newspaper advertising. The importance attached to a good reputation can be seen from the advertisements for second-hand houses in any local press: 'Built by Bloggs' and the Bloggs in question is usually a local rather than a national builder. However, for two decades after the abolition of building controls, marketing went little further than advertising: the promotional skills of the pre-war housebuilders were abandoned and forgotten. Tom Baron, founder of Whelmar and one-time advisor to Michael Heseltine, was a fierce critic of his industry's approach to marketing, and it was put trenchantly in his lecture on *Design and Marketing in the Eighties*: 'For 20 years up to 1974 we operated in a sellers' market . . . and we didn't need to work hard to sell our houses, our customers came and bought from us.' He described the industry's marketing principles as 'you can have any sort of house you want as long as it is the one I intend to build'.

Like all good generalisations, there were notable exceptions. This author remembers attending a conference in the mid-1960s where Neil Wates literally shocked the housebuilders in the audience by announcing that he would subcontract anything from the foundations to the roof but the one operation he would never subcontract was marketing. In the Midlands, McLean had a similar reputation for marketing innovation which 'contains a number of firsts . . . they have even been known to buy a prospective customer's existing house and help sell it for him'.[39] Also in the Midlands, Second City Developments, which built around 1000 units a year in the late 1970s, was run by Peter Pearce, a Fellow of the Chartered Institute of Marketing, who claimed that from the time he was appointed as housing managing director in 1969, the product was 'based on a design and pricing policy which was truly market driven . . . specific market research which defined needs and aspirations of potential purchasers'.[40]

Nevertheless, Baron's generalisation remains a fair assessment of the post-war period, and it was typified by Wimpey, the industry leader:

> 'They were very conservative, limited house types and it was just carrying on pushing, pushing; what happened was a culture that marketing didn't apply to housing. It wasn't just that it was a seller's market, I heard it expressed. . . . When Barratt came on the scene with their marketing techniques, Wimpey just said that's a complete waste of money'.[41]

Although, as mentioned above, companies such as McLean and Wates had paid attention to marketing in the late 1950s and 1960s, the sellers' market for housing that had pertained since the War had not encouraged the industry as a whole to be marketing oriented. It was not until the late 1970s that the industry as a whole afforded marketing the attention that it deserved and the leader of that change was Barratt: 'I'm always amazed at the way Lawrie Barratt has persuaded the rest of us that we are in a marketing business rather than a building business. He alone convinced the industry that it had to be market orientated'.[42] Precedents for many of the marketing schemes Barratt employed could be found in earlier periods (although it was surprising in the interviews, how many housebuilders were totally unaware of the marketing ideas prevalent in the inter-war period); what Barratt did was to implement them systematically and reinforce them by the creation of a national brand.

---

[39] Madden, 'Builders and their Businesses 7: John McLean & Sons Ltd. of Wolverhampton', p. 147.
[40] Interview with Peter Pearce, Nov. 2000.
[41] Interview with David Penton, Oct. 1999.
[42] Tom Baron quoted in *Housebuilder*, Aug. 1986.

Although Wimpey was a nationally known concern by virtue of its size, it was Barratt that pioneered the deliberate creation of a national brand; the Company advertised heavily on television in the 1970s and its oak tree, helicopter and Patrick Allan became familiar. This was associated with a period of undoubted commercial success for Barratt and it must be presumed that its national advertising played some part in this. However, when Granada Television screened two critical *World in Action* programmes in the early 1980s, the highly promoted Barratt name became a liability, and its sales collapsed from 16,500 in 1983 to 6800 in 1987. Since then, no other housebuilder has considered that the economics of scope merit the creation of a national housebuilding brand. At the end of the 1990s Bryant advertised on the Classic FM radio station and Berkeley Homes had a brief awareness advertising campaign on television, but with very little long-term benefit; these were no more than exceptions to the generally accepted practice of specific site advertising in either the property sections of the quality national papers or, more widespread, the local media. Indeed, over the last couple of decades, some housebuilders have actually adopted marketing policies that reduce the benefits of a nationally known brand name; Barratt itself has its KingsOak brand and a range of other examples are discussed below.

The need to stimulate consumer choice on large sites encourages land swaps between builders so that there can be a variety of brand names on the one site, and individual housebuilders have occasionally justified different brand names within their own organisation as it allows them that same diversity on large sites. 'We were helped by the fact that on a big tract of land we could have three of our own companies working – Tarmac, McLean, and Midland and General.'[43] Different names have also been used for different segments of the market: Countryside and Redrow introduced the Copthorn and Harwood names respectively for lower cost housing, while Beazer and then Persimmon retained the Charles Church brand for its luxury housing. However, the use of differing brands within the same housebuilder can go further. Housebuilders may retain existing local names where they are of long standing and of good repute: Kier trades under the names of Allison, Bellwinch and Twigden. Other housebuilders deliberately create new brands. NorthCountry Homes [sic] registered a series of names during the 1990s, provocatively using names that had been taken over by other housebuilders and abandoned – including Broseley, Clarke and Whelmar. Berkeley, as well as taking over Crosby and retaining its name for the Group's northern business, also created St George for the

---

[43] Interview with Eric Pountain, Nov. 2000.

London market, St Andrew and St David for Scotland and Wales, Beaufort for the west of England and St James for a joint venture.

For the housebuilding industry, marketing economies of scale could only be regarded as a significant influence on size if national advertising and the creation of a brand image was important in securing sales. The evidence of housebuilders' own strategies suggests that national marketing economies are not significant. No housebuilder has repeated the investment that Barratt put into the creation and exploitation of a national brand while some, albeit a minority, actually foster the use of separate brands within the same organisation. Marketing remains site oriented with the benefits available to large and small firms alike. This is not entirely illogical: the housing product is not moveable like a car or washing machine which can be brought to the customer; neither can it be utilised, like a petrol station or restaurant, by the customer temporarily moving to the point of sale. If the housebuilder does not have a site exactly where you want to live, down to the right side of the railway line, with the appropriate number of rooms, then no amount of brand creation will help.

Purchasing

Purchasing is an important economy of scale in some industries, but only recently has it been mentioned as a factor behind the increased consolidation within the housebuilding industry. In the pre-war and early post-war periods purchasing was generally through builders' merchants at a local level. The housebuilders themselves were local, and the building materials industry had a tradition and preference for dealing through merchants until at least the 1970s, as disclosed in assorted Monopolies and Price Commission Reports. For instance, at least 60% of all bricks were distributed through merchants, as were 95% of cement, all plasterboard, and almost all sanitary ware. As customers were progressively given the opportunity to deal directly with the manufacturers, there was increased opportunity to obtain purchasing economies but it was not until the mid-1990s that purchasing was given as even a minor benefit of an acquisition or merger, and that only in a few instances. Persimmon's offer document for Ideal in 1996 referred to 'improved buying power for building supplies' and its bid for Beazer looked for 'enhanced purchasing power'; the abortive Bryant/Beazer merger proposal of 2000 had mentioned 'procurement savings'; and a Wimpey press release instanced 'improved procurement' from the continued integration of McLean in 2001.

Apart from those examples, there was very little attempt to argue the merits of scale procurement. Interestingly, no contractor has numbered procurement as one of the benefits of owning a housebuilder; others played down the advantages. Berkeley's managing director responded to a specific question on group procurement at a December 2000 press conference:

'I don't believe that size would give us anything. I believe that a single owner-driver housebuilder, by and large, can buy most of the components for a single house as well as we can. We had a big team up to three years ago that did group procurement . . . It cost us more to run the system than gain in discounts.'

Neither did the interview process for the thesis produce strong support for purchasing economies as a material economy of size. Philip Davies thought that a firm of Linden's size (then around 700 units a year) could get effective buying through a large merchant who could probably get better terms than any housebuilder. Also, given the trend towards more complex urban schemes 'I can't see the advantage: materials are so varied that bulk rates do not represent a great saving'.[44] David Wilson, running a 4000 unit a year company, said that he was somewhat sceptical about the benefits of central purchasing for, although they did have such a facility, he thought that the local man could probably do the best deal.[45]

A thoughtful article on centralisation appeared in *Housebuilder*[46] as the final draft of this book was been prepared, and it was anxiously read in case it contradicted everything I had already written. In fact, it sat on the fence, producing arguments from both centralised and devolved buying proponents. Westbury had a preference for standardised house types (without which, bulk buying would be pointless) and asserted that 'there is no sense in buying 400 bathrooms from someone when we could buy 4000 and get a better deal out of it.' Bellway, in contrast, favoured 'almost wholly autonomous regions' and although there were national purchasing deals, the divisions could opt out. Their finance director admitted to regular debates on procurement but 'we do not think our method leaves us missing out too much. Local managements can still get good deals.' A sample of two is hardly representative but it is Bellway that has had the better profit margins. The debate will no doubt continue and really purchasing is only a part of the wider debate on centralised or autonomous management structures. At best it could be argued that procurement is one of the compensations rather than a reason for size. As an issue, it comes a long way behind the land buying decision and to put buying in perspective, this section concludes with the pithy observation of Swan Hill's John Theakston: 'If you

---

[44] Interview with Philip Davies, Feb. 2000.
[45] Interview with David Wilson, Feb. 2001.
[46] *Housebuilder*, Nov. 2005, pp. 27–8.

get the land decisions wrong, then no amount of discount on bricks is going to get you out of the hole.'[47]

Diseconomies of scale

Businesses experience organisational diseconomies as they grow in size, and this is well documented in the academic literature. For the housebuilding industry the issues extend beyond the increased costs of supervision and communication as, perhaps even more important, the increase in firm size may dilute the entrepreneurial flair that was responsible for creating the earlier growth. As early as 1937, Coase noted that 'there may be decreasing returns to the entrepreneur function, that is, the costs of organising additional transactions within the firm may rise.'[48] A contemporary view from Casson, specifically writing about enterprise and leadership, expressed similar concerns. Although not writing with housebuilding in mind, he described the weakening supervisory links as firms increase in size: 'jobs are increasingly delegated to people who are not personally known to the entrepreneur'.[49] It is only fair to concede that Penrose took a different approach, arguing that the once universally agreed concept of diminishing returns to management could no longer be supported and that 'single-minded direction' could now be achieved through 'an appropriate form of organisation'. She suggested that it was the capacity of the firm to alter its administrative structure that made it difficult to say that there was a point where a firm is too big to be efficiently managed.[50] This is not a view shared by those writing specifically about the housebuilding industry, nor supported by the evidence of the large housebuilders (10,000 plus) that emerged in the 1980s. However, there is evidence that today's large housebuilders are trying to adapt their structures to minimise the organisational diseconomies.

Those commenting specifically on the building industry have reinforced the views of the business historian. Harloe et al. argued that problems of site supervision increased as the companies grew, requiring more elaborate organisation and expertise.[51] Grebler made similar observations on US housebuilders, noting the conventional wisdom that the organisation of residential projects is so complex that 'the large builder is apt to incur

---

[47] John Theakston interview in *Housebuilder*, May 2001.
[48] Coase, 'The Nature of the Firm', pp. 394–5.
[49] Casson, *Enterprise and Leadership*, p. 75.
[50] Penrose, *The Theory of the Growth of the Firm*, p. 18.
[51] Harloe, *The Organisation of Housing*, p. 141.

incremental overhead expenses which tend to offset his other cost advantages'. The large firm had to extend its 'span of management' requiring a hierarchy of supervisors to ensure efficiency.[52] Although diseconomies of scale is discussed in this book as a late twentieth-century problem, there is some evidence that Ideal, then three times the size of its nearest competitor, was being affected before the Second War. Horsey argued that:

> 'Combines such as New Ideal Homesteads suffered from the relatively new problems of large size and loose organisation: notably, insufficient supervision of subcontractors or their own employees, leading to pilferage . . . short cuts in construction, and the sale of houses before proper installation of essential services.'[53]

The organisational problem in the housebuilding industry centres not on the individual operating unit but on the regional structures. The consensus is that the ideal size for one operational manager is 400–500 houses a year in a localised area, a rough and ready figure that has regularly been mentioned to me by managements since the 1960s; a recent public iteration was Wimpey's reference to its regional businesses being 'around the 500 units a year capacity of received housebuilding management wisdom'.[54] Increased corporate size requires not the doubling of the operating unit, but its replication and ultimately the introduction of additional layers of management. Given the limitations on the number of executives that might report directly to a group managing director, further increases in size require yet another intermediate layer of supervision. Not only does that incur a monetary cost but it also imposes a motivational barrier. The local managing director may now have two layers of management above him, yet if he is to produce acceptable performance he has to be of a calibre where he could have been, for instance, a main board director of a smaller company. In particular, the entrepreneurial land buying has to be delegated to individuals who can no longer be directly supervised by the group managing director; yet these subsidiary managements are competing against independent companies of similar size where the land buying may be personally directed by the controlling entrepreneur. It is in these subsidiary entities that the entrepreneurial flair can be lost: the then Redrow finance director commented that 'In any housebuilder there are a limited number of people at the top who add value, significant value, through land purchases. A large acquisition would dilute those skills – it is unlikely that there are people down the organisation who have them.'[55]

---

[52] Grebler, *Large Scale Housing and Real Estate Firms*, p. 65.
[53] Horsey, 'London Speculative Housebuilders of the 1930s', p. 151.
[54] Keith Cushen quoted in *Building Homes*, April 2001.
[55] Interview with Neil Fitzimmons, Aug. 2001.

Quoted company accounts provide some indication of the regional structure of a national housebuilder as the practice of listing the individual subsidiaries and the regions became increasingly common over the last decade or two. Such lists may not be totally accurate representations of the organisation (there may be area offices without legal form), but they do give an indication of the diffusion of management in a national housebuilder. In the pre-1990 period, three housebuilders exceeded annual sales of 10,000 units, and of these Wimpey's housebuilding structure, for so long integrated with its construction, was opaque. Barratt, however, was more informative: at its peak in 1983, it had sales of 16,500 and to manage that volume, the 1982 accounts showed that it required five UK housebuilding regions, in turn supervising 29 housebuilding subsidiaries, averaging just under 500 units each. By the end of the decade, Tarmac was building in excess of 12,000 units out of 21 subsidiaries, or just under 600 per subsidiary; its regional organisation was not stated.

These three firms stood head and shoulders above the rest of the industry by size; each went on to suffer substantial declines in volumes. Barratt fell from 16,500 in 1983 (with plans for 18,000) to under 5000 in 1993; McLean from 12,000 in 1988 to 6000 in 1994; and Wimpey from 10,700 in 1986 to 5500 in 1992. There was no single reason for these substantial declines. Barratt's sales were crippled by two critical Granada *World in Action* television programmes in 1983 and 1984. McLean's parent, Tarmac, had to contend with rising debt and problems across the group; in 1992 Neville Simms, previously managing director of the construction division, was appointed group chief executive with a policy to release capital by reducing the size of the housing division. In 1996 Tarmac sold its housing division to Wimpey in exchange for the latter's construction and quarrying. Wimpey, too, had recession-induced problems across a broad front, combined with managerial changes and was not sufficiently focused on housing to drive it forwards. Whatever the proximate causes, it remains the fact that three housebuilding firms, each of which was the industry number one for a time, not only failed to grow but actually experienced substantial volume declines. It is not necessarily a cause but, nevertheless, a common feature for all three was the dilution of the entrepreneurial flair which created the firms.

For a contemporary comparison, the year 2001 was the first ever that there were three housebuilders, Barratt, Persimmon and Wimpey, each building more than 10,000 units in the same year. There are differences between the firms (Persimmon, for instance, includes the low volume, high price Charles Church brand) but Table 9.1 demonstrates the large number of subsidiaries, each with their own managing director and boards, all reporting

Table 9.1   Housebuilders' regional structures, 2001.

Housebuilder	Units	Regions	Subsidiaries	Subsidiaries per region	Units per subsidiary
Barratt	11,310	5	29	5.8	390
Persimmon	12,051	7	33	4.7	365
Wimpey	11,537	3	23	7.7	502

Source: Company accounts.

upwards through regional chains of command, that are necessary to process large volumes. These management structures have yet to be tested by recession.

Managerial responses to the problems of control and motivation vary in the emphasis on either centralisation or delegation. The Barratt approach to controlling a large organisation during its growth phase was standardisation, both of the product and the development procedures; there was no doubt that edicts from Newcastle were to be followed. This was both a strength in providing a framework for growth and yet a weakness in that it inhibited local flexibility. In an interesting interview comment, John Cassidy, one-time deputy chairman, reflected on one man who ignored the system:

> 'Tony Fawcett was the finest managing director I have ever come across in the industry. He didn't like the Barratt philosophy; he liked to run his own business. The philosophy when I became involved was to build 70% for the first-time buyer, and in Manchester we were building 1000–1100 houses in the late 70s and making £3 m. profit. Tony, over in Yorkshire, ignored the first-time buyer market – he did 400 houses a year and he also made £3 m. profit. Because he was successful doing it his way, Lawrie was never in a position to challenge it.'[56]

Other housebuilders attempt to address the supervisory challenge by delegating as much authority as possible down to the local subsidiary whilst maintaining key supervisory controls at the centre. Berkeley probably took that as far as most, with its profusion of brand names and annual reports stressing 'the importance of autonomous operating companies'. Grebler quoted a similar philosophy from the chief executive of a large US housing company:

> 'The continuing struggle for a large company is to try to get the advantages of the relatively small, localised, hard-hitting firm and at the same

---

[56] Interview with John Cassidy, March 1999.

time get the advantage that a large firm has in financing . . . We are trying more and more to give our . . . division managers wide areas of lati-
tude and to encourage them to think as one does in running his own
business.'[57]

The disadvantage, of course, is that the housebuilder becomes more exposed to the mistakes of those appointed at a divisional level, a point made
by one of the most successful housebuilders of recent times, Redrow's
Morgan: 'The bigger you get the harder it is to control and anybody who
says different is not telling the truth. The further you get from head office
the more the cost overruns.'[58] The problems underlying regional expansion
are discussed further below.

The diseconomies of scale arise not from larger and larger sites but from
the need to introduce new operating units as the housebuilder expands geographically. The strategies for opening new regions vary. Some firms have
preferred the acquisition route, as did Barratt in the 1970s. Although there
is more than one motive for making acquisitions, they can provide a ready-
made nucleus of local management. For those who prefer to move into a
new location from scratch, there is a choice between recruiting a manager
from that new region, conversant with all the peculiarities of his area and
with an established network of contacts; or sending an existing manager,
already known and trusted by the group, to develop the new region. A more
cautious approach was to split an existing region in two and let the organisation creep out. There is no clear consensus about the best way to develop
regionally. Bryant in the 1990s and McLean in the 1970s and 1980s, both
believed in using their existing management: 'We [McLean] always sent in
one of our own people; we didn't go out and recruit. Our monthly management meetings were very intense and the men who could cope with the
heat were going to be good managers.'[59] Persimmon's Duncan Davidson
was a strong advocate of seeking out the right local managing director
before opening a new office; Redrow favoured splitting regions although it
also used the acquisition of Costain Homes in 1993 to move into the south-
east. Usually, new regions were contiguous with existing operations but
occasionally firms would make a more distant investment, as did the
Edinburgh-based Cala when it bought the Surrey Anns Homes in 1983.

Some firms found the organisational problems hit them very early in the
expansion phase. Allen Homes was part of the successful Allen construction

---

[57] Grebler, *Large Scale Housing and Real Estate Firms*, p. 68.
[58] Interview with Steve Morgan, April 2003.
[59] Interview with Sir Eric Pountain, Nov. 2000.

group. Its volumes had doubled to 250 in 1987 and its profitability encouraged Allen to move into new areas. 'They had a grand scheme to cover the whole country in the mid-1980s; we had to be a national housebuilder. We had planned out the regions.' In 1986, managers were recruited to start operations in Yorkshire, North Wales and the West Midlands. In the late 1980s, offices in Stoke, Leicester and Nottingham were being opened. 'So we had seven operating companies that were going to do 500 each. Yorkshire and Midlands were a disaster and Wales was only doing 12 a year.'[60] Allen had planned its expansion too late in the cycle, its resources were spread too thinly and not every subsidiary managing director appointment worked; in the event, the addition of these new regions added little more than 10% to housing volumes.

Invariably, when a UK housebuilder has experienced problems with a part of its operation, it is not in its home area: the managerial control is lost in the distant regions. Geoffrey McLean made the point as early as 1969 before his firm became part of the Tarmac expansion drive: 'there is a great difference between operating on an ever widening arc from a central management headquarters and establishing subsidiaries in other regions'.[61] Where there are problems, it is usually a recession that exposes them. One numerical example in the public domain is Bryant, where figures derived from its subsidiary company accounts filed at Companies House were published.[62] Table 9.2 contrasts the highly profitable home area (the Midlands), even in the difficult year of 1993, with the more distant regions.

Table 9.2   Bryant Homes divisional profits.

Division	Turnover £m.		Operating profit £m.		Margins %	
Year to April	**1993**	**1994**	**1993**	**1994**	**1993**	**1994**
Central	101	132	19.7	25.1	19.5	19.1
Northern	18	45	0.9	5.5	4.9	12.3
Southern	105	121	(3.1)	4.6	(2.9)	3.8
County Homes	5	22	(0.2)	(0.2)	(4.9)	(0.8)
Total	**224**	**302**	**17.3**	**35.0**	**7.7**	**11.6**
c.f. Divisional Total in Accounts	*224*	*306*	*17.4*	*33.9*	*7.8*	*11.1*

Note: Figures may be subject to rounding errors.

---

[60] Interview with Ian Hilton, Jan. 2002.
[61] *Building*, 16th April 1969.
[62] Wellings, *Forecasting Company Profits*, p. 119.

Many other examples can be found. Newcastle-based Bellway, one of the most successful companies of the 1990s, was in serious trouble in the mid-1980s with big losses in Scotland, north-west and Yorkshire.[63] The 1990 recession created problems for Westbury in its southern division: 'We opened an office in Fareham and started buying land at exactly the wrong time. When you look back we never had a write-off in Wales or in Gloucestershire which was our home patch.'[64] Trencherwood moved away in all directions from its solid west Berkshire base in 1987, the prime cause of its subsequent financial collapse. Cala, mentioned above, remained profitable in Scotland but incurred substantial losses in southern England. The chairman was frank in his annual report: 'Recessions generally highlight weakness in controls and in individuals and Cala has not been without its difficulties'. The Manchester-based Maunders maintained its north-west profits in the 1990 recession, but the south only broke even and East Anglia lost money. The north-east firm of Cussins diversified into the south-east from the mid-1980s and had to write off some £7 m. in 1991 and 1992 as it withdrew to its still profitable homeland.

Many housebuilders were fully aware of the problems of organising growth and chose not to expand regionally. Ben Bailey stayed in the north-east, modestly doubting its competence: 'One, we probably didn't want to and two, I'm not sure that we had the ability. I don't know really. We didn't do it so I suppose we hadn't got the ability'.[65] Roy Davies ran Bryant Homes from 1958 to 1987, keeping it at more or less the same size between 1975 and 1985, building around 2000 a year; his only regional move was to open a southern office. Davies said 'I didn't want to be bigger – we couldn't see the point. I wanted to see every site at least once every eight weeks.'[66] Fairview, one of the most consistently profitable companies in the industry, remained resolutely committed to the London area. It had refused to increase its regional coverage despite being encouraged to do so when taken over by Hillsdown in 1987. Dennis Cope, the founder of the business, had never wanted to become a national builder but Hillsdown thought it a natural progression.

> 'I can remember sitting down with Harry Solomon and him saying, "What's the potential for this business, why can't we become major housebuilders?"
> "Well, we can Harry if you want. I'll open a business for you in Glasgow, I'll open a business for you in Bristol and one in Birmingham but I will

---

[63] Interview with Howard Dawe, Nov. 2001.
[64] Interview with Richard Fraser, Sep. 2000.
[65] Interview with Richard Bailey, Jan. 2002.
[66] Interview with Roy Davies, Dec. 1999.

tell you now, we'll double the size and halve the margins so what's the point. Because once you get into these regional offices you are reluctant to delegate to people at those regions the authority to spend money on sites without planning permission, you are going to have to be extremely lucky to find the number of people you want that have got the skills and the judgements." [67]

As already mentioned, by 2001 there were once again three housebuilders with an annual output in excess of 10,000 – Barratt, Persimmon and Wimpey; whether they will avoid the fate that befell the big three of the 1980s (Persimmon now stands in place of McLean) remains to be seen. There is now evidence that some of the larger housebuilders are modifying the traditional regional pyramid structure as a means of combating managerial diseconomies. Persimmon recognised that if it wished to achieve significantly higher volumes it had to adapt its organisation to cope with the managerial strains. The 1999 chairman's statement laid out the new structure whereby, under the group chief executive, the national housing business, then building around 7000 units a year, was split into separate north and south divisions, each with its own board controlling ten operating companies. Two years later, the acquisition of Beazer almost doubled the size of the group to 12,000 a year. Asked why he thought Persimmon would avoid the mistakes of the other housebuilders who had reached 10,000 a year, founder Davidson explained,

> 'The biggest single reason is that we have split the Group into three main businesses – the North, the South and Charles Church. They are run completely separately and the only link with the head office is through John White and the finance director.'

Davidson argued that, in the past, Barratt, McLean and Wimpey Homes had been run in a more centralised manner: 'Also, our people have all been there a long time.' [68] More recently, in 2004, Wilson Bowden split its David Wilson housing subsidiary (5800 units) into a north and south division, each with its own chief executive. And at Barratt's AGM in November 2005, the chairman announced a 'New structure for growth' in which the heads of an 'extended and redefined' Barratt North and Barratt South would report directly to the Board. It is too early to judge the success of this strategy of dividing the country into two substantially independent entities, although it does implicitly recognise the problems inherent in continued expansion of the reporting lines.

---

[67] Interview with Dennis Cope, Sep. 1999.
[68] Interview with Duncan Davidson, Oct. 2002.

Do large companies earn superior rewards? A statistical comparison

It is in periods of takeover activity that the arguments in favour of the economies of scale are most frequently expressed, although their validity in a battle for corporate survival may be questionable. Equally, there have been some damning refutations, for instance in the late 1980s. English China Clays had claimed, when bidding for Bryant, that without a merger Bryant (then building 2000 houses a year) would find it increasingly difficult to maintain its growth without access to greater resources. *Building's* leader article called this:

> 'a moot point . . . The scale economies of volume building have become less important for the housebuilder pursuing the predominant trade-up market Local knowledge rather than financial muscle is the key to successful land buying.'[69]

Another rebuttal came from French Kier in 1986 following Beazer's claim that its bid would 'provide benefits of synergy and a savings of scale'. Chairman, John Mott, said 'There are economies of scale, but there are also costs associated with size'.[70] As the years passed, it could be seen that it was these buyers' strategy that was found wanting. Some ex-national housebuilders were also able to be more dispassionate when they looked back on their time running national businesses. David Calverley reflected on Ideal:

> 'To me, in the eighties, having a national coverage, the economies of scale were not that great; we were all firm believers that it was all about regional knowledge, knowing your patch, accountability; appoint good regional managers and let them run the business.'[71]

The empirical evidence offered in this chapter and the supporting arguments indicate at best that there is a body of successful housebuilders who do not believe there are economies of scale of sufficient size such that they are prepared to deliberately enlarge their business. The real world provides an imperfect laboratory in which to test hypotheses and one looks for other ways to indicate that economies of scale do not necessitate (and necessitate really is the key word) a remorseless increase in size. A reasonable question to ask is what other evidence might there be of the existence or otherwise of substantial economies of scale? What would a housebuilding world look

---

[69] *Building*, 2nd Jan. 1987, p. 4.
[70] *Building*, 10th Jan. 1986, p. 15.
[71] Interview with David Calverley, Nov. 1998.

like if significant economies did exist? Presumably it would contain larger companies consistently (not occasionally) earning superior returns to smaller ones. What would it not look like? It would not contain smaller companies competing side by side with the larger ones for the same customers, for the same resources and offering the same product at the same price: in other words, at the risk of overstating the point, the current structure of the industry could not exist if there were substantial economies of scale.

It is not conceptually difficult to formulate statistical comparisons of profit margins for companies of different sizes; indeed, mathematically inclined readers of this book might expect such statistical comparisons to play a central part in the debate. However, interpreting financial comparisons is a minefield; all too often, comparisons of accounting data are made without regard to variation inherent in companies' financial data and there is a greater degree of subjectivity in the compilation of the raw statistical material than most authors will admit. Individual housebuilders may contain different mixes of low margin social housing, high margin land dealing, low margin construction, or differing sales-capital ratios, all of which affect individual profit margins. But even if it is assumed that over a large sample, these individualities may even out, it will be seen that the comparative statistical evidence does not suggest a strongly positive link between size and margins. Even if it had done, there would remain question marks over the validity of any positive correlation. Forget the fact that the companies are not homogeneous; the difficult interpretational problems centre on the related issues of causality and sample selection.

Over a long period of time, it is the more profitable firms that can afford to expand the fastest. They generate returns that can be reinvested and have stock market ratings that facilitate acquisitions. If large firms do earn higher returns, is it their size that has enabled them to achieve those returns or is it the high returns that have enabled them to expand? At the other end of the scale the causality between low volume and perhaps low margins is even harder to disentangle. There are without doubt small firms on low margins but not because they lack economies of scale. Sometimes they are firms that once were larger, but poor performance has led to lower profits and a reduction in the size of the firm.

Despite these qualifications, some basic comparisons have been made to see if there is a recognisable relationship between volume and margins. If there is, the qualifications may need to be readdressed; if not, they are of passing interest only. In the thesis, the *PHA 2002* was used to compare profit margins in year 2001; it happened to be the latest year available at the time of writing but it did, in fact, represent almost the maximum concentration achieved within the housebuilding industry (the peak was reached in 2002). If economies of scale were being achieved, that is the time when superior returns should be most evident. To check that the year 2001 was not in some way aberrant, the same calculations were performed for companies in 2000 with almost identical results; to update the results for this book, the year 2004 was also tested, with similar effect. To test a significantly earlier period, the year 1987 was selected, although slightly different size boundaries had to be used; like recent years, that year followed a sustained period of rising prosperity and was relatively free from the distortions that can arise during a recession. Again, the results were not inconsistent with those of contemporary years. It was not possible to perform the same tests on periods prior to the 1980s as there is insufficient corporate data.

The total number of companies in the 2001 *PHA* was 84, from which six were removed; two were predominantly social housing companies (on which margins are very low) and the financial data for the remaining four was either not available or unrepresentative. Figure 9.1, comprising housebuilding companies ranging in size from 50 to 15,000 units a year, shows an almost horizontal line with a low coefficient of determination. (R^2 was 0.008 for 1987, 0.004 for 2000 and 0.003 for 2004.) A chart which eliminated the very small companies (those below 500 units) would have shown a line that was almost equally horizontal, although R^2 did rise from 0.001 to 0.008. (Eliminating the very small companies gave R^2 of 0.002 for 1987, 0.005 for 2000 and 0.021 for 2004.)

In an attempt to find some range of companies where there would appear to be a recognisable difference between the smaller and the larger, the size

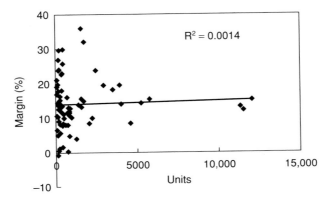

Figure 9.1 Housebuilders' margins, 2001, 50–15,000 unit companies.
Source: *PHA* 2002.

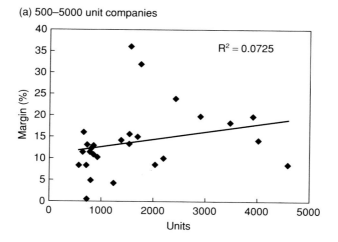

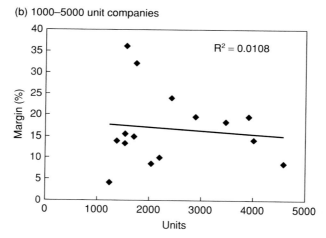

Figure 9.2   Housebuilders' margins, 2001.

Source: *PHA* 2002.

range 500 to 5000 units was taken. This has some logic in that 500 units is the size of operation generally regarded to be around the optimum for one managing director to control. Figure 9.2 (a) shows this grouping and a slightly more positive relationship between size and margin is found, but R^2 remains at no more than 0.072. (R^2 was 0.002 for 1987, 0.057 for 2000 and 0.047 for 2004.)

If the figures were to be taken at face value they might suggest that as firms increased from the single division structure of around 500 units towards a multi-division 5000 (say, a semi-national), some improvement in margin can be detected. And when the volumes are pushed higher to the large national size, that advantage disappears. However, the high variation of margins around the average and the small number of companies in the larger size category does not suggest that the data provide any convincing statistical evidence that significant benefits accrue to size. Just to illustrate what appears to be an almost random distribution of profit margins, the size group 1000–5000 was also taken and this actually shows a negative correlation (Figure 9.2 (b)). (The line for year 2000 also sloped downwards with a very low R^2 of 0.011; for 1987, the line was horizontal with R^2 infinitesimal. And for 2004 it sloped upwards with R^2 of 0.017.)

An alternative approach was considered, taking the largest companies and comparing the change in their margins over time. However, the further back chronologically the data are taken, the smaller the percentage of companies that have survived. If an historic group is taken, many (generally the poorer performing ones) will have fallen by the wayside and their data is not available for the later years; if only the survivors from the historic control group are used, then there is an inbuilt bias towards success. The same effect is true in reverse: if a contemporary control group is selected, that too has an inbuilt bias towards success as it consists only of survivors. The second difficulty is the considerable cyclical variability of profit margins; changing the base by only one year can make a large difference to the comparisons. This approach was therefore not considered helpful although, out of interest, the statistics did not support the contention that size improves margins.

The final exercise was to compare selected small companies with the returns made by large companies. Figure 9.1 showed that there was a very wide variation in margin within the smaller companies and it has been stated that the causality is harder to determine for the small than the large company. Poor financial performance, that is low or non-existent margins, does have a strong negative effect on growth. Many of the small companies are where they are because of their low margins, and not the other way round. A further complication is that more of the small companies are private and there are other ways of extracting value from a family business than by creating taxable profits. It is probably unfair to name the particular example but there is one housebuilder in the 100–500 unit size range where the owner/managing director has chosen to take over £4 m. a year more remuneration in 2003 and 2004 than he did in 2002. The published trading margins averaged 9% in these two years but adding back the owner's remuneration increases the average margin to 24%. This may be an extreme example but it does suggest that the true average margin for small companies is probably higher than the published figures suggest. It also illustrates the dangers of using simplistic statistical comparisons in corporate analysis.

Table 9.3   Best five profit margins in 2004 by size of builder.

5000–15,000 (6)	Units	Margins %
Persimmon	12,360	23.3
David Wilson	5588	21.8
Bellway	6610	19.5
Wimpey	12,232	17.8
Barratt	14,021	15.7
Average		*20.6*
1000–5000 (16)		
McCarthy & Stone	2055	46.0
Bovis	2700	26.7
Fairview	1990	20.5
Bloor	1916	19.9
Redrow	4284	19.6
Average		*26.5*
300–1000 (19)		
Wainhomes	327	35.5
Abbey	385	30.7
Strata Homes	310	27.0
Jelson	327	25.7
Ben Bailey	527	22.5
Average		*29.7*
100–300 (34)		
Chartdale Homes	158	35.3
Urban Splash	140	31.7
Oakdene	180	29.8
Churchill Retirement	112	28.8
Cavanna Group	140	28.4
Average		*31.4*

Having made that point about the averages, a final comparison of margins is made by taking the five highest trading margins from four different size groups, as shown in Table 9.3. As each size group reduces, so the average margins of the top five increases. There is a statistical weakness in this comparison in that the chance of having extreme values increases with the size of the cohort, which is why averages were used earlier. However, that is not the point that is being made; Table 9.3 is merely intended to show that in the smaller size ranges there exist groups of housebuilders that are capable of consistently high margins, higher than their larger competitors, having apparently forgone the benefits of scale. Let it be clear that this chapter is not trying to prove that small companies are inherently more profitable than large ones; only that the need to create large housebuilders in order to exploit economies of scale does not seem to be supported by the corporate data.

This chapter has examined the standard explanations for growth in corporate size and found them less than convincing. The production economies of large sites were regarded as modest and often conflicted with capital utilisation requirements; moreover, site size is largely outside the control of the housebuilder. There were more substantive arguments for economies of scope accruing to the multi-sited large housebuilders but they did not necessitate national businesses, although one could argue that they enabled companies to finance the costs of growth. The ability to acquire land because of greater financial strength, marketing and purchasing were addressed. Access to finance may assist in the purchase of very large sites but there was no evidence that finance was a constraint to either entry into the business or to the growth of smaller firms. Indeed, if there is a criticism of the financial sector it is that it is over-relaxed about lending to speculative housebuilders. Marketing tended to be localised and site oriented and the one attempt to promote aggressively a national brand (Barratt) proved counterproductive. More recently, some of the major acquisitions have been accompanied by claims of purchasing economies but not all housebuilders are convinced.

Such advantages that accrue to scale may be matched, to a greater or lesser extent, by organisational diseconomies. After a certain size (typically 500 units) housebuilders become larger by replicating their original structure on an ever widening regional basis. This introduces additional layers of supervisory and administrative costs; equally important, it dilutes the entrepreneurial flair of the business leader. Businessmen may want to expand, indeed may have many reasons for wanting to grow their firms, but it does not appear that it is economically necessary that their firms should expand. The statistical comparisons that closed this chapter show that highly profitable small firms can be found operating side by side with large firms, offering the same product, in the same marketplace.

Those who believe in the economies of scale and scope in the housebuilding industry should ask, as local housebuilders became regional and then national concerns, if the industry consolidation was economically inevitable, why did it still remain relatively easy for new entrepreneurs to continue entering this industry, compete effectively with national concerns, and then become significant businesses themselves? Although there are recognisable competitive advantages that accrue to the larger firm, this book argues that any economies that do exist in the speculative housebuilding industry are apt to be exaggerated, not of sufficient amount to necessitate the creation of large firms, and are frequently offset by organisational diseconomies. Chapters 10 and 11 concentrate on the reasons why housebuilders decline or fail, before concluding with an alternative explanation of why housebuilders seek to grow.

10

The Decline of the Private Housebuilder: a Chronology

Introduction

Picking up from the quotation from Devine in the Introduction suggesting that the analysis of growth cannot be divorced from that of decline, this chapter begins the examination of the reasons for corporate decline or failure by analysing the fate of the leading housebuilders. Rather than take them as a group, the housebuilders have been divided into three time periods: the leading firms from the 1930s; those at the end of the post-war boom; and the leading firms at the end of the 1980s. The immediate fate of the top ten was touched on in Part I, Tables 4.5, 5.4 and 6.6 but in this chapter, each period is analysed in more detail, with a summary table listing the leading housebuilders and their size; their industry ranking in 2004 if they survived; and a brief description of the reason for their departure. The predominant cause of decline amongst the pre-war housebuilders is attributed first to the cessation of housebuilding during the War and the immediate post-war period, and to succession. For the pre-1974 list the departures were a result, first, of attractive offers from acquisitive companies in the late 1960s and early 1970s; then financial failure as a result of the 1974 recession; and then succession issues. During the third period, the leading companies in the late 1980s suffered from a combination of the 1990 recession and an unwinding of earlier diversified structures; it is too early to judge the importance of succession. These companies provide the raw material for the themes that are brought together in Chapter 11.

The pre-war housebuilders

Table 10.1 returns to the list of the large pre-war housebuilders and shows that the names bear little relationship to the large housebuilders at the end

Table 10.1 The pre-war housebuilders: corporate outcome.

Company	1930s output	Fate by year 2004	2004 rank
Ideal Homes	5000	Taken over by Trafalgar House 1967; and by Persimmon 1996	
Henry Boot Homes	1500–2000	Sold to Wilson Bowden 2003	
Wates Homes	1500–2000	Independent: *c.*70 p.a.	100+
Taylor Woodrow[a]	1200–1500	Independent: 9050 p.a.	4
Davis Estates	1000–1200	Taken over by Wood Hall Trust 1957, parent acquired 1982 and withdrew from housing	
Wimpey	1200	Independent: 12,200 p.a.	3
Mactaggart & Mickel	1000	Independent: *c.*200 p.a.	60+
Costain Homes	1000+	Housing sold to Redrow 1993	
G.T. Crouch	1000	Collapsed 1984	
Laing Homes	800	Sold to Wimpey 2002	
T.F. Nash	750–1000	Vanished early post-war years	
Dares Estates	800	Rescue bid 1971 after construction losses; later withdrew from housing	
R.T. Warren	750	Taken over by Bovis 1967	
Comben & Wakeling	600	Taken over by Carlton 1971 (reverse)	
Janes	600	Taken over by Barratt 1976	
Miller	500–600	Independent: 2500 p.a.	12
Morrell Estates	500?	Collapsed 1937–39	
Mucklow	500	Withdrew from housing 1980s–90s	
William Leech	500	Taken over by Beazer 1985	
N. Moss	500?	Taken over 1946 and withdrew from housing	

[a] Taylor Woodrow's UK housing now trades as Bryant.

of the century and not much to those of even the 1970s. Their decline can be almost entirely attributed to two factors: the hiatus of wartime and building controls, and problems of succession. The table contains 20 pre-war housebuilders and summarises what happened to each individual company. Of the 20, only five names survived to 2004; Wimpey had returned as the largest private housebuilder in the second half of the 1990s, a position that it had occupied for longer than any other company. That apart, only two others (Taylor Woodrow and Miller) ranked in the top 20 in year 2004 and the other two names (Mactaggart & Mickel and Wates) can be described as no more than small housebuilders by today's standards. Even the three firms that were still in the top 20 had only reached their respective positions after experiencing long periods of decline. Wimpey built no more units in 2004 than in 1972 and its output had halved between 1972 and 1992; it was only the merger with the similarly sized McLean Homes that restored its volumes. Taylor Woodrow, having recovered rapidly to around 1200 units in the mid-1950s, had lengthy periods at around 500 a year and did not surpass 1200 a year again until 1996; it was only the purchase of Bryant in 2001 that took Taylor Woodrow back into the top ten. Miller did regain its pre-war output levels in the mid-1950s but it was not until

40 years later that its housing output began to grow. It is only fresh generations of management that allowed these three housing businesses to
recover and then expand. Not one single pre-war housebuilder, therefore,
has avoided long periods of decline; the best that can be said is that a few of
them survived long enough with their other interests to regroup and focus
once more on their original housing businesses.

The hiatus of 15 years of war and post-war controls meant that businesses
were run down, founders passed through what would have been a conventional retiring age without being able to restart, succession patterns were
broken and, crucially for many of the larger firms, other activities came to
dominate. Fifteen years can represent a whole generation of employee
directors; include a few more years for rebuilding the original business and
it does literally represent a business generation. Some of the pre-war housebuilders turned into national, even international, contractors. As outlined
in Part I, this was particularly true of Wimpey, Laing, Taylor Woodrow and
Costain. The wartime effort of building airfields, defence works and the
Mulberry Harbour created a massive resource of construction and civil
engineering expertise. Unable to resume private housing, the directors
capitalised on their wartime experience by creating national or even
international construction businesses. By the time building controls were
removed, the parent company boards were dominated by contractors and
engineers. Taylor Woodrow and Wimpey were two that rapidly resumed
their pre-war housing operations, but only Wimpey really grew the business for a significant period of time. One cannot criticise, merely note,
those companies that created substantial non-housing businesses. However, nearly all the remaining companies (and many outside that list) became
shadows of their former selves – if they survived at all.

Companies which had done little more than put their pre-war operations
on a care and maintenance basis, or had only a mild flirtation with construction, frequently found that the eventual resumption of their mainstream activity was all too often impeded by the ageing or death of the
pre-war driving force. Succeeding generations opted for a quiet life, perhaps
shifting the balance of the business towards investment, often using the
stock of pre-war rented housing as a base. Mactaggart & Mickel is a typical
example, continuing to build modest volumes for a long time on sites
which had been acquired before the war, whilst at the same time amassing
a considerable investment portfolio. George Ball Estates converted itself
into a wholly investment company; the Warren and Gough-Cooper families are others that still carry on a property investment business having
sold out the development arm of their groups; while Hilbery Chaplin is
once more an estate agent. For some of the established pre-war firms
little is known other than they rapidly departed the housebuilding scene.

Nathaniel Moss' son sold the firm in 1946; London builders such as T.F. Nash, F. & C. Costin and Newman Eyre vanished without trace and Companies House records have been destroyed; Ellis Berg appears to have sold E. & L. Berg to a property company in around 1971. Whether these founder-managed businesses 'departed' for physical lack of family succession, want of second generation interest, or ineptitude is dulled by the passage of time and a lack of data.

Succession issues link nearly all the companies in Table 10.1, whether they were survivors, taken over, or sold by their parent company. Some of the succession issues are easily identifiable: the dominant individual falls ill or dies. Illness prevented Ideal's Leo Meyer from attending board meetings after 1959 and he died in 1961; by then, his eldest son, Jimmy, was firmly established running the independent Federated Land. Non-family succession failed and Ideal succumbed to a takeover by Trafalgar House in 1967. Arthur Davis had a severe car accident in the 1950s and the business was sold to Wood Hall Trust, a conglomerate with interests in Australian pastoral trading, food, property and building; in turn, Wood Hall was taken over by the Australian Elders group and private housing was progressively wound down. Tom Warren died in 1964 leaving seven family shareholding groups. 'All the son-in-laws got involved – there was internecine strife.'[1] The trading business was sold to Bovis in 1967.

Less dramatic was when the dominant individual reached retirement age or, to be more precise, the age at which he no longer wished to run the company; it was not unknown in the building industry for this to be a generation after the conventional retirement age. Sir Herbert Janes was 78 before he resigned as chairman in 1962 and although volumes increased modestly thereafter, succession ultimately became a problem. In 1976, Janes accepted a bid from Barratt, prompted, it is said, by friction within the family. The relationship between Leslie Sell (Sir Herbert's son-in-law), then 76, and Robert Janes (Sir Herbert's son) had deteriorated to such an extent that they no longer conversed at all, with every communication being by way of memo through intermediaries. Similar family dissension affected Wates. Norman Wates died in 1969 but his son, Neil, appeared equally capable of driving the firm forward. However, there were several other third generation Wates in the firm and Neil Wates resigned as chairman and managing director in 1975 after a celebrated boardroom row:

> 'Neil Wates had been managing director since 1964 and the strong and intensely felt opinions and ambitions he held about and for the Group made it increasingly difficult to accept the chairmanship of his uncle

---

[1] Interview with R.T. Warren (Junior), Nov. 2001.

Ronald. The graceful charade of 1973 masked the determination of Neil Wates that Ronald Wates should go and in February of that year Neil Wates became chairman as well as managing director. Now Ronald's son Michael is to become chairman and there is to be no new chief executive.'[2]

There were dominant individuals that managed to pass on control to another generation but rarely with the success that they had enjoyed. The second generation of Comben & Wakeling had taken the Company public in 1964 but the profit performance was poor and after a loss in 1970, the firm succumbed to a takeover bid from Carlton Industries.

Despite their initial post-war successes, the four large contractor-housebuilders still had considerable difficulty with succession. For two of them, it was almost the longevity of the founders that caused the problems. Wimpey is synonymous with Godfrey Mitchell whose regular presence in the office until he died in 1982, 63 years after he had bought the Company, prevented the establishment of strong successor leadership. Less well known at Wimpey, however, was F.W. McLeod, a bricklayer who concentrated on driving forward the private housing volumes. His death in 1969 marked the end of a focused housebuilding operation and it was probably not until the mid-1990s that housing momentum was again resumed. Taylor Woodrow, too, was to suffer from a founder who stayed overlong, inhibiting the task of his successors. However, Taylor Woodrow's decline as a UK housebuilder has to be put in context: it was a decline in one part of the business, not in the business as a whole, which enjoyed consistent success through the 1960s and 1970s. Taylor Woodrow had resumed housebuilding as enthusiastically as any firm and by 1955 its target was up to 1500 but by 1958 its sales had almost halved to 658; the 1956 level of output was not seen again for 40 years. The management team lost its focus; Frank Taylor 'visited' the housing board but he was running an international construction company. Whereas Wimpey had McLeod, Frank Taylor still had Tommy Fairclough, a man who had only been an operational manager and who was facing ill health.

For Costain and Laing, succession presented challenges much earlier in the post-war period. Richard Costain had suffered increasingly from illness and after his death in 1966 his brother opted to concentrate on his career as an MP. After a second attempt at bringing in management from outside, leadership passed to John Sowden, one of Costain's civil engineers. The remarkable success achieved by Costain in its Middle East contracting

---

[2] *Building*, 11th April 1975, p. 51.

meant that housing had become almost irrelevant and when eventually Costain did try to rebuild its housing it was without clear control or understanding from the parent board. Unit output rose from 400 a year to 2200 in the five years to 1987 with the Company widely rumoured to be one of the highest bidders for land; in the recession years Costain Homes lost a total of £137 m. before being sold. John Laing had been succeeded by his two sons after the war but they had wider interests and the administration of the Company was in the hands of Ernest Uren. After ill health forced his retirement in 1971, housing output dwindled to just a few hundred a year. David Holliday became managing director of Laing Homes in 1980 and increased sales from under a thousand to 3400 in 1988. In contrast to Costain Homes, Laing's housing profits stood up reasonably well in the recession but losses in the construction division of £183 m. in 2000 and 2001 weakened the whole group and Laing Homes was sold to Wimpey in 2002.

Straightforward financial failure accounted for only two of the companies, Morrell and Crouch, a smaller proportion than will be seen in later lists in this chapter. Morrell Estates was distinguished by being the first quoted housebuilder to fail, when it placed its only trading subsidiary into liquidation in 1937, just two years after flotation. Its involvement in the celebrated Borders case[3] came too late for that to be blamed for its financial difficulties which will probably remain forever unexplained. The Crouch failure had its origins in the sudden death in 1973 of John Crouch, aged 41. In 1978, a private company controlled by Ronald Clempson acquired a substantial shareholding in Crouch Group and Clempson was elected chairman. Injudicious investments in property, particularly in the USA, led to losses in the early 1980s. Following a further review of the US properties, Clempson was removed from the Board in 1983; however, it was too late to prevent Crouch failing in 1984. Financial failure was not, of course, always absolute. Dares was subject to a rescue bid in 1971 following large construction losses, and further rescues followed that before it eventually withdrew from housing.

The early 1970s

Table 10.2 shows the 30 housebuilders that had completed 1000 units in at least one year of the housing boom of the 1960s and early 1970s. It contains more companies than Table 10.1; the passage of years had given time for

---

[3] For background, see Cleary, *The Building Society Movement*, pp. 218–23.

Table 10.2   The pre-1974 housebuilders: corporate outcome.

Housebuilder	Peak units[a]	Fate by year 2004	2004 rank
Wimpey	12,500	Independent: 12,200 p.a.	3
Northern Developments	4000	Failed 1975	
Whelmar	3200	Sold in five parts 1986/87	
Bovis Homes	c.3000	Taken over by P&O 1974; floated 1997: 2000 units p.a.	10
Ideal Homes	2000–3000	Taken over by Trafalgar House in 1967 and Persimmon in 1996	
Barratt	2500	Independent: 14,020 p.a.	1
Broseley	2200	Taken over by Ideal 1986	
Leech	1888	Taken over by Beazer 1985	
Bryant	1600	Taken over by Taylor Woodrow 2001	
Bardolin	1500	Taken over by London & Northern in 1973 and Raine in 1987	
Bellway	1500	Independent: 6610 p.a.	5
Francis Parker	1400	Withdrew from housing mid-1970s	
Orme	1357	Taken over by Comben 1978	
Comben	1269	Taken over by Ideal 1984	
Page-Johnson	1200–1500	Taken over by Bovis 1971	
David Charles	1200	Failed 1977	
Greaves	1200	Failed 1976	
Wates Homes	1000–1250?	Independent: 67 p.a.	100+
Hallmark	1250	Taken over by Spey Westmoreland 1970 and sold	
Gough Cooper	1050	Taken over by Allied London Properties 1980 and run down	
Bacal [Fell]	1300	Failed 1975	
E. Fletcher	c.1200 (1965)	Taken over by Bardolin 1969	
Janes	1000–1200	Taken over by Barratt 1976	
Galliford Estates	1000–1200	Taken over by Sears 1974; Prowting 1994	
McLean	1000+	Taken over by Tarmac 1973; Wimpey 1996	
Federated	1000+	Failed 1990	
Costain Homes	c.1000?	Sold to Redrow 1993	
Davis Estates	c.1000?	Taken over by Wood Hall Trust 1957, parent acquired 1982 and withdrew from housing	
John Lawrence	800–1200	Housing sold to Lovell 1986	
Whittingham	c.1000	Taken over by Comben 1983	

[a] Early 1970s unless otherwise stated. Note: when a company is listed as being taken over twice, it means that it continued to trade as an identifiable entity after the first takeover, for example Ideal and Trafalgar House.

larger firms to develop and make acquisitions. There is an overlap with the pre-war section in that the larger pre-war housebuilders have already been discussed but these are included in Table 10.2 for the sake of completeness. As with the pre-war corpus of companies, what stands out is how few survived as independent entities, only five, and of those Bovis had been taken over only to re-emerge 20 years later. The companies in Table 10.2 exhibit recognisable differences from the pre-war housebuilders in Table 10.1. One of the more quantifiable is that the majority of the companies in Table 10.2 were quoted. Ignoring housebuilders that represented a small part of larger unrelated quoted entities there were some 24 quoted housebuilders, which facilitated acquisitions, driven by the buyer's desire to expand and not just the seller's inability to continue.

The causes of departure are not always simple or singular but it is possible to identify three groups of housebuilders with common characteristics: those that departed before the recession struck, predominantly at attractive prices; those that failed, directly or indirectly, as a result of the 1974 recession; and those for whom succession issues predominated. Financial failure, principally the 1974 recession, is a significant cause of departure. Whereas decline in the pre-war list had partially centred around the failure to provide a comparable successor to the dominant individual, it can now be seen that the mistakes are just as easily committed by the dominant individual himself as by his successor. Succession problems may take years to unravel but the overconfidence of the dominant individual can produce precipitate departure from the industry's ranks.

Six companies from Table 10.2 departed before the 1974 recession: Ideal, Page-Johnson, Hallmark, E. Fletcher, Bardolin and McLean, and they left for entirely different reasons from most of the post-recession departures: Ideal has already been discussed and its problems were attributed to succession. Page-Johnson and Fletcher, both run by dominant individuals with controlling shareholdings, were interesting in that they are the first examples of large housebuilders selling out, not because they had been unsuccessful, but because, to quote a phrase, they were made an offer they couldn't refuse; other acquisitive housebuilders were prepared to use their quoted shares to accelerate their growth.

Johnnie Johnson's sons had never joined the business (it could be argued that he anticipated a succession problem but there is no evidence either way): 'He wasn't that old – he liked the finer things in life, he'd got to the fun stage, he'd got a boat, property in Australia, farms, an estate in Northumberland. And he got a hell of a price.'[4] The acquisition of Page-Johnson, made at the same time as the land-rich Warren, immediately propelled Bovis into the ranks of the leading housebuilders. Bardolin's acquisition of

---

[4] Interview with Bill Gair, Nov. 1998.

Fletcher was the archetypal Stock Exchange driven transaction: Jock Mackenzie, a colourful barrister and financier, became chairman of the small quoted housebuilder, Bardolin, in 1968 with the specific objective of creating a national housebuilding group. Edward Fletcher had formed his company in 1935 and second generation Geoffrey Fletcher had become managing director in 1960. Fletcher was by far the largest of Bardolin's acquisitions and the Fletchers were, in effect, running the enlarged Company. (Bardolin, in turn was acquired in early 1973 by Jock Mackenzie's London & Northern Securities as a piece of corporate reorganisation.)

Geoffrey McLean, a second generation owner, floated the family Company in 1963 but subsequent growth was disappointing. In March, McLean acquired Midland and General Developments, founded and run by Eric Pountain. Later that year McLean incurred substantial losses on local authority housing contracts and, after a boardroom coup, Pountain became managing director. In 1973, McLean was taken over by Tarmac who wanted Eric Pountain's management team to revitalise its own housing operation and by the late 1980s it had become the largest housebuilder in the country. Asked why he sold it Pountain replied: 'I don't know, I must have been mad, but it was an opportunity at the time. It seemed a lot of money.'[5]

Lower down the size range, more quoted housebuilders received good offers from larger companies. In addition to the ones mentioned above, there were another eleven between 1967 and 1973 – nine of them going in 1972 and 1973 as the housing cycle was coming to its peak. In total, 15 quoted companies succumbed to attractive offers before the recession, as can be seen in the Appendix. Only Hallmark and Ideal (mentioned earlier) departed for other reasons. Hallmark was a financially driven holding company, a 'shell' that had been used to acquire Alan Draycott's housing business in 1957. Further housing acquisitions were made, particularly of A.J. Wait in 1963, but Hallmark was also diversifying into commercial property, banking and manufacturing and by 1965 housing accounted for less than a quarter of profits. In 1970, Hallmark was acquired by Spey Westmoreland for its property interests and the housebuilding division was considered not relevant to the mainstream business and sold.

Nine companies from Table 10.2 failed financially, either completely in that receivers were appointed, or they were so severely weakened that housebuilding operations came to an end anyway; all bar Federated Land

---

[5] Interview with Sir Eric Pountain, Nov. 2000.

were victims of the 1974 recession. Reference has already been made to the failures in Chapter 5, which discussed the changes in market share. Northern Developments, David Charles, Greaves, and Bacal (previously Fell) all went into receivership; all were being run by a dominant individual and, whatever the cause of failure, it was not succession. Northern Developments' Derek Barnes continued buying land through the early 1970s using bank debt:

> 'At the end, he was buying land without even seeing it half the time. Someone would ring him up with the offer of land on the telephone and he would ask: 'Who are you? Where are you? What's your land? Are there any roads near? Any sewers near? Is it flat? How much do you want for it? Send me the details.'[6]

At David Charles, Robin Buckingham refused to consider the possibility of a cyclical downturn: 'Mr Buckingham does not subscribe to the current pessimism surrounding the housing sector. He believes that this side will continue to expand for a good few years and, as a mark of confidence, he is raising output from 1200 to 1500 houses this year'.[7] Greaves, too, had entered the recession with a high level of borrowings and other house-builders remember Greaves buying land 'at astronomical prices'. Fell had bought Adkins and Shaw shortly after its 1962 flotation and changed its name to Building and Contracting Associates (later Bacal) in 1965 when Eric Adkins assumed control. The firm expanded into civil engineering and the losses reported in the first half of 1974 were attributed to the impact of inflation on fixed-price contracts; a subsequent accountant's report indicated that the losses had been substantially understated and the group was heavily in debt. Federated was the one company from the list that managed to postpone its failure until the 1990 recession, again through overambitious expenditure on land at the wrong time in the housing cycle. However, succession issues could be cited here. Federated was run successively by Leo Meyer's two sons, Jimmy and Peter; the latter managed to combine the roles of chairman and managing director while being non-resident. Of the remaining bankruptcies, Budge Brothers, Lawdon and Joviel were all run by business founders, whereas Greensquare Properties and Lewston found themselves part of financial conglomerates.

Those for whom the financial impact of the 1974 recession also meant the end of an independent housebuilding existence, although falling just short of receivership, were Bovis, Francis Parker, Galliford Estates and Orme.

---

[6] Unattributable interview.
[7] *Building*, 3rd Nov. 1972, p. 112.

Once again, the dominant individuals responsible for creating the housing business were at the helm at the moment of crisis; succession was not the cause. Frank Sanderson's business had been bought so that he could expand Bovis' embryonic housing division; he became group managing director in 1970, instituted a string of housing acquisitions and attempted an audacious reverse takeover bid for P&O. In between, he had bought a Section 123 banking company, Twentieth Century Banking, which fell victim to the secondary banking crisis; it was supported by the Bank of England 'lifeboat' only long enough for Bovis to be rescued – by P&O. Galliford Estates, too, had to agree a sale for modest consideration to a stronger partner, as borrowings on a £40 m. European property development programme forced a rescue bid from Sears. The newly amalgamated Francis Parker group, building 600 houses in 1972, was planning 2500 for 1975; it had also diversified into construction, aggregates and other building materials. Losses on fixed-price contracting and the collapse in land values led to the cessation of dividends and the housing business was gradually phased out – failure due to over-rapid expansion, diversification and fixed-price contracting. Orme's case is a little less clear cut. It had been specifically formed in 1970 by two financiers to be a vehicle for assembling a national housebuilding business and sales approached 1400 units. The increase in the land bank strained finances, profits fell for five years in succession and Messrs Whitfield and Tanner finally sought a purchaser in 1978.

The remaining names in the list of departures in Table 10.2 include housebuilders covered under the pre-war grouping, Costain, Davis Estates, Leech and Janes, whose decline was attributed to succession problems. That leaves Broseley, Comben (in its new form), Gough Cooper, John Lawrence, Whelmar and Whittingham and the same conclusion is predominately true for this second group, that the main reason for their departure was succession, although manifesting itself in different ways. Broseley and Whelmar, run by close friends from the same part of Lancashire, are excellent examples of two large housebuilders (both top five companies in their heyday) with corporate owners that recognised that their housing business was only as good as its founder. Whelmar had been moved out of Metropolitan Railway Country Estates and into Christian Salvesen, all the time being run by Tom Baron. When Salvesen floated as a public company in 1985, Tom Baron retired and Salvesen offered Whelmar for sale in five separate tranches. Broseley had gradually moved into the ownership of Royal (later Guardian Royal) Exchange. In the mid-1980s its founder, Danny Horrocks, suffered heart attacks; by then just past 60 he asked GRE what it wanted to do with the business. The association between GRE and Danny Horrocks had lasted over 25 years; without him the directors felt that there was little sense in owning a business that they did not understand, which they had never managed and which no longer had any common link with the insurance industry. A buyer was to be sought and in 1986 the housing side of Broseley was sold to Trafalgar House where it was incorporated into Ideal Homes.

In contrast to Broseley and Whelmar, whose owners made a clean break with the business, Gough Cooper provides another example of the slow deterioration that can occur after the departure of the founder. Harry Gough-Cooper, a qualified civil engineer, first started building houses in the early 1930s, expanded rapidly in the late 1950s and by 1962 was building around 800 units a year. However, Gough-Cooper emigrated to South Africa in 1967, appointing John Boardman, who had joined in 1939 as a buyer, as chief executive. 'No member of the family was involved with running the building company or had any aspirations to manage it.'[8] By 1972, Harry was terminally ill (he died three years later). A public flotation was seen as the answer to the succession issue but housing volumes were later reduced to conserve debt; the Company diversified into contracting to compensate for the decline in private housing but this pushed the group as a whole into loss in 1979/80 and Allied London Properties made a successful bid.

Whereas most succession can be anticipated, Whittingham had to contend with two sudden deaths. The dominant individual was the second generation William David Whittingham who had created a solid West Midlands housebuilder by the early 1960s. However, in 1965, only one year after flotation, William became seriously ill and third generation Tom, aged 26, became managing director. He expanded output to around 1000 units a year by the early 1970s, moved into commercial property and bought a photographic processing company (Colortrend). The group entered the recession highly geared but survived; profits were gradually recovering when Tom died in 1977 aged 38. Joint managing directors were appointed (one from outside) but Colortrend moved into losses in the early 1980s, housing volumes were down to 400 and in 1983 the chairman arranged an agreed bid from Comben. Here, succession, diversification and the impact of recession were all contributory factors.

John Lawrence, which became Scotland's largest private housebuilder in the 1960s, skipped a generation after his death in 1977 although, despite numerous enquiries, it has not been possible to find the reason. His grandson diversified into the leisure trade, purchased Rangers Football Club and

---

[8] Correspondence with Jennifer Gough-Cooper.

property in Nevada. Housing was run down and volumes were only 150 a year when it was sold to Lovell in 1986. The group went into receivership in 1997. The final company in the list is Comben, really Carlton Homes, having reversed into the quoted Company. For reasons too convoluted to explore here, Comben became a partially owned, and still quoted, part of Max Rayne's industrial empire and then, in 1982, of Hawker Siddeley. Hawker supported the Comben expansion strategy but commercial logic inevitably ruled and Hawker was a willing seller when Trafalgar House approached in 1984.

The late 1980s

For the final time period, a cut-off of around 1000 units has again been chosen to examine the fate of the industry leaders; for nearly all the companies, the peak volume was achieved in 1988 except for Wates (1987) and Fairview (1984). Table 10.3 contains 30 companies above the 1000 level, exactly the same as in Table 10.2; it excludes Broseley, Comben and Leech, all taken over between 1983 and 1984. There is a shorter time interval between the late 1980s grouping and the year 2004; therefore there is a higher proportion of survivors. Nevertheless, of the 30 companies producing 1000 units or more before the recession started in 1989, 16 of them did not survive year 2004 as continuing entities, although Bovis, Fairclough and Lovell did continue under new ownership. Furthermore, some of those that did survive experienced declines in volumes – Bovis and McCarthy & Stone, for instance, out of the top ten and Croudace, Abbey and Wates from those building around 1000 a year.

Financial difficulties is a recurrent cause of withdrawal or decline in this period. However, a new theme emerges: a realisation that focus is critical to the success of a housebuilding operation and the consequent retreat from the industry by non-housebuilding groups, particularly the contractors.

In comparing the departures from the pre-1974 and the pre-war lists, there were noticeable differences in explanation between the two periods; so it is again with the pre-1990 companies. The first difference is that none of the departures from the pre-1990 list were the direct result of financial failure (that is receivership), compared with nine in the previous period. There were many small housebuilders that did have to face receivership; the docklands developer Kentish Homes (c.200 units) was one of the first casualties of the recession when its shares were suspended in July 1989. However, the financial system was more supportive of the larger firms in the housebuilding sector than it had been in the previous recession. In part

Table 10.3   The pre-1990 housebuilders: corporate outcome.

Housebuilder	Focus	Units 1988	Units 2004	Fate by year 2004	2004 rank
McLean	G	12,165		Housing sold to Wimpey 1996	
Wimpey	G	9087	12,232	Independent	3
Barratt	F	7000	14,021	Independent	1
Beazer	G	6276		Taken over by Hanson 1991 and Persimmon 2001	
Ideal Homes	G	5150		Sold to Persimmon 1996	
Laing Homes	G	3436		Sold to Wimpey 2002	
Lovell Homes	G	3060	2051	Housing sold to Morgan Sindall 1999	14
Bovis	G	3000	2700	Housing floated 1997	10
McCarthy & Stone	F	2596	2050	Independent	13
Wilcon	F	2160		Taken over by Taylor Woodrow 2003	
Westbury	F	2415	4400	Independent	8
Bryant	F	2150		Taken over by Taylor Woodrow 2001	
Persimmon	F	2043	12,360	Independent	2
Fairclough Homes	G	1942	1547	Sold to Centex 1999[a]	19
Costain Homes	G	1872		Housing sold 1993	
Bellway	F	1640	. 6610	Independent	5
Clarke Homes	G	1610		Sold to Balfour Beatty 1995	
David Wilson	F	1592	5588	Independent	6
Raine	G	1502		Taken over by Alfred McAlpine 1997	
Crest	G	1429	2524	Independent	11
Alfred McAlpine	G	1350		Sold to Wimpey 2001	
English China Clays	G	1289		Housing run down 1991–95	
Mowlem Homes	G	1200		Sold to Beazer 1994	
Galliford Sears	G	1109		Sold to Prowting 1993	
Redrow	F	1104	4284	Independent	9
Croudace	F	1100	543	Independent	30
Abbey Homesteads	F	1027	385	Independent	38
Taylor Woodrow	G	998	9053	Independent	4
Fairview [1984]	F	1113	1990	Demerged from Hillsdown 1998	15
Wates Homes [1987]	G	1100	67	Independent	>100

F = focused housebuilder. G = general group see text below. [a] Sold to Miller 2005.

that was due to the absence of extensive reliance on the secondary banks that had themselves collapsed in the early 1970s, thereby compounding the problems facing housebuilders; and also because the bankers realised that their best hope of realising their loans was through a controlled exit rather than distressed sale. In talking about the rescue of Charles Church, the deputy chief executive of the Royal Bank of Scotland said that:

> 'a decision on whether to support a debt/equity swap depends upon the strength of a company's management as much as the underlying quality of its assets and its position in the marketplace . . . it is not in our interest to have a fire sale. We would probably be looking at a substantial losses if residential and commercial property assets were sold in the current depressed market. It obviously is preferable if companies can continue trading while prices recover.'[9]

Lovell needed two debt reconstructions and Beazer, Mowlem, McCarthy & Stone and Raine Industries all needed assistance when they breached banking covenants. Excellent examples of bank support can also be found among housebuilders just outside the list above: Charles Church (700 units), Fairbriar (300) and Trencherwood (500) were all given continuing bank support in the early 1990s despite having net asset deficits of around £50 m. apiece. Other smaller companies to be assisted with reconstructions included Anglia Secure Homes, the smaller quoted rival to McCarthy & Stone.

If financial difficulties were not the direct cause of change of control or departure from the industry, then they were undoubtedly a substantial indirect cause. Eight companies were sold, sooner or later, by their parent companies as a result of losses made during the early 1990s: Ideal (again), Beazer, Lovell, Fairclough, Costain, Clarke, Raine and Mowlem. Each of these was sold by a group that, at the minimum, ranged across construction and commercial property development as well as housebuilding. In Costain's case there was also extensive coal mining in Australia and the USA, Beazer had US roadstone, while Trafalgar House (Ideal's parent since 1967) included shipping and hotels. The losses which created a weakened group balance sheet were not necessarily confined to the housebuilding subsidiaries but also occurred in other parts of the group, particularly commercial property and construction. That it was the housebuilding part of the group that was sold reflected a combination of factors. The capital requirements of rebuilding the land bank meant housebuilding represented the greatest future drain on scarce capital resources (compared with, say, construction); it was often the simplest part of the group to sell (again, a contrast with construction where there was a much greater problem in identifying ongoing liabilities); and, as the housing market recovered, there was a body of competing firms (nearly all quoted) that were keen to expand.

---

[9] *Financial Times* 17th Aug. 1991.

In the case of Raine Industries (which included Hassall Homes and Hall & Tawse), it was the whole group that was bought by Alfred McAlpine.

With the possible exception of BICC's Clarke Homes (whose losses were not disclosed) the size of the losses made by these groups was a significant contributor to the eventual sale of their housing subsidiaries. Trafalgar House lost £347 m. in 1993, largely due to provisions that were actually greater in commercial property than housing. Y.J. Lovell, relative to its size, was the most severely affected by both commercial property and housebuilding and by 1997 it had a £32 m. deficit on shareholders' funds and its second debt restructuring. Fairclough Homes, part of the Amec construction and process engineering group, lost £155 m. between 1990 and 1992, with further losses on commercial property. Costain Group lost over £200 m. in 1992 with construction, mining, property and housing all contributing; its housing land provisions through the recession totalled £113 m. Mowlem followed up £58 m. losses in 1991–92 with a £124 m. loss in 1993, primarily in construction and its SGB scaffolding subsidiary rather than in housing. Beazer was the only group that actually contained a successful UK housebuilding subsidiary, but the parent company had bought a US aggregates and wood treatment business for $1.8 billion cash just before the recession and faced colossal environmental liabilities. The group was rescued by Hanson and the housebuilding business was subsequently floated as an independent entity. That leaves only four other departures to consider – McLean, Galliford Sears (previously Galliford Estates), English China Clays and Bovis which was sold by P&O but continued as an independent entity. These four lead into a discussion of 'focus'.

One of the features that stands out from Table 10.3 is the contrast between the focused (F) and the general companies (G). Focus or concentration is a useful shorthand expression to indicate that, whatever other activities may be carried on within the group, housebuilding is the dominant activity, the managing director would regard himself as a housebuilder, and the majority of the main Board are housebuilding related rather than representing other interests. Whereas the pre-1974 list largely comprised companies that were focused housebuilders, the pre-1990 list contains 18 mixed groups against only 12 focused housebuilders. All 12 of the departures from the industry between 1989 and 2000, including the eight attributed to financial failure, were parts of general businesses; not one of the focused companies left the industry in that period. Those that were forced to sell their housing divisions, or where the whole company was sold as result of overwhelming financial pressures, were discussed above. Four other general companies also disposed of their housing businesses. Sears, a retailing business, sold its Galliford subsidiary to the management, whereupon it was almost immediately sold on to Prowting; Tarmac, also an aggregates and construction business, swapped its McLean Homes for Wimpey's construction and quarrying assets; English China Clays decided to withdraw from housing, building out much of the land and then selling the rump; and P&O floated Bovis on the Stock Exchange.

There was an acceptance, rightly or wrongly, of the argument that businesses are more efficient and more in tune with Stock Exchange fashions when they focus on their core activity. Weaknesses in business strategy are more likely to be exposed when trading is difficult, rather than easy, and it is no surprise therefore that the recession of the early 1990s acted as a catalyst for many companies. Change in the ownership of the business, or a change in the chief executive (often themselves products of the recession) were additional causal factors.

The change in corporate control is exemplified by Beazer and Ideal Homes. Beazer fell to the Hanson Group in 1991; Hanson disposed of the construction business almost immediately and then waited for the housing market to recover before floating Beazer as an independent company on the Stock Exchange. Hongkong Land took indirect control of Trafalgar House in the mid-1990s and, with no commitment to housing, sold Ideal Homes to reduce debt. Sears, having experienced its first major housing recession, presumably decided there was no overwhelming reason for a retailer to own a housebuilder. English China Clays recruited a new chief executive from Rugby Cement in 1990 and decided to focus on its core clay interests. Tarmac's chief executive, Eric Pountain, a housebuilder who had made McLean Homes the largest in the country, was replaced by Neville Simms, a contractor with little historical interest in housebuilding. He was more than pleased to swap Tarmac's housing for Wimpey's construction. Amec (Fairclough Homes) and BICC (Clarke Homes) both had management changes at the top and decided to concentrate on what they knew best, or, to be realistic, on where they lost least money.

There is a circularity in some of these explanations. Extreme financial pressure forced or encouraged the sale of housebuilding subsidiaries; but so did takeovers and so did management changes. However, all three were often, although not always, the interconnected result of below average financial performance. The close control needed over any form of speculative development has been discussed earlier and the evidence suggests that this is harder to achieve in a group setting or following periods of management change.

If 12 of the 18 unfocused housebuilders were departures, did the remaining six display any characteristics that detract from the simplistic observation that unfocused becomes unsuccessful? The answer is that, with the exception of Wates, they all adopted a focused strategy. Crest gradually sold its industrial and construction interests and became a successful focused housebuilder. Wimpey also turned itself into a focused housebuilder by its asset swap with Tarmac in 1996: its volume sales in 2000 were only half that achieved by the two components in 1988 and it was only after several management changes that Wimpey's profit margins began to approach those of the industry average in 2001. Laing moved from number six in the industry to number 26; its construction losses at the end of the 1990s crippled Laing financially and in 2002 it sold Laing Homes to focus on its PFI business. McAlpine put increasing emphasis on its housing rather than construction, substantially increased its volumes through the acquisition of Raine, and reached number six in the industry by 2000. It looked a successful mixed business until in 2001 it, too, decided it needed to focus and its new construction-oriented group managing director sold the housing company to Wimpey. Taylor Woodrow's group leadership oscillated between the construction and the development-oriented subsidiaries and it had difficulty in deciding what type of business it wanted to be. By the end of the 1990s Taylor Woodrow was already describing itself as an international housing and property company before the acquisition of Bryant in 2001 substantially increased its UK housebuilding operation. Finally, Wates' numbers tell their own story, with volumes down below 100 by the end of the 1990s, and the housing subsidiary suffering several changes in leadership under the overall control of the Wates family.

To suggest that lack of focus in a speculative development business is a poor recipe for success does not automatically prove the opposite, that focus inevitably produces success; it only suggests less chance of failure. Earlier periods have shown that dominant individuals, capable of dynamically expanding their business, can also preside over failure. It is now appropriate to make a distinction within the ranks of the focused housebuilders. Of the focused housebuilders, six had the same dominant individual throughout the period from the late 1980s to the year 2000: Bellway (Howard Dawe), Fairview (Dennis Cope), McCarthy & Stone (John McCarthy), Persimmon (Duncan Davidson), Redrow (Steve Morgan) and the eponymous David Wilson. All but the first were the founders of their business. (Towards the end of this period, the dominant individuals were appointing chief executives or managing directors under themselves as chairmen, as they prepared for their own retirement.) Of the 12 focused housebuilders identified in Table 10.3, it is this group that has shown the superior financial performance compared with their pre-recession levels. The exception is McCarthy & Stone, a special case as it was entirely dependent on the sheltered housing market and it was only the tenacity of its founder that enabled it to survive. This comparison is discussed below.

Performance comparisons between individual companies are easier to make than to interpret. To test the assertion that the continuous presence of a dominant individual produced superior results compared with those companies where managements had been changed, a comparison was made of growth in trading profits between 1989, the last year before the recession, and year 2000 (Figure 10.1). Acquisitions have some impact on the absolute level of growth but have not materially affected the comparison. The 'continuous companies' were taken to be Bellway, Fairview, Persimmon, Redrow and Wilson Bowden; their profits index stood at 375 in year 2000 versus 190 for those companies where managements had changed. Four of the five continuous companies were being run by their founder in 1989 (Bellway was the exception); they had been there for at least a decade so there was no suggestion that these more successful companies had assumed control at a propitious moment (that is when returns were below average); they achieved growth upon growth.

Did the companies that changed managements underperform because they had lacked continuity, or was it poor performance that caused the management change? The reality was a little of both. The new management generally came in during the recession, but even when they had been embedded and the recession ended, there was still a superior performance by the continuous companies; based on 1995, the profits index for the continuous managements was 353 versus 296. Furthermore, Figure 10.2 shows a continued superiority in profit margins, which were a full three points higher in 2000.

The focused housebuilders where managements changed were Abbey, Barratt, Bryant, Crest, Westbury and Wilson Connolly. Their unit volume figures tell a mixed story. Barratt, Crest, Bryant, Wilson Connolly and Westbury all achieved sufficient growth in unit sales over the period to look successes on that measure. However, in one way or another, all experienced the departure of chief executives in, or near the beginning of, the period and all took the best part of a decade to regain the profit levels enjoyed in 1988. None of these five companies could be regarded as companies in decline over the 1988–2000 period but they took longer to begin their recovery and Bryant and Wilson Connolly so lost their direction at the end of the period that they were later taken over.

This chapter has been divided into broad time periods, partly to replicate Part I, but also because the balance of the reasons for corporate decline

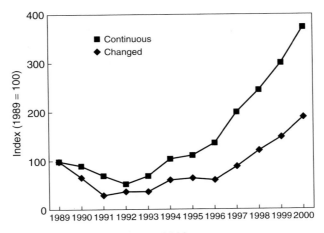

Figure 10.1 Trading profit growth, 1989–2000.

Source: *PHA*s and author's analysis.

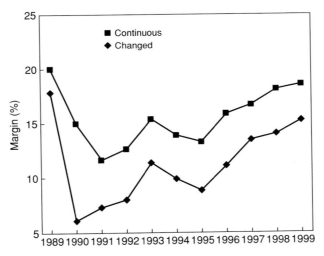

Figure 10.2 Profit margins, 1989–2000.

and failure has differed. The main cause of decline in the cohort of pre-war firms was unique to the period – 15 years of war and building controls which destroyed the continuity of the original housebuilding businesses. In some cases, firms switched their emphasis to more productive areas, particularly construction; in others, founders retired or scaled down their activities. Of those firms that did continue, the inability to manage succession contributed to decline – one factor that was common to later periods.

The next cohort of firms to be examined was that from the pre-1974 recession. Acquisitions at favourable prices, as proprietors took advantage of competitors' desire to expand, had removed many companies before recession struck. Financial failure then accounted for others, either quickly in the form of bankruptcy or slow decline in the face of weakened balance sheets. This contrasted with the pre-war period when there was only one quoted company failure and no acquisitions. Succession, however, continued as a contributory cause and its impact may have been greater than it first appears for it could have been an explanation for vendors' willingness to sell.

For those companies that were the industry leaders in the late 1980s, it is too early to assess the influence of succession. However, there were extensive departures from the industry and they were the direct and indirect result of the second major recession to afflict the industry. Although there were fewer immediate bankruptcies than in post-1974, as the banks were more supportive, the financial walking wounded were gradually sold to stronger competitors. At the same time, the recession prompted a realisation that the focused housebuilders had tended to be more successful and the non-housebuilding groups, particularly the contractors, retreated from the industry.

11

Decline: an Overview

Introduction

This chapter draws together and further develops the three common themes that underlie the decline and failure of housebuilders: succession, lack of focus and housing recessions. It will be argued that succession to a dominant individual plays an important role in decline, easily identifiable in over 20 of the quoted company departures but present in a much wider number of companies that have quietly agreed a sale. Paradoxically, decline has sometimes occurred because the dominant character has stayed too long, or where the family has not been sufficiently ruthless in arranging succession. To the extent that succession is a contributory factor, it appears to be a second generation, not the proverbial third generation, problem; and it applies whether succession be family or managerial. The underlying reasons for succession failure are explored: the entrepreneurial and single-minded characteristics which are necessary to create a successful and expanding housebuilder do not appear to create the conditions where a 'number two' can easily follow.

One of the strongest themes to emerge from this chapter is the near universal failure to marry a successful housebuilding business with other forms of activity and it examines housebuilding when married with construction, commercial property, conglomerates and then with overseas diversification. The pairing of speculative development and construction has been an almost unmitigated failure, primarily because it was based on the similarity of physical process and not intellectual and temperamental complementarity. There would appear greater synergy between the development of speculative housing and commercial property sites but, again, there have been numerous failures of this business model: in particular, the retention of property assets by housebuilders has not found favour in the quoted arena and such combinations have been invariably dismantled. Housebuilders' attempts to diversify into unrelated activities have universally failed: in contrast, there have been a few conglomerates that have run successful housebuilding subsidiaries for periods of time but even where operationally successful they tend not to be supported in recession and rarely survived changes in management in the holding company. Finally, housebuilders' diversification overseas, particularly in France and the USA, is considered and it is noted that only Taylor Woodrow and Wimpey have been able to sustain such ventures. By the end of the 1990s, the pitfalls of diversification appear to be generally recognised and the top ten housebuilders were all focused firms with little in the way of non-housing interests.

The third important explanatory role in decline is the two deep housing recessions centred around 1974 and 1990, which have played an overwhelming part in the downfall of individual housebuilders. Around 40 quoted housebuilders left the industry as a result of those recessions, and over half of those were run by a dominant individual at the time. However, despite their high absolute failure rate, the focused housebuilders, particularly those with a lengthy control by a dominant individual, were the least likely to fail and provided most of the long-term successes in the housebuilding industry.

To provide a context for this chapter, the total number of departures from the quoted sector are plotted in Figure 11.1, although not all of these are failures. In total, the chart includes 129 transactions, and the individual

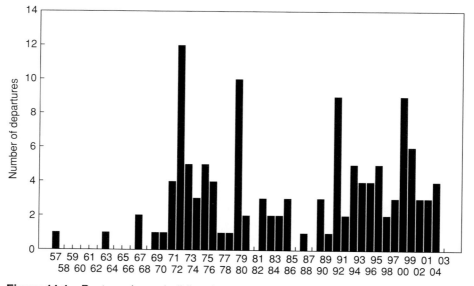

Figure 11.1   Post-war housebuilding departures: the quoted sector, 1957–2004.

names, dates and suggested causes are contained in the Appendix. The majority are companies where the business was totally or largely housebuilding, but it also includes the sale of the housebuilding divisions of larger quoted entities and there is therefore some (although not much) subjectivity about what is included. More recent years also include a number of MBOs where the housebuilder has left the quoted arena but the management continuity has not changed. For a number of companies, departure was spread over a period of years; a date has therefore been allocated arbitrarily. Thus, companies that wound down in the late 1970s have been included under 1979. Such is the nature of corporate life that some companies have exited more than once, hence the reference above to transactions rather than companies.

Succession

Family succession

This book contends that succession issues have been an important cause of the decline or departure of firms; however, its extent is not easy to quantify as the causes of corporate decline are rarely singular, and external judgement on management is frequently highly subjective. Nevertheless, succession has been an easily identifiable contributory factor in over 20 of these departures. However, this will not represent the full measure of the problems caused by succession: there are housebuilders where the reason for departure has been given as an 'attractive offer' that might not have been agreed as a takeover if there had been an obvious family succession, for example Page-Johnson. Moreover, amongst those quoted firms that survived, succession problems have contributed to long periods of decline, sometimes where the founder has stayed too long, for example Wimpey, and sometimes where succession was handled smoothly but to a less effective leader, for example at the firm of Henry Boot after the death of Charles Boot in 1945. There are also many unquoted companies that sold out or closed down because of perceived problems in organising succession, and this was particularly true of some of the successful inter-war housebuilders like Moss and Nash, while the housing operations of Mactaggart & Mickel and Wates went into substantial decline.

Casson observed that just because many firms are run by families this 'does not imply that family firms require a special theory of their own'.[1] Family and managerial succession are both subsets of a common problem – the

---

[1] Casson, *Enterprise and Leadership*, p. 220.

transition of power from a dominant (and successful) character. As the family or personally owned firm has played a pivotal role in the development of the housebuilding industry it should be asked first, how extensive was family succession in the housebuilding industry? The quantitative data must be treated with caution as there are a number of borderline attributions, for example family succession before housebuilding was acquired (Bovis), or succession from a nominal business only (for example David Wilson). Neither of these has been counted as family succession. There have been 38 companies that, at one point or other in their history, have been in the industry's top ten (Table 7.2); of these, 15 involved family succession in one form or another. Family succession is slightly understated because two or three of the 23 housebuilders not deemed to have had family succession still had their founder at the helm.

One of the commonest management aphorisms centres around businesses built up in the first generation being lost in the third, although, as Roy Church put it, 'The view that . . . the third generation of a founding business family typically experienced failure or extinction is not now widely shared'.[2] Providing that first generation is not taken literally but refers to the first dominant individual, then a few examples of significant third generation decline can be found in the housebuilding industry, namely in the histories of John Lawrence, Wates and Laing. However, the reality is that substantial decline has occurred more often under the control of the second generation, while founders themselves have frequently been the instrument of their firms' failure, an observation supported by David Jeremy's response to the question, 'Why do small firms die?' His conclusion was that: 'Contrary to those who blame the second and third generation in the family firm for its collapse, the evidence shows that founders, not successors, have been the most widespread instruments of firm failure.'[3] The extent to which founders become the instrument of their firms' subsequent failure is explored later in the chapter under 'Demand and the housing cycle'.

There is no shortage of explanations of the problems inherent in passing on a business to the second generation, nor are they difficult to perceive.[4] It is hard to better Jonathan Boswell on the father-son relationship: 'Who is to disentangle the subtle web of heredity or environment, of subordination or affection, of obedience crudely enforced or, more probably, cumulatively ingrained?' He went on to say that when the forcefulness and strong

---

[2] Church, 'The Family Firm in Industrial Capitalism', p. 25.
[3] Jeremy, *A Business History of Britain 1900–1990s*, p. 338.
[4] Even as a 20-year-old, this author did not need economic theory to put 200 miles between himself and his father's business.

character of founders are added, the conclusion that inheritors have less chance to develop along fresh and distinctive lines is inescapable.[5] Similar views were expressed in a *Financial Times* article on family businesses which argued that few founding entrepreneurs were easy to get on with: their children can find them a fearsome act to follow, 'if, that is, they ever retire.'[6] The housebuilding histories do contain excellent examples of failure to achieve father-son succession: Peter Prowting joined his father's firm in 1948 but their working partnership was not a great success: 'Because I couldn't get on with my father, I persuaded him to buy a business over in Windsor called Burfoot and Son, a similar type of business to ours.'[7] Peter Prowting ran Burfoot until 1952, only moving back to the family firm as his father was due to retire. Another short, and more recent, experiment in family succession was at the Berkeley Group, founded in 1976 by A.W. 'Tony' Pidgley, which in 1998 bought Thirlstone Homes, owned and run by Tony K. Pidgley, the founder's son. Three years later, T.K. Pidgley resigned from the Group: the father's on-the-record comment was 'If I ever made one mistake, it was buying my son's business: nepotism doesn't work'.[8]

Family conflict may involve more than just father and son, as Janes, Wates and Abbey illustrate. In 1976, Janes accepted a bid from Barratt as the relationship between Herbert Janes' son and his son-in-law had deteriorated to such an extent that communication was by way of memo. The family dissension could be both public and protracted. Neil Wates was forced out as managing director of Wates in 1975 after a public row with the rest of the family. The dissension could be seen even more starkly at Abbey, an Irish registered company operating predominantly in the UK, where the family conflict was worthy of a long running soap opera. Charles Gallagher, one of four brothers, failed to gain control of the Company and left in 1975 to start his own housing company, Matthew Homes. In 1983, brother James died suddenly and Patrick Gallagher became acting chairman. 'All eyes are now on Charles Gallagher, who James thwarted for years when the former attempted to gain control of Abbey.'[9] At the next AGM, Charles, supported by the James Gallagher family shareholding, stood against Patrick and replaced him as chairman. Two years later, French Kier launched a takeover bid for Abbey, having already received acceptances of 36% of the shares, being the family stakes of the late James Gallagher and the company president, Patrick Gallagher.

---

[5] Boswell, *The Rise and Decline of Small Firms*, p. 127.
[6] *Financial Times*, 'Inside Track', 14th Aug. 2001.
[7] Interview with Peter Prowting, Dec. 2000.
[8] Interview with Tony Pidgley, May 2001.
[9] *Irish Business*, July 1983, p. 6.

The damage that can be done by family conflict stands out from the examples above, but it could rightly be pointed out that such public airing is kept to a minimum. Many instances of sons leaving their fathers' businesses may pass unnoticed by the wider public and, at the least, untroubled by any analysis of the underlying reasons. The inclusion of the following examples is not meant to imply that conflict was the cause of their departure, merely that sons do come and go at early stages in their careers without undue external analysis. John McCarthy (managing director of McCarthy & Stone) had his three sons in the business, who left aged 19, 22 and 28, respectively; Spencer and Clinton McCarthy went on to form a rival sheltered housing company. John Maunders had one son working for him for a short time. John and Russell Bell, the founding brothers of Bellway both had their sons on the Board briefly in the 1970s. Other second generation sons never entered the business at all with little to indicate whether the reason was a genuine lack of interest, perceived lack of ability, or an assumption that there would be conflict. Ideal Homes founder Leo Meyer financed his son Jimmie to start Federated Homes in 1959; John Lawrence of Glasgow passed the business on to his grandson when he died in 1977; Stan Clarke's son preferred to go into agriculture; Johnnie Johnson of Page-Johnson had two sons who 'had no interest in the business'.[10] It is not possible to know the extent to which the 'official' reasons reflect the underlying reasons, which represents a major limitation in the ability of outsiders to analyse the family firm. At the beginning of this section, it was stated that over 20 of the departures from the quoted sector could easily be attributed to succession issues. The Appendix also shows, for instance, that in the late 1960s and early 1970s there were another ten or so companies that left the industry due to 'attractive offers' and these, too, could have had potential succession as a causal factor. The paragraphs below also touch on companies that might, paradoxically, have prospered from a little more succession confrontation, and those where succession led, not necessarily to departure from the industry but to periods of prolonged underperformance.

It should not always be assumed that family conflict has adverse effects; it sometimes allows a more dynamic second generation to assert itself to the longer-term benefit of the firm. Peter Prowting was mentioned above and Geoffrey McLean was instanced in Chapter 4, as having demanded control of the firm at the end of World War II. It could even be argued that a little more conflict, from whatever source, would have prevented other companies from quietly going to sleep. Charles Boot had taken the small firm of Henry Boot and created one of the largest of the inter-war housebuilders.

---

[10] Interview with John Swift, Nov. 1998.

He died in 1945 and was succeeded as chairman by his brother ('not a very strong leader'),[11] then his son, then his nephew. It was not until 1986, when his great-nephew Jamie Boot became managing director, following substantial group losses, that the firm began to grow its housing business again, contrary to the three generations' aphorism – although Boot Homes was eventually sold in 2003. Laing suffered when John Laing's sons, Kirby and Maurice, began to take more interest in public affairs during the 1960s; similarly, when Richard Costain died in 1966, his brother Albert, previously joint managing director, stood down in favour of his parliamentary career as MP for Folkestone and Hythe.

Managerial succession

This section must open by expressing some dissatisfaction with the term 'managerial', which is frequently used to distinguish it from family control, but it inappropriately implies that family firms lack management. Successful entrepreneurs do not always find it easy to plan for their replacement, particularly if there is no obvious male succession. Two of the best known construction entrepreneurs had no sons – Frank Taylor (Taylor Woodrow) and Godfrey Mitchell (Wimpey). Both created businesses which were among the most successful of their type in the twentieth century, yet both stayed too long, thereby causing difficulties for their successors. Frank Taylor resigned as chairman in 1974 telling the *Financial Times*: 'It is really sad to see older men hanging on at the head of companies after they should have retired'.[12] However, he remained as managing director and appointed Brian Trafford, his son-in-law, as deputy managing director with a clear indication that he would soon succeed as managing director. In the event, that presumption ended and in 1978 three more assistant managing directors were appointed. In 1979, aged 74, Taylor finally stood down as managing director but remained on the board as a director until late 1990, having seen in his third successor as chairman. 'After he retired as managing director he continued to have a strong influence on the business . . . This was not always to the advantage of the Company as it sought to reorganise.'[13] At Wimpey, Godfrey Mitchell had retired as chairman in 1973 but he, too, continued as a director and, by all accounts, remained a dominant figure within the group. His successors, R.H. Gane, and in 1976, R.B. Smith, had worked all their lives under the shadow of Mitchell and ruled under his influence; operational control was shared amongst four joint managing directors. Godfrey Mitchell finally retired in November 1981,

[11] Unattributable interview.
[12] *Financial Times*, 5th Jan. 1974.
[13] Ibid., 16th Feb. 1995.

following his ninetieth birthday, although he remained as president and continued to come into the office until his death in December 1982, some 63 years after he had bought the Company.

If family succession has proved hard to achieve, it does not imply that non-family (or managerial) succession has been any more successful. When the Laing family's right-hand man, Ernest Uren, retired through ill health in 1969, the firm formally appointed an outsider as managing director; Fred Catherwood had previously been chief executive of Costain, managing director of British Aluminium and director-general of NEDC, but he only lasted three years at Laing. Wilson (Connolly) provided an example of failed succession from a dominant managerial chief executive when Mike Robinson died unexpectedly in 1990; a succession of replacements in the 1990s turned one of the most successful housebuilders into one of the industry's least successful larger companies (see below). Costain had both success and failure as it tried to marry professional management with family control; Fred Catherwood was no more successful there than at Laing. Other names have been mentioned in earlier chapters. Ideal's management, following the death of Leo Meyer, became totally separated from the founding family and the firm slowly declined before being taken over. Gough Cooper did not survive the illness and then death of its founder even though John Boardman had appeared a successful managing director under Harry Gough-Cooper's chairmanship.

One of the most high profile transitions was the retirement of Lawrie Barratt and the succession of John Swanson as chairman and chief executive in 1989, after a year as managing director. The author has the advantage of contemporary observation and of interviews, often sharply contradictory, several years after the event, but providing a definitive judgement still remains difficult. In July 1991, in the depth of the recession, the Company announced that losses would approach £100 m.; John Swanson resigned and Lawrie Barratt came out of retirement to 'rescue' his company. How easy was it to succeed the most well known figure in the industry and one who had ruled the Company for 30 years – especially at such a critical time? There is no question that Lawrie Barratt's return was portrayed as a rescue. The author himself was able to ask Sir Lawrie at the time, how much of the provisions dated back to land bought under his own tenure and was left in no doubt that, in his view, he had left the Company in perfect health. It was perhaps a harsh verdict on his successor. Looking back, John Swanson did not think the task of following a dominant personality was impossible, but neither was it easy.

'Perhaps if Lawrie had stayed on as chairman and I had become chief executive for a longer period through that transition, that would have helped. There is no doubt at all that I missed Lawrie's counsel when he left the Company. I think in that turmoil and the problems the Company had at that time, and they weren't all market driven, it would have helped to have had someone there'.[14]

The new managing director, Frank Eaton, who succeeded Lawrie Barratt as chairman five years later, did have a much more successful tenure as chief executive, albeit without having to face an industry downturn.

Another succession following a strong leader was at Wilson Connolly when Mike Robinson died in a swimming accident in 1990 after 20 years as chief executive; his successor was the finance director, Ian Black. The comment on missing the advice of the elder statesman made by Black was remarkably similar to Swanson's: 'Mike had been a guiding light and in some ways the guru of the industry, so it would have been nice to have had him around to advise during the recession but, as it was, we faced situations that we had never faced before.'[15] Black was not helped by the succession coming without any transition period (and the problems faced by both men in succeeding dominant leaders were exacerbated by the sudden onset of recession).

Housebuilding entrepreneurs themselves were not unaware of succession problems. Smaller firms wishing to retain family ownership may adopt a more cautious approach to expansion: Hubert Leach, founded in 1933 and building around 100 units a year, specifically attributes the management of family succession to their willingness to contain the size of the business.[16] Alan Cherry, founder of Countryside, also accepted that housebuilding was a difficult business to pass on.

> 'I did not want my sons to come into this business . . . I've seen too many problems with fathers and sons. In the early days of Bairstow Eves, I had also specialised in receivership work and most of the businesses that I dealt with were builders and I saw a lot of this father-son problem.'[17]

(Notwithstanding those generalised reservations, he did bring both sons into the business and Graham Cherry became chief executive in 1996, although still under his father's chairmanship.) There are owners of businesses that have so strongly believed that succession poses potentially insurmountable problems that they have sold the business rather than seek a successor; Broseley's Danny Horrocks and Whelmar's Tom Baron have

---

[14] Interview with John Swanson, Oct. 1999.
[15] *Building Homes*, Nov. 1996, p. 19.
[16] Interview with Paul Leach, July 1998.
[17] Interview with Alan Cherry, Jan. 1999.

already been mentioned as examples of founders who continued to run their companies when absorbed by larger organisations, Guardian Royal Exchange and Christian Salvesen respectively. Both men had been in control of their firms since the 1950s and both retired in the mid-1980s. Neither GRE nor Christian Salvesen contemplated appointing successor managements and the two housebuilding companies were sold. These sales were well publicised but there were probably other sales, particularly those before the 1974 recession, where the unpublicised reason for accepting a takeover bid was concern over succession.

Why is it so difficult for long-standing dominant individuals to pass on the reins of control to the, presumably competent, lieutenants that help them run the business? There is, of course, the obvious reluctance of entrepreneurs to hand over the custody of the fortune they have created to anybody else, however talented they may appear. That apart, there are other reasons. There may be a substantive difference between a leader, with whom the proverbial buck stops, and a number two, a difference admirably expressed by one of the twentieth-century's great business leaders, and one with particular knowledge of the construction process, Weetman Pearson, later Lord Cowdray, who took the family firm of S. Pearson and created what was probably Britain's largest international construction firm before and after the First War. 'A great many men are invaluable assistants who could never run a great firm. Men who can achieve success by ability and character are rare. Most of the successful men of the day have seized success as it was passing.'[18] Even in those instances where it is possible for the successor to replicate the founder's ability, what is indubitably difficult to achieve is the same interpersonal relationship with the key team members that was enjoyed by the founder. One of the frequent anecdotes in the interviews is where the interviewee relates with amusement, and almost a degree of pride, how he was given an almighty telling-off (usually put more strongly) from the founder, but how well they still got on. The successor may have been no more than *primus inter pares* or perhaps even recruited after some of his boardroom colleagues; his ability to control powerful subordinates may have to depend more on persuasion than the natural authority of his predecessor. A football analogy makes the point:

> 'The last time United tried to replace a long-serving and hugely successful manager – Sir Matt Busby – it went into such a tailspin that it was relegated into the old second division in 1974 . . . Gary Neville . . .

---

[18] Spender, *Weetman Pearson*, pp. 278–9.

recently pointed out that players who have known Sir Alex since they were little more than children will not feel the same bond with a new manager.'[19]

The succession problems at Taylor Woodrow and Wimpey related above illustrated the particular problems of a founder staying too long, but they also illustrated the general difficulty in organising the succession from any dominant individual that had been in control of the business for decades; it is this that underlies both family and non-family succession. Corley has commented that only recently (that is the early 1990s) have business historians properly addressed the question of how a firm is likely to be affected when its leader hands over to a successor; in particular, he draws attention to Mary Rose's contention that a firm's capacity to survive may derive from the failure of the first generation to prepare, as well as any faults of the successors.[20] Those who have served under a dominant individual for long periods of time may not possess the necessary leadership or decision making qualities; equally, the organisational structure that is bequeathed may be inappropriate for the personal qualities of the successor management. Unfortunately, when case studies are examined, it can be difficult, sometimes impossible, to properly identify cause and effect. Any reader will be aware that even within one's own organisation, it can be difficult to form a consensus on the leadership qualities and decisions of individuals: how much more difficult when analysing companies using only the limited self-censored public material and interviews with participants who have their own particular viewpoints to stress.

This section has argued that, in varying ways, succession within the house-building industry has been hard to achieve. There is no intent to be dogmatic for it is a relative and not an absolute contention, and it is instructive to look at the few instances where succession worked, sometimes to great effect. Examples include Leech's John Adamson (1936); Laing's Ernest Uren (1950s); Bryant's Roy Davies (1958); Wilson Connolly's Mike Robinson (1970); Bovis' Philip Warner (1973); and Bellway's Howard Dawe (1985). However, what was distinctive about these examples is that none was a simple case of the dominant family man retiring and then handing over a thriving business to an employee successor. Uren, Davies and Robinson were all managing directors within a continuing family environment – in each case there was a family chairman for the whole of their tenure. Who knows how these three would have succeeded with complete

[19] *The Economist*, 10th Feb. 2001, p. 34.
[20] Corley, 'The Entrepreneur', pp. 22–3.

independence, but there is a hint that a family presence was needed in the background. Laing 'wouldn't be what it was today without Uren's contribution – he was a brilliant organiser but couldn't carry people along with him.'[21] In Bryant, there was almost a love-hate relationship but it worked for 25 years:

> 'There was a tremendous partnership between Roy and Chris [Bryant], both of whom knew their place in the scheme of things. Chris used Roy and let him have his head to run the homes division. Roy would do a lot of things behind Chris' back but Chris tended to be aware of them. The only problem was that if you tried to get them together they would have a discussion about something, then they would tend to have a go at each other. But in practice it was a very good working relationship.'[22]

The most successful partnership of all was between Lynn Wilson and Mike Robinson, but even here there was a suggestion that the family chairman played a moderating role.

> 'At the time we interviewed him there was almost electricity between us, within five minutes, but I know other people found him odd and peculiar. He knew exactly what he wanted; he had a very analytic mind although there were times that one had to pour oil on troubled waters. He was a fantastic operator and ahead of his time by miles.'[23]

In each of these examples, the key to success lay in the relationship between the family and the managing director.

The other three large company examples mentioned above were Leech, Bovis and Bellway, and in each case the new managing director took over not from a successful predecessor but when the business was in difficulty. William Leech hit financial difficulties before the war with a substantial stock of unsold houses; the banks insisted that John Adamson, the firm's accountant, be put in charge and he was responsible for developing the Company into a sizeable post-war housebuilder. In 1972, Philip Warner took control of Bovis Homes under P&O's ownership after Frank Sanderson had led the former to virtual bankruptcy and Warner ran it successfully for 25 years, although always within the strict financial disciplines laid down by the parent. Howard Dawe, Bellway's technical director, became managing director in 1985, under family chairmanship, having previously run the housing division. 'In many ways I don't know how we survived. We had to get rid of all the peripheral businesses. There were losses in the

---

[21] Interview with Sir Maurice Laing, April 2000.
[22] Interview with Michael Chapman, April 2001.
[23] Interview with Lynn Wilson, Sep. 2000.

north-west, Yorkshire and Scotland.'[24] He went on to become executive chairman with no family representation on the board, and under his leadership Bellway became one of the most successful housebuilders of the 1990s.

Relay succession

There are many ways in which succession problems have manifested themselves and they are not unique to the speculative housing industry, although it is doubtful whether the information available could be standardised in such a way as to facilitate an intra-industry comparison. However, the characteristics of the industry which have been stressed throughout the book make the entrepreneurial function especially important, and it is this attribute that does not appear to have been readily transmitted to successor managements. To date, the speculative housebuilding industry has not been producing a succession of firms wherein one dominant (and successful) character has been followed by another. For the avoidance of ambiguity, the criteria applied in that comment have been that each dominant individual should have enjoyed at least ten years of success and that the firm should have been handed on without obvious sign of problems. Nevertheless, it may be that there is now a greater recognition of the problems associated with succession. Earlier in the section, there were references to Barratt's Swanson and Wilson Connolly's Black missing the support of their predecessors. In a recent article on 'relay succession', or the controlled handover of executive authority to an internal successor, Zhang and Rajagopalan commented that there had been few empirical studies on the benefits of relay succession, but their research on US chief executives indicated that there were compelling arguments in its favour.[25] It is ironic that this approach to controlled succession is frowned on by City corporate governance.

By the end of the 1990s, there was some evidence of UK housebuilders adopting a more formalised and public process for managing internal succession: the approach of three of the most successful housebuilders, Bellway, Persimmon and David Wilson, involved long periods of successor grooming. At Persimmon, founder Duncan Davidson appointed John White as chief executive in 1993; White, then managing director of the Midlands region, had joined the Company in 1979. Davidson moved to the post of executive chairman, becoming non-executive chairman in 2002 and due to retire in 2006 (as life president). Another founder, David Wilson of

---

[24] Interview with Howard Dawe, Nov. 2001.
[25] Zhang, 'When the Known Devil is Better than an Unknown God', p. 483.

Wilson Bowden, appointed Ian Robertson, the finance director from 1994, as deputy chief executive at the beginning of 2001 and chief executive in 2003. And at Bellway, John Watson was appointed chief executive in 1999, 21 years after he joined the firm, and Howard Dawe moved to executive chairman, becoming non-executive chairman in 2004. Thus, all three of the 'predecessors' were still on their respective boards in 2004, exercising a watchful eye as chairmen: it is not yet possible to judge the performance of their successors when in sole control but such controlled handover periods must offer the best prospect of avoiding the succession problems that have characterised the second half of the twentieth century.

Focus versus diversification

Neither the firms that diversify into speculative housebuilding nor those housebuilders that diversify extensively out of their core business appear to have been as successful as were the focused housebuilders, and this book identifies lack of focus not only as one of the most important causes of decline in housebuilding firms but also one of the most easily avoidable. Sometimes lack of focus was a direct cause of failure, at others a drag on the business. John Kay argued that corporate success is based on 'the distinctive capabilities of the firm – those things, often the product of its particular history, which competitors cannot reproduce even after others realise the benefits these capabilities bring to the company that enjoys them';[26] the comment on distinctive capability could, and should, be applied to the whole of the speculative housebuilding industry.

The inter-war period saw little more than some construction companies moving into housebuilding and vice-versa; the merger wave in the 1920s passed by the housebuilding industry, and there was virtually no overseas housebuilding. The immediate post-war period of building controls and dislike of the socialist government encouraged some limited expansion of housebuilding in winter climes and a further development of wartime construction skills, but the unrelated or conglomerate diversification, as elsewhere in the economy, came later, the mid-1960s for the housebuilding industry, and it is discussed in the latter part of this section.

In this chapter, diversification has been divided into four broad categories. Some may regard the first more as integration than diversification: investment into (or from) what appear to be the related areas of contracting. Despite the physical similarity of the process, the different temperaments

---

[26] Kay, *Foundations of Corporate Success*, Foreword.

and skill sets of their proponents has meant that the association with construction has almost always ended in failure for one party or the other. There is a greater degree of overlap with the underlying economics of commercial property but, in the quoted sector, the mix of housebuilding and commercial property has not been liked by the investment community, particularly when completed properties have been retained as investments. Unrelated diversification, usually through acquisition, into businesses that have no particular operational synergy with housebuilding have been an unmitigated disaster but there have been some notable successes in the opposite direction when it was the unrelated businesses that owned housebuilders; however, none has survived change of personnel at the top. There has also been what for most companies has been a passing flirtation with housebuilding overseas. There were two waves of expansion, in continental Europe prior to Britain's entry into the EEC in 1973, and North America in the late-1970s and 1980s; little was profitable and only Taylor Woodrow and Wimpey now have substantive overseas housing.

Housebuilding and construction

Because of the physical similarity between speculative and contract building, this is a common area of overlap; housebuilders diversify into contracting and, more frequently, construction companies diversify into housebuilding. A financial argument was also advanced, in that the cash generated by construction advance payments could be invested in the capital-intensive development business. At times, there was an even more holistic justification advanced. Lovell's Norman Wakefield was not untypical in 1981, arguing that: 'To be a totally viable business now, one has got to be developer, owner and client as well as being builder. And what the recession has done is to take the better organised, more substantial companies further into property development'.[27] As late into the cycle as 1987, Robert Douglas' new chief executive planned to re-enter the housing market for 'without a housebuilding arm, we are not integrated properly'.[28] Or Mowlem's acquisition of Unit Construction in 1986: 'Diversification was the way of the world at the time. Contracting was highly volatile and we thought housing and construction would be both complementary and counter cyclical'.[29]

The mix of housebuilding and construction has now ended for all the large housebuilders but Miller, and a few of the medium sized firms; although

---

[27] *Building*, 31st July 1981.
[28] Ibid, 21st Aug. 1987.
[29] Interview with Brian Watkins, Oct. 2001.

the latter's synergy arguments (discussed below) have some validity, the profitability of the contractors' housebuilding operations remains below average. The economic differences between speculative housing and construction were addressed in the Introduction ('What is the speculative housing industry?'). The contractor builds in accordance with the contract terms, usually at a predetermined price, and his primary risk is on the cost side; he is paid as the contract progresses, requires little capital and operates on low profit margins. In contrast, the private housebuilder is a developer, buying his land and executing much, or all, of the building work without the benefit of a contract with the purchaser; his primary risk is on the sales side. The capital requirement is high and, therefore, profit margins also need to be high. Chapter 3 outlined the reasons for the biggest shift from housing into construction (war and controls) and the adverse effects that it had on those companies' housebuilding businesses. Albeit on a smaller scale than the contractors' investment in housing, housebuilders themselves continued to be attracted to construction as a means of diversification.

Some firms that were predominantly housebuilders at the start of the 1960s either entered or substantially increased their commitment to local authority contracting. Local authority housebuilding was once again a rapidly expanding market for, having fallen to 114,000 units in 1961, it rose to a short-term peak of 192,000 in 1967. Many of the owners had started as builders and the firms frequently had their own building departments. In the post-war boom, local authority building had been a profitable occupation; however, in the late 1960s and early 1970s, losses on local authority contracts became commonplace. The rapid rise in construction costs in the early 1970s inevitably impacted on fixed-price contracts but losses were also being made before the rate of inflation accelerated, suggesting poor estimating or cost control. Looking back, it was easy to be wise after the event: 'I made the foolish mistake, as we all did'.[30] Six examples can be provided of quoted housebuilders that suffered so severely from construction losses that, sooner or later, they lost their independence: Five Oaks, Comben, Dares, Drury, Fell (Bacal) and Jackson. The impact was most noticeable in the period between 1967 and 1971 when construction contract losses exceeded housing profits for five of these companies.

Five Oaks suffered a loss of £1.3 m. in 1967 and after a further loss in 1968 there was a deficit of net assets; the Company did no more than limp along under changing management before confining itself to commercial property. Comben & Wakeling's group loss in 1969 was the result of problems

---

[30] Interview with Eric Grove, May 2001.

on just one contract but it was sufficient for it to lose its independence to Carlton Industries a year later. Dares incurred its first losses in 1969 and suspended dividends in 1970; after further losses it was 'rescued' by the Stern Group and ceased housebuilding in the north and Midlands. Drury's losses on contracts started in 1969 and 1970, but were not recognised until 1971, leading to its purchase by Francis Parker at the end of the year. Jackson had been the only one of these five examples to avoid a group loss; it 'merely' halved its group profits in 1971 due to large losses on a GLC contract. Under pressure from its principal shareholder, Jackson was encouraged to merge with Bob Francis' private companies to create Francis Parker. Following the departure of its founder in 1965, Fell changed its name to Building and Construction Associates (Bacal) and significantly expanded its construction activities. Although Bacal's construction losses were first disclosed in 1971, it was the first half of 1974 before group losses were reported; the shares were suspended in March 1975 and a receiver appointed in May.

Later on, the 1974 housing recession also encouraged some companies to diversify into construction, although rarely with advantage. One example was Gough Cooper, but once again fixed-price contracts made insufficient allowance for inflation and the construction division proved a substantial loss maker from 1978, pushing the whole group into loss in 1980, when it succumbed to a takeover. The temptations offered by contracting appealed to those housebuilders that had previous experience or perhaps even started as builders, such as Ben Bailey, a north-east housebuilder. Ben Bailey, a bricklayer by trade, started building houses in 1933, diversifying into contracting during the war and continuing with contracting until building controls were removed. When it found itself with spare capacity in the early 1960s as a result of planning delays, Bailey had returned to contracting, with a negative impact on group profits. Again, when spare capacity was created by the 1974 recession, Ben Bailey formed a public works division, which was followed three years later by losses on fixed-price contracts.

In case it is thought that it was only the housebuilders who were relatively new to contracting that suffered problems, there were also housebuilders with long-standing construction arms that suffered as well. Losses on fixed-price contracts in 1971 and 1972 necessitated provisions at Bryant's construction subsidiary; in 1977 summonses were issued against the Company and certain directors regarding corruption on construction contracts in Birmingham, leading to an Old Bailey trial; and in 1978 Bryant had to make provisions against a Saudi Arabian gunnery contract (not helped because the army insisted on using the range before it had been finished). Bett Brothers had enjoyed the post-war council housing boom, but it had to withdraw from competitive tendering in 1983 when losses reduced profits to £0.4 m. after a peak of £2.3 m. in 1980. Elsewhere, Francis Parker required provisions of £4.5 m. on fixed-price local authority contracts which contributed to its decision to withdraw from both contracting and housebuilding.

Whereas the housebuilders that moved into construction in the 1960s and early 1970s tended to be drawn from the ranks of the smaller and medium-sized firms, when the reverse movement took place and construction companies (including those that had originally been predominantly housebuilders) moved into, or increased their investment in, speculative housebuilding, they included more of the larger companies. Contractors were attracted by the high returns on speculative housing but just as the housebuilders had experienced difficulties with the disciplines of fixed-price contracting so in turn the contracting dominated firms struggled to come to terms with the different management approaches required by the two disciplines. At first, some contractors even appeared ashamed to be associated with their old market. Laing, as mentioned in Chapter 3, did not use its own name but restarted private housing in 1953 as John and David Martin Ltd (family Christian names). According to Sir Maurice Laing, 'We were trying to get major civil contracts and the potential clients were saying "you are just housebuilders."'[31] Also after the War, Costain used the Dolphin Development Company for its private housing, only changing its name to Richard Costain Homes in 1966. Even in the mid-1960s the Manchester firm of Arthur Wardle used a separate name (Cookson Wigan) for its housing business: John Cassidy remembered the managing director telling him that 'people still retained this idea of housebuilders from the thirties as a bit of a nasty type of trade – we don't want people to know we are involved in this one.'[32] The expression 'cottage bashers' was not the only term used to belittle those who wanted to build houses rather than enjoy the more glamorous world of large civil engineering contracts.

The parent company appointment of directors to the main board was particularly revealing of the attitudes held by contractors to speculative housebuilding: the pre-war housebuilders that became the international contractors of the post-war period had little housebuilding representation on their parent company boards. For instance, Costain never had its housing managing director on the parent board throughout the post-war period. At Laing, David Holliday was the first housebuilding managing director to

---

[31] Interview with Sir Maurice Laing, April 2000.
[32] Interview with John Cassidy, March 1999.

be appointed to the main board in 1984. Taylor Woodrow had to wait until 1998 before it had a full-time housing director on its main board. It took Taylor Woodrow 40 years to regain the housing volumes it had achieved in 1956. Asked what mistakes he had made, Frank Taylor said 'he concentrated so intensely on construction that he feels he may have missed opportunities; he should perhaps have invested more in land much earlier.'[33] Wimpey was mentioned in the previous chapter as not putting its housing into a separate subsidiary until 1978, and even then requiring the construction companies to do most of the building. Speculative housing did not prosper when it was not given unconditional support. Gleeson had been a housebuilder before the war but its post-war success was in public works: 'We certainly thought of ourselves as above all else contractors and in those days people would view the housebuilding arm as a regulator or safety valve, something we turn on and off depending on how the contracting is going.'[34] This was a not unreasonable corporate strategy, but it did mean that Gleeson's housing volumes never rose much above 100 until the late 1980s.

A widespread problem was the organisational conflict within a mixed construction and housing group both in the way that contractors thought that the building process should be organised on a housebuilding site, and the insistence that the construction subsidiary should be responsible for that building process. Housebuilders that were forced to use fellow subsidiaries for their construction rarely found it satisfactory. Wood Hall Trust, which had bought Davis Estates in 1957, also owned the Fairweather construction company and amalgamated the two businesses under a common board in the early 1970s. However, when Davis was forced to use Fairweather, 'It was a disaster. You don't apply the same disciplines when you are both part of the same group.'[35] When David Holliday moved from the construction division to be managing director of Laing Homes in 1980 he found that the construction company did the work for the housebuilding company: 'I said this was not the right way to do it. At that time my appointment was still a construction appointment rather than a developer appointment. I dropped my contractor hat very early on.'[36] Mowlem, one of the oldest established contractors in the country, started building flats for sale in Glasgow and Edinburgh in the early 1970s. However, it was conducted on a very low key basis and was not overly successful: 'The contracting people were always interfering and although the houses were good quality, we were unable to

[33] Jenkins, *On Site 1921–71*, p. 112.
[34] Interview with Dermot Gleeson, Jan. 2002.
[35] Interview with Brian Hewitt, Oct. 1998.
[36] Interview with David Holliday, Dec. 1998.

make money.'[37] Many will have observed from their own experience that human relationships within organisations are not perfect. Sadtler et al. put it colourfully: 'If you ask a room full of managers how many prefer doing business with sister units rather than external businesses, they will vote one and all in favour of external relationships'.[38] It would be surprising if readers had not had similar thoughts from time to time.

Gray's history of Alfred McAlpine is revealing in its description of a contractor coming to terms with the different management skills required for speculative housing:

> 'Bobby McAlpine believes that because they were contractors they made a big error in believing that the important element in private housing development was the building of the houses. What they didn't realise, then, was that the real factors are the site and its architectural planning on the one hand, and the marketing of the houses on the other: the least important element is the actual construction of the houses.'

There was a frank admission that none of the top management had any professional experience in housing: 'They had not, for example, been able to acquire the flair, the ability to size up a site and know instantly the difference between a good and a bad one.'[39] A legitimate question would be, why were the contractors so slow to realise that their housing activities required a different managerial approach? What is obvious with hindsight is less obvious at the time and there is validity in Jeremy's comment that 'existing organisations are governed by a specific set of codes which may prove extremely difficult to change, even when new personalities are installed'.[40]

Another cultural difference between construction and speculative development was the disparity of financial reward that accrued to the individuals, which became acute when the housing market boomed. At Laing:

> 'One of the internal difficulties was that you had a contractor who employed 11,000 people and a housebuilder who employed 600 people – what is the salary rise going to be? You get all this looking across the fence and the jealousies and what have you – not particularly at the top level but lower down. It is very difficult to weld it into the same culture.'[41]

---

[37] Interview with Brian Watkins, Oct. 2001.
[38] Sadtler, *Break up!*, pp. 14–15.
[39] Gray, *The Road to Success*, p. 141.
[40] Jeremy, *A Business History of Britain 1900s–1990s*, p. 188.
[41] Interview with David Holliday, Dec. 1998.

This clash of temperament between the traditional contractor, employing a small group of entrepreneurial developers, more highly paid and more profitable, found an almost exact parallel in the 1980s when the clearing banks bought specialist merchant banks and stockbrokers. Because the pairings of construction and housebuilding, and banking and broking, appear so similar, the larger business assumes that it understands the smaller; the lesson from both industries is that they rarely do.

Some of the construction firms that had never had a history of speculative housing did recognise the need for specialist skills and purchased dedicated housebuilders. Tarmac, a quarrying and construction group, had tried speculative housing without success and there appeared little understanding of the development process. Alan Osborne, Tarmac's construction managing director, remembered 'We were always doing quite a lot of public housing and the message came back "yes you can go into private housing, providing you don't buy any land." '[42] Tom McMillan, another Tarmac director, frankly admitted that when they started 'they hadn't a clue' and Osborne also conceded that 'when we first were in private housing it was true that we had a more construction led method of building'. Ron King, later to become managing director of the enlarged McLean, remembers Tarmac's Bill Francis telling him during the negotiations: 'The way you market and present your houses leaves us standing. That's what we are buying you for.' The McLean team had a poor view of what they found:

> 'They were just building box type houses, poor quality construction, no design appeal, no selling appeal and nearly a thousand houses built and not sold. Our philosophy was we sell them and then we build them. Whereas they were just totally construction oriented, building houses.'[43]

Despite all the problems enumerated above, many of which where plain to see, the contractors continued to make significant housing acquisitions in the 1980s, particularly towards the end of the decade as the housing cycle was reaching its peak. Alfred McAlpine bought Finlas in 1982 and Canberra in 1988; Mowlem bought Unit Construction in 1985; there were three acquisitions in 1986 when Amec formed a joint venture with Hammerfine (buying the rest in 1988), Higgs & Hill bought Southend Estates and Tilbury Contracting bought Whelmar's Scottish subsidiary; and in 1987 Balfour Beatty bought Clarke Homes. In a period of only two or three years, Balfour Beatty increased its volume from 100 to 1600; Fairclough from 600 to 1500; Mowlem from nominal levels to 1200; Higgs

---

[42] Interview with Alan Osborne, Feb. 2000.
[43] Interview with Ron King, Nov. 1999.

& Hill from 150 to 550; Tilbury from around 200 to 750; and McAlpine's sales rose from 360 in 1982 to 1350 in 1988. In general, the management teams were left to run the day-to-day business, but the contractor dominated top management rarely felt it necessary to accord the housebuilders representation on the parent company board; the housebuilders would, therefore, have had less influence than before on strategic issues.

At the same time, other contractor-housebuilders were significantly increasing the scale of their private housing divisions: between 1982 and the peak pre-recession year, Costain's volumes rose from 400 to 2200, Laing's from 1000 to 3400 and Lovell's from 1200 to 3100. In 1989, six out of the top ten housebuilders and 12 out of the top 20 were part of groups which also contained large contracting businesses, and by the late 1980s private housebuilding was accounting for a significant part of their group profits – as much as 60% for Higgs & Hill and Alfred McAlpine and 70% for Laing. Few contractors totally resisted the pressure to diversify into housing. From a list of 19 UK owned contractors with a turnover over £200 m. in 1991,[44] only three, Kier, Wiltshier and Sir Robert McAlpine, did not have a private housebuilding division and even Kier, which demerged from Beazer after the latter's purchase by Hanson, later went on to acquire housebuilding businesses. Sir Robert McAlpine had been the largest speculative housebuilder on the west coast of Scotland in the late nineteenth century, but he went bankrupt and the firm never went back into housebuilding. Sir Robert's grandson said that it had been looked at from time to time but they had always turned it down: 'if you build houses, you get people complaining that the drains don't work and it is very cyclical.'[45]

The examples given in the text so far, supported by the histories in the companion volume, indicate a much greater degree of underperformance by the contractor-led housebuilders than the focused housebuilders. In an attempt to quantify this, an analysis of those pre-1990 recession firms that had built over 1000 units in any one year (Table 5.3) was undertaken. The Introduction has already warned about the problems of inter-company comparison and the first step was to exclude those housebuilders that clearly did not fit into one category or the other, for example those that were owned by conglomerates, or those where the decision on whether to describe them as contractor-led was too subjective (for example Lovell); McCarthy & Stone was also excluded as its total concentration on sheltered housing made it a special case. This left 18 companies which, fortuitously, divided into nine focused and nine contractor-led housebuilders.

---

[44] Wellings, *Construction Equities*, p. 172.
[45] Interview with Sir William McAlpine, March 2001.

Table 11.1 The relative performance of contractor-led vs. focused housebuilders.

Company	Units			Trading margins %		Provisions 1989–93	
	Pre-1990 peak	1995	% change	1988	1995	£m.	per plot £
Contractor-led housebuilders							
Tarmac/McLean	12,165	6140	−50	26.6	7.8	132.1	5081
Wimpey	9581	7609	−21	23.1	6.2	71.3	2910
Laing	3436	1675	−51	20.9	13.0	66.7	9529
Costain	2212	410[a]	−81	14.0	−5.5	113.3	37,767
Amec/Fairclough	1942	1811	−7	22.5	0.5	107	21,400
BICC/Clarke	1610	405	−75	n/a	−34.9	n/a	n/a
McAlpine	1350	1645	22	16.6	7.0	11.6	2578
Mowlem	1200	560[b]	−53	20.0	−7.1	16.3	7409
Wates	1100	227	−79	24.5	12.0	23.5	n/a
Total/average	**34,596**	**20,482**	**−41**	**21.0**	**−0.1**	**67.7**	**12,382**
Focused housebuilders							
Barratt	7000	6601	−6	17.5	10.9	65.1	3829
Westbury	2415	2678	11	25.4	8.5	36.7	4893
Wilcon	2600	3870	49	35.4	8.7	10.4	680
Bryant	2150	3733	74	21.5	11.5	23	3194
Persimmon	2043	3593	76	28.6	10.3	5.5	567
Bellway	1720	3813	122	17.9	13.5	9.3	2325
David Wilson	1592	1916	20	29.0	12.6	0	0
Redrow	1208	2258	87	18.6	14.3	0	0
Abbey	1027	444	−57	23.1	13.5	15.3	9563
Total	**21,755**	**28,906**	**33**	**24.1**	**11.5**	**18.4**	**2783**

[a] 1992 [b] 1993

The first comparison in Table 11.1 was of the change in housing volumes from the pre-1990 peak to 1995, the point where the industry had begun to emerge from recession. The unit volumes were shown in each period (or in the year of sale for Costain and Mowlem) and the percentage change calculated. As a class, the contractor-led housebuilders experienced a 41% fall in unit volumes whereas the focused housebuilders increased volumes by a third. Of the contractor-led housebuilders, only McAlpine achieved a volume increase; in contrast, of the focused housebuilders, only Barratt and the Dublin quoted Abbey suffered falls in volume.

The next test was to see whether, regardless of the movements in their volumes, the profit performance of the contractor led housebuilders compared unfavourably with those of the focused housebuilders. Using the figures from the *PHA*s, the trading margins of the two groups were compared. In

1988, the focused housebuilders averaged margins of 24%, higher than the contractor-led housebuilders but not substantially so (figures for Clarke were not published). However, it is times of difficulty that most test management, and in 1995 the focused housebuilders achieved margins of 11.5%, whereas the contractor-led housebuilders did no more than break even. Only two of the contractor-led housebuilders achieved margins of over 10%: only two of the focused housebuilders failed to achieve 10% margins.

Trading profits are before financing costs, which are not easy to ascertain in diversified groups. They are also before exceptional charges, and the early 1990s saw substantial write-offs against the pre-recession land banks. The final columns in Table 11.1 show the size of the land provisions; because, other things being equal, the larger companies will have the larger absolute provisions; the provision per land plot is also shown. (The provisions for Clarke were never disclosed, neither was the pre-1990 land bank for Wates.) The absolute provisions for the contractor-led housebuilders was higher, but they were building more houses at the peak. However, in relation to their land holdings, the write-off per plot was some four times that of the focused housebuilders. Thus, it would appear that on the three criteria of volume growth, trading margins and land write-offs, the focused housebuilders fared substantially better than the contractor-led housebuilders.

Most of the companies operating a construction/housing business eventually chose to concentrate on one or the other. As mentioned above, the housebuilders that had diversified into, or increased the scale of, contracting in the 1960s and 1970s not infrequently lost their independence. The construction companies, often those who had bought their way into housing in the 1980s, divested one business or the other. Amec (1999), BICC (1995), Birse (1995), Mowlem (1994), Amey (1998) and Tilbury Douglas (2000) all sold their housing as did longer established companies like Costain (1993), Lovell (1999) and Tarmac (swapping its housing for Wimpey's construction and quarrying in 1996). In the opposite direction were Higgs & Hill selling its construction in 1996 (renaming itself Swan Hill), and Wimpey's sale of its construction was the corollary of the Tarmac deal. The divestment of housebuilding was often (though not always) caused by the scale of group losses during the recession (instanced in Chapter 10); housebuilding may or may not have been the major contributor to the group loss, but the housing land bank was usually the most realisable asset. Even if financial necessity did not require a sale, the realisation that housing did not represent the easy way of making money that had been assumed in the 1980s, and a reluctance to countenance the capital commitment that would be required to grow the business, produced the same result. Indeed, contractors were not just concerned about the capital commitment inherent in the housebuilding industry; they had also realised that their supposedly cash-generative construction businesses were less so in recession – Mowlem's finance director admitted that 'none of us recognised the inability of housebuilding to spin off cash when it really matters.'[46] The attitude of investors had also changed in that they wanted managements to be focused on the businesses they knew best; moreover, they were not prepared to accept the risks of what they perceived as a volatile construction business. Whilst this comment is based on my own City experience, it is supported by Toms and Wright who discussed the pressures for, and rewards to, corporate divestment.

Amidst the widespread jettisoning of the contractor-housebuilder model during the 1990s, a few (predominantly medium-sized) firms continued to argue for the retention of both construction and private housebuilding. Six companies actively promoted both their construction and their speculative housing, namely Henry Boot, Galliford Try, Gleeson, Kier, Miller and Morrison; with the exception of Miller, all had housing volumes of under 1000 units a year. (Also, in 1999, Morgan Sindall bought the partnership housing activities of Y.J. Lovell.) Other than Kier, which diversified into housebuilding following its management buyout from Hanson in 1992, these firms were following inherited strategies, dating as far back as the 1930s for Boot and Gleeson, and the wartime for Miller. Nevertheless, those strategies did clearly recognise the problems that have existed in the construction-housing hybrids and they sought to minimise the disadvantages and exploit the skills common to both through the 1990s.

At the very least, there had to be a strict separation of functions, as Fraser Morrison of Morrison Construction recognised:

> 'In relation to running an integrated housing and construction business the key in my view was to ensure that the housebuilding division was a separate entity run by housebuilding professionals because it rarely worked to have construction people involved in the selling of houses. We tried on various occasions to have our construction division involved in building the houses . . . but that did not work well in my view.'[47]

In effect these companies were adopting a balanced portfolio strategy with Kier, in particular, being successful in investing its positive construction cash flow into a succession of small housebuilding acquisitions. There

---

[46] Interview with Brian Watkins, Oct. 2001.
[47] Fraser Morrison correspondence.

were occasional arguments drawing on the synergy of overlapping skills, particularly by the Scottish Miller Group whose privately owned status undoubtedly helped it pursue a different strategy to its quoted peers. Keith Miller, interviewed in 1999, argued that there was a wider synergy between construction, housing and commercial development:

'There are big local authority land holdings and you can't unlock it just through housing because it does not make enough money – except for down south. We have the ability to unlock commercial value from sites which will then in turn unlock residential value: [it] is a skill which gives us a slight edge.'[48]

Justifications can be found for combining construction and housing under the one corporate ownership, but they do sound defensive on occasions. Gleeson accepted that it might entail an acceptance of lower returns:

'Whether it is the case that Gleeson Homes will always be somewhat less efficient than a pure housebuilder, I don't know. I can't see why it should be so but supposing you persuaded me that up to a point it must be so, I would still, for strategic reasons, want to keep Gleeson Homes. I don't think that the return on Gleeson Homes compared to its peers is the only consideration.'[49] As this book was going to press, Gleeson announced a strategic review, concentracting activity on housing regeneration and commercial property.

Keith Miller also agreed that the companies that had been most successful in the housing sector were the focused ones: 'I guess our housebuilding company, whilst it's been successful, is by no means an upper quartile performer – I accept that'. Indeed, the evidence suggests that the operating margins of the housebuilding subsidiaries of the six companies above were some four to five percentage points below the average of the 20 largest housebuilders in the three years to 2000, as shown in Table 11.2.

Table 11.2   A comparison of housebuilding profit margins of hybrid construction-housebuilding companies: six in 1998–2000, four in 2003–2004.

Margins %	1998	1999	2000	2003	2004
Contractors	8.5	9.0	10.6	12.8	14.3
Largest 20 housebuilders (2004)	13.0	13.6	14.7	17.2	18.2
Difference	−4.5	−4.6	−4.1	−4.4	−3.9

Source: *PHAs* and underlying data.

---

[48] Interview with Keith Miller, Feb. 1999.
[49] Interview with Dermot Gleeson, Jan. 2002.

Subsequently, Morrison Construction became part of AWG, a water util-ity, and there have been abortive attempts to sell the diminishing housing business; in 2003, Henry Boot sold its Homes subsidiary and Galliford Try rebutted a takeover approach by a construction company that was partly predicated on the sale of its housing division. Galliford has, however, remained positive on its housebuilding division, appointing the latter's managing director as group chief executive in 2005; Kier has continued with bolt-on acquisitions; and, in 2005, Miller bought Fairclough Homes from Centex. Having said that, when the margins of these four remaining companies were compared with the top 20 housebuilders' margins for the years 2003 and 2004, the disparity was much the same as in the earlier years.

This book has continually stressed the difference in the business models of construction and speculative development, and it is this that underlies the difficulty that the two physically similar businesses have in coexisting under the same management. Although contemporary views are not unan-imous, most housebuilders and contractors now accept that the two busi-nesses do not sit easily together. Peter Mason was responsible as chief executive for the disposal of Clarke Homes from Balfour Beatty (1995) and then Fairclough Homes from Amec (1999). He argued that the only synergy between housebuilding and contracting was cash, as the contractor norm-ally generated cash and the housebuilder required funding.

> 'You can't hand it back to the shareholders because it weakens the overall balance sheet. Historically, contractors have invested it in housebuild-ing – it seemed a good idea. But if the contractor invests in housebuild-ing, it needs a continual increase in capital to grow the business or it becomes moribund and the best people go elsewhere'.[50]

Peter Costain looked back at the place of a housebuilding operation within a publicly quoted contractor and argued that one of the problems was that the contractor was not investing at the right point in the cycle – at the bot-tom there were usually other commitments for the funds and at the top of the cycle they were short of land and therefore had to buy it at the wrong price.[51] Laing suffered from exactly the same problem: in June 1992 the directors announced that their policy was to take £70 m. out of housing worldwide over the succeeding three years; by 1998 volumes had fallen to only a third of the level achieved ten years earlier. Lynn Wilson took a broader view: 'I think construction is an entirely different business – a very low-margin high-risk business run by people who are only in it because they like constructing interesting buildings. Developers are a different

---

[50] Interview with Sir Peter Mason, April 2002.
[51] Interview with Peter Costain, Sep. 1991.

breed'.[52] The Costain/Mason contractor attitude is valid but it is Wilson representing the housebuilders who points to the real temperamental difference between the two industries.

Housebuilding and commercial property

Commercial property development has probably been as common a stablemate for speculative housebuilding as construction. As so often in this book, the classification of companies into one category or another can become arbitrary at the margin, but of the companies that appear in the league tables of leading housebuilders, almost exactly half have had a property development or investment business for a period of time, although not always as a separately constituted entity. From that number have been excluded firms that did have an occasional commercial property development and the pre-war developers that put arcades of shops or a cinema onto their large estates. Indeed, if the four companies that had only a limited post-war existence are excluded, then the proportion of housebuilders that have involved themselves with commercial property, or been in larger groups that have included commercial property, rises to 54%.

The assumed synergy with construction failed because it was based on the similarity of physical process and not intellectual and temperamental complementarity. However, if development skills lie at the core of a successful housebuilder, so do they also for the commercial property company. The pre-war estate developers mentioned above provided commercial property, usually retail and leisure, as a part of the whole estate; the more recent trend towards urban redevelopment has led once again to mixed use development, typically shops and restaurants at the bottom of apartment blocks but sometimes on a larger scale. The entrepreneur who considered himself an opportunistic developer may be equally predisposed towards housing or small commercial schemes; firms like Broseley and Fairview, whose founders came from an estate agency background, did both with equanimity. The site opportunity that was unsuitable for housing would not be turned down if it would make money as a retail development. The temperament and business inclination of those at the top was important and some developers had a preference for one part of the market or other; Fairview, for instance, increased its commitment to commercial property when Ken Oliver joined the Board in 1969. Other housebuilders may have moved into commercial property simply because they saw it as a related way of making additional profit: Beazer admitted that in the early 1970s,

---

[52] Interview with Lynn Wilson, Sep. 2000.

'We perceived that money was to be made in property and had seen other companies making good money'.[53] Sometimes, like English & Continental in the early 1970s, there were specific financing reasons for running commercial property with housebuilding: 'The investment property did not generate revenue while it was being refurbished and let; there was, however, an interest charge which would have produced an unutilised tax loss but this could be covered by the profits of the housing company'.[54]

Although, in general, completed property developments were sold to create trading revenue in much the same way as houses were sold, some companies retained completed properties as investment assets, considering that their rental income gave stability to an otherwise fluctuating trading business and the assets supported a sound balance sheet. This was a post-war phenomenon, but it repeatedly gave rise to problems at publicly quoted companies as investors tended to value trading companies at a multiple of profits but value property companies in relation to their asset value. As the *Investors Chronicle* pointed out in 1978, 'at a time when the earnings yield on the construction index is nearly 20% and that on the property share index under 3%, it looks as if the market is ignoring the property assets of the builders.'[55] An entity combining both was rarely worth the sum of the component parts, leading to pressure from shareholders to split the businesses to realise full value. Laing demerged its property company in 1978, and its shares rose by 70% in the six months following its announcement. Bellway and Fairview followed in 1979 and 1982; Clarke Homes separated out St Modwen Property in the 1980s prior to the former's possible flotation, and more recently Banner Homes demerged its property business in 1997.

If housebuilders wished to disengage from property investment, the alternative to the formal separation discussed above was to run down one part of the business or the other: those whose property businesses had prospered naturally tended to exit from housing and become property companies. Percy Bilton (1970s through 1980s), Mucklow (late 1970s/early 1980s), Five Oaks (1970s), M.P. Kent (late 1970s/early 1980s) and Allied London (early 1990s) were all examples of businesses that had become predominantly property oriented but were less successful at housing, which was duly built out. Federated Land announced a phased withdrawal from housing in 1981, which was accelerated the following year when the British Steel Pension Fund bought the Company for its property assets. Sunley actually got other

[53] Interview with Alan Chapple, Aug. 2000.
[54] Interview with Ramon Greene, April 2001.
[55] *Investors Chronicle*, 4th Aug. 1978.

housebuilders to build out their housing assets for them. In contrast, firms that had been more successful as housebuilders chose to run down the commercial property side, notably Bryant, Wimpey and Wilson Connolly in the 1990s, and Taylor Woodrow is currently doing so. It was also illustrative of attitudes that when disposals of whole groups were being considered, commercial property was never included with housebuilding; either the buyers did not consider it fitted with their business or the vendors considered that they could realise more by selling the two parts separately. Thus, the sales of Broseley (1986), Costain Homes (1993), Galliford Estates (1993), Ideal Homes (1996) and McLean Homes (1996) all excluded the associated property assets, as did the re-flotations of Beazer (1994) and Bovis Homes (1997).

Not only were investors averse to mixing housebuilding profits and property assets, the recessions of 1974 and 1990 also made them apprehensive about large-scale commercial property development even when it was for sale, not retention. These recessions had sometimes caused more difficulty for the property than the housing businesses. It was usually possible for houses in the course of construction to be built out and sold; at a price, there would be a purchaser. In contrast, large commercial schemes were unsaleable if a tenant had not been secured. Galliford Estates and Beazer were brought to the brink of collapse in the 1974 recession by their commercial arms and David Charles did fail:

> 'When the recession came [Charles] was able to cut back [on housing] and more or less kept up the repayments on the bank loans. It was the commercial property side which caused the problem: one couldn't cope with the borrowings on a half built office block; they weren't pre-let.'[56]

It was the larger schemes that again proved difficult in the 1990 recession and Roger Lewis, chief executive of Crest, contrasted the difference between large and small developments:

> 'Property had been one of the driving forces of Crest through to 1989 and I think that one of the things which we did wrong was that we bought a couple of big sites at the wrong moment; until then we had always had a policy of remaining in smaller developments – in market towns which we understood.'[57]

Erostin, having correctly anticipated the 1990 housing recession with extensive sales of land in 1989, failed in 1991 with ten unsold commercial properties on its books.

---

[56] Interview with M.J. Deasley, Jan. 2002.
[57] Interview with Roger Lewis, July 2001.

There is a recognisable complementarity between speculative housebuilding and speculative commercial property, not in the construction process but in the development skill sets and attitudes. At first glance, it is not easy to see why the twin operation is not more common. In the quoted arena, the failure of a business model that combined lowly rated trading profits and highly rated investment property assets can be understood, because it was a mixture that investors valued less than the sum of their component parts. However, that should not have been a constraint where both houses and commercial property were developed for onward sale. There is some evidence that the two are just regarded by the participants as inherently different, whether rationally or not.

Scott, in *The Property Masters*, specifically excludes residential property, 'since the economic, and other, factors determining conditions in these markets are very different from those influencing commercial property', although his book traces many of the themes that are covered in this book.[58] Victoria Mitchell, a director of the Savills agency, suggested that until recently, commercial developers did not want to know about residential: 'They thought, quite simply, that it was "beneath" them,'[59] a comment reminiscent of the contractors. There is no doubt that the marriage of housebuilding and commercial property development for sale could be made to work as, for instance, at Wilson Bowden which specialised in industrial parks. However, it is noticeable that these were developed in much the same way as large housing estates. Perhaps the essential difference between the two forms of development arose where the size of the project was larger (for instance office blocks), when the capital commitment and the time scale required a different management philosophy, and the unevenness of the profit flow again caused concern to investors, who preferred to value a more sustainable stream of income.

Housing and conglomerates

It was argued above that speculative housebuilders tend not to succeed when part of a construction group, despite the apparent similarity of the businesses. The evidence suggests that housebuilders achieve little more long-term success when part of an unrelated group or conglomerate; even where the housebuilding subsidiary did perform well, changes in parent company strategy invariably led to it being sold. There was almost no merger activity of any kind in the housebuilding industry in the inter-war period; managerial objectives could be achieved through organic growth.

---

[58] Scott, *The Property Masters*, p. 4.
[59] Victoria Mitchell, correspondence with the author, Dec. 2002.

However, housebuilders did feature in what has been termed the third merger wave, between the mid-1950s and 1973 when, according to Jeremy, conglomerate mergers 'appreciably increased'; Channon stated that diversified firms had risen from 24% of the largest 100 firms in 1950 to 60% by 1970; Toms and Wright also refer to 'diversification, conglomeration and the multi-divisional 1950–80.'[60] By the onset of the 1974 recession, conglomerates or non-related owners were well represented in the top ten housebuilders: there were Salvesen's Whelmar (number 3), P&O's Bovis (4), GRE's Broseley (6) and London & Northern's Bardolin (9) totalling over 10,000 units, or about 30% of the top ten output. By 1980, the top ten included Broseley (4), Bovis (5), Hawker's Comben (8), Trafalgar House's Ideal (9) and Whelmar (10) with output approaching 9000 or 25% of the top ten output. Mention should also be made of English China Clays which began to actively expand its private housebuilding in the early 1970s and the relationship between food group Hillsdown and Fairview which started in 1987.

When housebuilders diversified into construction and commercial property (or vice versa) an underlying logic could be recognised; in contrast, the unrelated diversification was largely a product of financial engineering and fashion. The contemporary intellectual justification for diversification used by its proponents was 'a belief that the managers of the predator companies had greater ability and expertise than the incumbents',[61] a qualitative claim that goes further than the mere quantitative exploitation of managerial economies of scale as set out by Penrose.[62] Moreover, to the extent that the predator philosophy was accepted by investors, and their shares accorded a high rating, earnings per share could be increased by the simple expedient of buying companies on lower ratings; success bred success and reached its apogee in the Slater Walker era of the late 1960s and early 1970s.

In assessing the influence of conglomerates on the British housing market, there are definitional problems with the very concept of diversification: Penrose suggests that it is neither possible nor desirable 'to establish any "absolute" measure for such words.'[63] For example, diversified construction

---

[60] Jeremy, *A Business History of Britain 1900–1990s*, pp. 209–10; Channon, *The Strategy and Structure of British Enterprise*, pp. 237–8; Toms, 'Corporate Governance, Strategy and Structure', p. 93.

[61] Toms, 'Corporate Governance, Strategy and Structure', p. 98.

[62] Penrose, *The Theory of the Growth of the Firm*, pp. 92–5.

[63] Ibid, p. 107.

and building materials groups such as Tarmac could or could not be defined as a conglomerate according to preference. Some companies had interesting explanations of why their apparently conglomerate structure was really a focused business: Crest considered that it was not what the businesses had in common that mattered, but it was the approach that you took to those businesses – in their case a marketing philosophy which could be applied to tennis courts, boat building and housing. For the purpose of this section, conglomerates are taken to be unrelated owners, groups with interests that extend well outside the wider construction industry, or companies that actually have a focused mainstream business but who own a housebuilder.

As in the section on construction, housebuilders differed according to whether they were initiating the diversification, that is creating the conglomerate, or whether they were the subject of it, that is being acquired. The housebuilder that became part of a conglomerate is considered first, as these tend to include the larger housebuilding entities: the chronology of the more important acquisitions is outlined first with the conclusions being presented at the close of the section. Table 11.3 lists these conglomerate acquisitions.

The first true unrelated acquisition of a housebuilder came in 1957 with the purchase by Wood Hall Trust of Davis Estates, one of the pre-war top ten, and still on the fringe of that group at the time of acquisition. Although Wood Hall Trust installed its own financial systems at Davis, it left the management in place for a few years. However, Wood Hall was more interested in the cash flow from Davis than growing the business, and volumes were allowed to decline. In 1983, Wood Hall was in turn taken over by

Table 11.3 Important conglomerate acquisitions of housebuilders.

Year	Housebuilder	Conglomerate	Conglomerate activity
1957	Davis Estates	Wood Hall Trust	Australian pastoral trading, food
1967	Ideal Homes	Trafalgar House	Construction, newspapers, hotels, ships
1968	Whelmar	Christian Salvesen	Food distribution
1960s	Broseley Estates	Guardian Royal Exchange	Insurance
1970	Comben	Carlton Industries	Batteries, whisky, plant hire, housebuilding
1974	Bovis	P&O	Shipping
1974	Galliford Estates	Sears	Retailing
1978	Comben/Carlton	Hawker Siddeley	Engineering
1984	Bradley Estates	English China Clays	China clay, quarrying, housebuilding
1984	Comben	Trafalgar House	As above
1986	Broseley	Trafalgar House	As above
1987	Fairview Estates	Hillsdown	Food

Elders and the housing was gradually run down. It was another decade after Davis was bought before there were any more unrelated acquisitions when in 1967 Trafalgar House bought Ideal Homes. Ideal's David Calverley had three powerful figures above him – Nigel Broakes (himself a developer), Victor Matthews and Eric Parker, and Trafalgar's control was more than just financial monitoring. 'All land purchases had to be cleared by Eric Parker, and if they were above a certain size, then Victor Matthews.'[64] It took time to stabilise the business but Trafalgar encouraged growth in the 1980s, financing the substantial acquisitions of Comben then Broseley; by 1987 annual output was over 5000 and Ideal was number five in the industry. However, when the 1990 recession came, it hit a number of Trafalgar's divisions at the same time, culminating in a £347 m. group loss in 1993, a rundown in Ideal's volumes and its eventual sale.

There were two housebuilders that have already been mentioned under 'succession'. Whelmar, run by Tom Baron, was bought in 1968 by Christian Salvesen. A series of small acquisitions helped take it up to number three in the industry prior to the 1974 recession, but after that volumes were allowed to decline and when Baron retired in 1985, the business was broken into five and sold piecemeal. Broseley had been founded by Danny Horrocks and control gradually passed to the Royal Exchange during the 1960s. By 1982, volumes had reached 4500 and it was number four in the industry but on Horrocks' retirement in 1986 the housing business was sold to Trafalgar House. In both cases, the parent company managements recognised the difficulty of replacing the entrepreneurial founders from their own ranks and the incompatibility of a development business within a food distribution or insurance company.

In 1973, Bardolin was acquired by London & Northern, and Bardolin's managing director and founder of the principal operating subsidiary resigned immediately; in 1975, housing losses were incurred in the Midlands and in 1976 in the south as well. By 1982, combined public and private housing sales were down to 400 compared with around 1500 at the time of Bardolin's acquisition. In 1986, London & Northern itself fell to a bid and the housing was eventually sold on to Raine. Comben was a more complicated story and it retained a quoted minority throughout. In 1970, it became part of Carlton Industries (itself run by developers). In 1978, Carlton was sold on to Hawker Siddeley which retained Comben as an autonomous quoted subsidiary until it was sold to Trafalgar House in 1986.

---

[64]   Interview with David Calverley, Nov. 1998.

Bovis had been rescued by P&O in 1974 and was held for over 20 years until it was floated in its entirety in 1997; throughout that period it was run by Philip Warner, one of the industry's longest serving managing directors. Warner brought Bovis Homes back to profitability and it finished the 1970s as one of the most profitable in the industry. However, it was never able to achieve long-term growth in volumes. Although there was little, if any, operational interference by P&O, the constraint from the parent company was financial. 'Our growth aspirations were curbed by what P&O was prepared to invest in the business. We were always bidding for funds in competition with the other divisions . . . our horizons were always a bit bigger than we were allowed to achieve.'[65] Bovis might not have been allowed to grow but the managerial independence that it was given enabled it to become one of the more profitable housebuilders.

Another 1974 rescue was that of Galliford Estates by the retailing firm of Sears. In the early 1970s Galliford had rapidly expanded its commercial property division, which included a European development programme of some £40 m. There was an underlying logic in the acquisition, for Sears was controlled by Charles Clore, one of the great names in property development. Sears was able to build out Galliford's commercial developments but housebuilding remained a peripheral activity: David Brill remembered that, 'The day I took over as managing director, Maitland-Smith told me that housing wasn't regarded as a core activity'.[66]

It is arguable whether English China Clays should be regarded as a conglomerate. It had a long-standing involvement with the building industry through the use of waste as a base for building materials and it also moved into local contracting after the war. In the late 1940s it was successful with its Cornish Unit House for local authorities and in the 1960s began private development in its local region. In 1972, it recruited John Reeve from Janes to provide specialist expertise and he was appointed housing managing director in 1980.

> 'There was a belief by a majority of the main board that land for development represented a suitable investment for cash being generated by the mainstream clay business. It was considered that housebuilding was not so diverse from the mainstream business of extraction since their successes were all dependent upon land acquisition and planning permissions.'[67]

---

[65] Interview with Philip Warner, June 2001.
[66] Interview with David Brill, May 2001.
[67] John Reeve correspondence with author.

Reeve was successful in developing the housing business on a semi-national basis and the acquisition of the West Country firm of Edwin H. Bradley (Bradley Estates) in 1984 took it to over 1000 units a year. In 1986, ECC narrowly failed in its bid for Bryant but volumes continued to increase, reaching almost 1300 in 1989; moreover, margins were the highest of any large housebuilder. However, new management arrived in 1990, and English China Clays decided that more focus was needed on its core clay business and that private housing did not fit into the mainstream activities; in particular, 'it was considered that our involvement in housing was having a depressive effect on the share price'.[68] Volumes were sharply reduced and controlled land sales were made to other builders over a four-year period, with the rump of the business acquired in 1995 by Wainhomes.

If there was ever to be an exception, it was Fairview Homes. Fairview, one of the consistently most profitable housebuilders, had taken itself private in 1982 but the death of one of the shareholders led to a search for an exit route in 1987; thus started one of the most unlikely partnerships – between a food conglomerate and a housebuilder. While plans were being made for a quotation on the USM, Victor Blank of Charterhouse suggested a meeting with Harry Solomon, just taking over as managing director of Hillsdown Holdings. 'We met Harry and within 7–10 days we had done a deal. They wanted anything that made money. They were in the business of issuing dear paper for cheap assets but in our case they didn't get cheap assets – they got good management.' Fairview's success can only be a tribute to the relationship between Cope and Solomon. Dennis Cope described it:

> 'It was all about one man, Harry Solomon. I can remember we completed the deal on the Friday and I rang Harry on the Monday morning and I said "Harry, I can't tell you how pleased I am this has gone through, what do you want me to do now, do we need a meeting or something?" He said, "It's very simple Dennis, I want you to run it like it's your own." End of conversation. I don't think we could have done it with anyone else. He left us to run it ourselves . . . They didn't come down and look at the sites, they didn't have a man on the Board.'[69]

Ten years later, Solomon had gone and under a new chairman Fairview was demerged.

The arguments about mixing housebuilding with unrelated activities are similar when it is the housebuilder that is doing the diversifying. However, it is hard to find housebuilder-led diversification into unrelated activities

---

[68] Ibid.
[69] Interview with Dennis Cope, Sep. 1999.

Table 11.4   Illustrative diversification by housebuilders.

Period	Housebuilder	Diversification
1960s	Hallmark	Property, banking and brassware
1960s	Bellway	Kitchens to container ports
Late 1960s	Bunting Estates	Engineering and chemicals
Late 1960s	Whittingham	Environmental engineering and photographic processing
1971	Bovis	Banking
1970s	Crest Homes	Boat-building, tennis courts, spectacles, engineering

that did not lead to either failure or the downgrading of the original housing business. Table 11.4 gives some illustrative examples of the diversification. Sometimes the problems were caused by the businesses acquired; sometimes by the indirect impact on housing from neglect and a diversion of capital. Hallmark diversified away from housing in the early 1960s with interests ranging across property, housebuilding, Twentieth Century Banking (the finance house that was later to do so much damage to Bovis) and manufacturing – primarily Barking Brassware. Arthur Wait, who had been running housebuilding, left the group four years after his own business was acquired. 'Complete disillusionment; they kept nicking his cash! He was a disillusioned man'. Although there was no direct interference from the main board in the running of housebuilding, financing became a problem. 'The problem was that we were the cash cow of the business; all of the profit, all of it, went out of the window into Hallmark to use for commercial property investment.'[70] When Hallmark was bought in 1970, housebuilding was immediately sold.

Bovis, mentioned above as part of P&O, had previously been brought to the verge of bankruptcy in 1973 by the secondary banking crisis; in 1971 it had bought Twentieth Century Banking and significantly expanded its activities. Bellway had a diversification strategy in the 1960s, from kitchens to container ports: 'Ken Bell was fascinated by anything that was not central to the housebuilding business.'[71] Bunting Estates, shortly after its flotation in 1965, was used as a vehicle for the acquisition of Gas Purification and Chemical from related directors; losses were made in housing and then in engineering, and housing activity had ceased by 1980. At the end of the 1960s, William Whittingham moved into environmental engineering and photographic processing; the latter business was expanded and became one of the top ten in the country. In consequence, the original housebuilding was not expanded and, after a period of high profits, photographic losses

---

[70] Interview with Brian Wait, Aug. 2001.
[71] Interview with Howard Dawe, Nov. 2001.

were incurred in 1982. A weakened Whittingham fell to a takeover bid the following year. Perhaps one of the simplest admissions was made by Ben Bailey's son, Richard, looking back on his company's long flirtation with distribution: 'We didn't know enough about merchanting. We were OK when it was small but once it got larger with big premises it started to chase us around. I didn't know enough about merchanting – I'm a house-builder.'[72] Peter Prowting was clear that the mainstream business suffered in the 1970s and early 1980s from the Group's attempts at diversifying:

> 'I was getting involved in other things; I wasn't driving the business. In those days conglomerates were the flavour of the month. We bought a Ford main dealer in Croydon; a sock factory in the Midlands; a coal mine; I set up a swimming pool contracting company; we bought a builders merchants in Hereford and Wellington.'[73]

Almost all these were sold by the late 1980s.

Crest Homes had what it regarded as a focused attitude to diversification, acquiring Camper & Nicholson, Britain's leading yacht maker (hence the name change to Crest Nicholson) in 1972. 'The logic of the merger lay in Bryan Skinner's unconventional view of the role of the housebuilder. He saw housing not as an adjunct of the building industry but of the leisure industry. In that light both houses and boats are places in which leisure time is spent.'[74] Skinner outlined his housing and leisure concept in the 1973 Annual Report:

> 'It is our aim to appeal to the rational investor by demonstrating historic growth and good future prospect . . . we try to observe business struc-tural and sociological changes arising from such items as increasing leisure time, affluence, inflation, speed of innovation and obsolescence, consumer power and social accountability . . . Our business activities are linked together by certain common themes. They all have strong marketing elements, and we consider ourselves to be the market leaders in terms of quality, reputation and value for money.'

However, a later managing director suggested that Crest had been no more than a child of its times: 'The reality was that, at that stage, conglomerates were much more acceptable and Bryan believed that the common theme could be in the approach to business as opposed to the industry in which that business was engaged.'[75]

---

[72] Interview with Richard Bailey, Jan. 2002.
[73] Interview with Peter Prowting, Dec. 2000.
[74] *Building*, 1st Feb. 1974, p. 104.
[75] Interview with Roger Lewis, July 2001.

The acquisitive nature of conglomerates, frequently predatory, never made them universally popular; indeed, at the end of the 1960s, a *Times* editorial stated that there was a danger of the word 'conglomerate' becoming 'a term of criticism'.[76] The financial pressures of the 1974 recession exposed the fragile structure of many conglomerates and, although successful diversified groups could still attract a following, by the late 1970s that wave of conglomerate philosophy had largely run its course. A movement took place in the opposite direction and the period 1980–2000 was described by Toms and Wright as one of 'divestment and restructuring',[77] although that did not stop a revival of 'fashionable' conglomerates like Hanson and BTR. Toms and Wright went on to argue that improved corporate governance prevented firms from buying unrelated business to satisfy directors' aspirations and forced them to refocus.[78] However, having practised in the City throughout the period, this author's own judgement is that the conglomerate fashion ended because it failed to produce consistent growth, shares underperformed, and conglomerates were unable to obtain the support for further share issues: Toms and Wright refer to the 'conglomerate discount'[79] and a contemporary view was typified by the *Independent*'s comment that: 'In recent years conglomerates have been disappointing investments as they struggle to perform in a market which became more appreciative of the more focused approach.'[80] Those conglomerates that did re-emerge in the 1980s came under pressure following the 1990 recession and their structures were once again criticised. In their 1997 polemic, Sadtler et al. concentrated on exposing 'the value destruction that lurks in many diversified companies'.[81] More recently, a *Financial Times* article reflected on the changing fashion for conglomerate structures arguing, *inter alia*, 'that the intellectual fashion moved decisively against conglomerates'.[82] It followed that once investors came to believe that focus was good for corporate performance share prices could be increased by the disposal of unrelated businesses.

The descriptions of the distinctive and entrepreneurial nature of the development process that have been given throughout this book will have anticipated the specific problems faced by housebuilders within diversified structures, but for an independent comment Grebler's discussion of conglomerates in

---

[76] *The Times*, 9th Sep. 1969, p. 23.
[77] Toms, 'Corporate Governance, Strategy and Structure', p. 93.
[78] Ibid. p. 106.
[79] Ibid. p. 108.
[80] *Independent*, 31st Jan. 1996, p. 19.
[81] Sadtler, *Break up!* p. xii.
[82] *Financial Times* 8th March 2000, p. 25.

his housing work is apposite. He regarded the foremost difficulty as 'the idiosyncrasy of the businesses compared to the normal operations of manufacturing, financial and most other corporations'. He stressed the continual non-routine decisions of the developer, the irregularity of profit flow, the front-end loading of the investment, and the length of the product cycle compared with manufacturing. He concluded with what this author regards as the most important problem, the integration of management skills and practices, and the harnessing of the developer's entrepreneurial talent and experience. Grebler pointed out that the acquirer attempted to retain those skills through management contracts but so often the seller became disillusioned and left, leaving a gap which could not easily be filled: 'His equivalent usually prefers to be an independent operator. If the replacement was drawn from the executive staff of the parent company or from second rank real estate specialists, the seller's spark and finesse were usually missing.'[83]

By the end of the 1990s, there was no housebuilder over 1000 units that was owned by an unrelated owner. Indeed, in the *PHA* 2004, it was only the unwanted housing interests of utilities company AWG that came into that category. There was also only one large housebuilder with an unrelated activity, Bloor owning Triumph motorcycles, but that is more a private company using its cash flow to fund the owner's personal interests. This does suggest that, as a business model, unrelated ownership of housebuilding companies has been found wanting, and where the management succession is mishandled, as with Bardolin, then immediate problems follow. But to say that operationally unrelated ownership has never worked is too simplistic. The examples above indicate that where the acquirer has sustained a relationship with the founder, the business can continue to operate successfully – Tom Baron and Danny Horrocks had enjoyed long-standing ties with their purchasers before being bought. Professional management could also be successful when it was given operational independence and enjoyed a strong long-term relationship with the parent managing director. Bovis under Warner, Ideal under Calverley, ECC's housing under John Reeve and Fairview under the ownership of Hillsdown are good examples of profitable housebuilding subsidiaries.

However, even these examples of operational independence were only successful within limits: there were still important constraints in the long-term business model of a housebuilder as a conglomerate subsidiary. First, the parents were generally reluctant to see sustained growth in the

---

[83] Grebler, *Large Scale Housing and Real Estate Firms*, pp. 140–5.

housebuilding subsidiary, sometimes because they just wanted it to generate a cash flow, sometimes because, as for Bovis, it was competing for capital within the rest of the group. Second, success depended on the original personal relationship: when housing managing directors retired at Broseley and Whelmar, the parents sold the housebuilders; when the parent company managements changed, as at Hillsdown and ECC, they took one quick look at the housebuilding business, wondered what it was doing there, and sold it. Finally, the unrelated parent was not supportive during recession: in theory, the diverse product portfolio should have strengthened the parent's ability to support the housebuilding business but, in practice, recessions catch most businesses at the same time; ECC's decision to run down housing was influenced by the fact that it was depressing the share price. Sears took money out of Galliford Sears through land sales in the early 1990s, before selling the business. Even where there was a will to retain housebuilding, there was not the same will to invest contra-cyclically. Ideal's Calverley recognised that one of the disadvantages of being part of a large group was that it was unable to take advantage of the recession to reinvest at the bottom of the land market: 'The tragedy was that with other parts of Trafalgar also being hit by the recession there weren't the resources to take advantage of the opportunity to replenish the land bank at what by then were historically cheap land prices.'[84]

This inability to provide financial support at the bottom of the housing cycle suggests that even the best run conglomerate becomes a fair-weather friend. This was a marked contrast with some of the specialist housebuilders in the early 1990s who were able to persuade investors to provide new capital through rights issues. The ability of successful housebuilders like Bellway, Berkeley and Persimmon to raise new money is understandable, but there can be no better example of the benefits of focus than McCarthy & Stone, the sheltered housing specialist. McCarthy & Stone had been crippled by the recession: volumes had fallen from 2600 to 1000, for several years its debt averaged 150% of a diminishing equity base, and it was dependent on bank support to continue trading. Yet in 1991 it raised £13 m. from a rights issue and, despite the level of debt, the banks allowed the firm to purchase new land at what were exceptionally depressed prices. This provided the basis for a prolonged recovery and by 2004 McCarthy & Stone's volumes were back over 2000, pre-tax margins were 44% and there was over £50 m. cash in the bank. The reason the firm survived and succeeded was because it had dedicated management, not the least being founder John McCarthy, with no alternative but to fight for the firm's

---

[84] Interview with David Calverley, Nov. 1998.

survival. I find it impossible to believe that if McCarthy & Stone had been part of a diversified group, it would have been supported by the central management.

Overseas housing

A considerable number of housebuilders diversified overseas but only Taylor Woodrow and Wimpey can claim to have achieved any degree of long-term success; both have earned substantial profits in the USA in recent years on the back of the American housing boom. The reality is that all the other housebuilders, and there were many, eventually closed their overseas operations, either voluntarily or of necessity. The reasons for expanding overseas in a service industry are limited, some would argue non-existent. Channon suggested that it occurs in response to limitations in the home market: 'Like product diversification, therefore, geographic diversification appears to take place when high quality domestic opportunities in the firm's original business area are no longer available.'[85] However, if the economies of scale and scope are limited in the domestic housing market, they are all the more so internationally. There is no international branding of houses; there are no falling exports to protect through overseas production. Among the requirements of a successful housebuilder are detailed local market knowledge (of land resources and customer preferences) and an ability to keep tight managerial control; if the housebuilder possesses these skills at home, they are difficult to take overseas. (Indeed, many English housebuilders were nervous of even going north of the border.) It was rare to find a housebuilder claiming that it was bringing anything to the overseas markets that the local companies were not already doing – and probably better.

Although there is a long, indeed noble, history of contractors operating overseas through the nineteenth century, there is little evidence of speculative housing overseas before the Second War. In 1937, Taylor Woodrow, in partnership with Owen Aisher (Marley), Leo Meyer (Ideal) and Norman Wates, as individuals, began developing in New York State, but with little gain. In the immediate post-war period, a few housebuilders went to South Africa, understandable in the absence of domestic opportunities, a Labour government they feared and, in some cases, a desire for winter warmth on ageing limbs; there were also occasional forays into Australia and Canada. However, with the growth in the home market, the need for overseas diversification became less pressing. When it did come, the two most popular

---

[85] Channon, *The Service Industries*, p. 42.

areas for overseas investment proved to be France and then the USA, the latter being the more substantial and enduring. These were not exclusive for, apart from the old dominions, a number of companies flirted with Mediterranean developments, and there were even a couple of housebuilders that were undaunted by the prospect of entering the German housing market. In 1989, Lovell was reported as 'leading a consortium that plans to revolutionise the West German housebuilding industry,'[86] and Costain also had a joint venture in the late 1980s. Nevertheless, it is the wider interests in France and USA that will be addressed here.

Nearly all the French investments started within the narrow timeframe of 1969 to 1972 and it was probably the hopes engendered by the prospect of Britain's entry into the EEC in 1973 that provided the catalyst. Lawdon in 1968 and Page-Johnson and Bovis in 1969 were the first, followed by Bellway, Bilton, Comben, Higgs & Hill, Ideal, Rush & Tompkins, Taylor Woodrow and Wimpey. These investments had largely been abandoned by the time (1979) that Federated decided to build in central Paris, and the only subsequent French investment was by McCarthy & Stone in the late 1980s when it tried (unsuccessfully) to export its sheltered housing concept. It does not appear that any of the French investments showed a profit and no firms persevered for more than a few years, circumstances that were not conducive to providing much information on the structure of these operations.

The reasons for failure go to the heart of the development process, understanding the local culture and knowledge base, as the following examples illustrate. After initial small profits from building in the Paris region, Bellway incurred 'huge losses . . . The French decided that we were too big and worked against us';[87] The French subsidiary was closed in 1979 after combined losses in France and Australia of £1.8 m. Terry Roydon had also tried building in Paris for Comben and although he was fluent in French and had a bilingual managing director he was still unable to make a success of it: 'It seemed a wonderful opportunity to give English expertise – not English houses, just English estate development skills, which didn't exist very much in Paris at that time. What got us was that we could never get our hands on sufficient land to make a go of it.'[88] Wimpey had French staff running the operation but had no more success; while Bovis found the demands of the local communes too expensive.[89] McCarthy & Stone also

---

[86] *Building*, 23rd June 1989.
[87] Interview with Howard Dawe, Nov. 2001.
[88] Interview with Terry Roydon, Jan. 2000.
[89] Cooper, *Building Relationships*, p. 112.

found the system too difficult: 'We couldn't get the margins up – too many fingers in the pie on land and the employment laws were horrendous.'[90] More recently, the American Centex, which owned the British Fairclough Homes until 2005, looked at the French market as part of its European strategy but decided not to invest: 'We walked away from one French company as we got three different answers from three different lawyers on a major planning point.'[91] Culture plays an important part and the most common comment the author has heard over the years is to the effect that if you do not get on with the mayor, there is no point in bothering.

The most substantial overseas commitment was made in the USA and that was predominantly, although not exclusively, initiated in the 1980s. Was there a common denominator behind these investments? One pointer was that the period when the housebuilders went to America was after the home market had gone ex-growth (and exporting, obviously, was not an option); from the late 1970s housebuilders had also been studying the US market to learn new ideas, primarily marketing, which then gave them a familiarity with the country and, human nature being what it is, it probably looked like fun. Federated Homes had built a few houses in Ohio in the mid-1960s but the first significant post-war housing investment in the USA was in 1975 when Frank Taylor personally visited Florida and bought a large tract of land. This was followed by more than a dozen other housebuilders in the 1980s with a flurry at the beginning of the decade. Barratt bought two Californian housebuilders in 1980 and 1981; the business survived the recession but was eventually sold in 2004. Charles Church, Comben and Westbury started from scratch in the Houston area but neither venture lasted more than a few years. Wimpey bought an existing Texan company in 1980 and, after two decades, eventually managed to develop a substantial business. In joint venture, Prowting bought an apartment block for refurbishment in Virginia with the intent of building a substantial US business but was soon disenchanted. Bovis formed a joint company in Georgia in 1981 with an ex-Bovis employee, then working locally; Texas was entered in 1983 but both companies were closed in 1986 and Bovis bought a Florida company the following year. Some companies were just inept, or worse. In 1982, Crouch bought a 270-acre leisure and residential complex in Florida, but construction was halted the following year following the failure of the American partner to produce its half of the development money. Crouch had also bought land in California which, in the words of the 1983 interim statement 'has been found to be valueless,

---

[90] Interview with John McCarthy, Sep. 2001.
[91] Interview with Stewart Baseley, March 2002.

and is being sold at a price less than it was purchased for': Crouch lost £3.5 m. despite UK housing being profitable.

Further into the decade it would become progressively more difficult as the housing recession gave less and less time for a new operation to establish itself. In some respects, Beazer could be regarded as an exception. It bought existing housebuilders: Cohn Communities of Atlanta in 1985, building around 300 houses a year; and Randall Phillips of Nashville in 1986 (around 400 a year). Beazer's strength was that Jerry Cohn stayed on to run it and 'we had no major problems with it'.[92] It did not survive as part of the UK Beazer following its takeover by Hanson but, given its independence, it did go on to become a successful quoted company in its own right, building over 16,000 houses in 2004. Laing entered the Californian market in 1984, to build affordable houses in the Los Angeles region; a strategic review in 1995 led to its closure. Alfred McAlpine also bought a couple of house-builders in 1985, in New England, but these did not survive the recession. In 1987, Costain formed a California subsidiary and in that same year Lovell bought extensive tracts of land in New England in joint venture with local partners, a source of substantial losses a couple of years later.

The final purchases were made as late in the cycle as 1988 by the large Tarmac (McLean), medium-sized Walter Lawrence and small Egerton Trust. Tarmac established a couple of new companies in Virginia and Maryland and these ticked over until the asset swap with Wimpey, when the US sub-sidiaries, then building around 230 units, were excluded from the transac-tion. Walter Lawrence bought a 51% holding in a Californian housebuilder, West Venture Developments, but the latter incurred substantial losses and contributed to the downfall of Raine Industries after it had bought Lawrence. Frank Sanderson had taken hold of Caparo Properties in 1985, renamed it Egerton Trust and embarked on a series of acquisitions. In the USA they included the Peters Hartel Corporation, which was principally involved in the creation of an 'English Village' of 172 units on Cape Cod and in 1988 the purchase of Foxwood Homes of New Hampshire; adminis-trators were appointed to Egerton in 1991.

Table 11.5 gives an approximate indication of the scale of the UK com-panies' North American operations at the point just before the market crashed. Capital investment and profits are not generally available; more-over, the table probably understates the commitment as tracts of land were being purchased for future development. For instance, by 1990 Lovell had

---

[92] Interview with Allan Chapple, Aug. 2000.

Table 11.5   UK housebuilders' North American volumes, 1989.

Company	1989 units America	c.f. UK unit sales
Wimpey	*c.*2000[a]	7100
Taylor Woodrow	1389[ab]	468
Beazer	1120	6066
Barratt	900	6600
Trafalgar House (Ideal)	500–600	3402
Walter Lawrence	500	856
Laing	388	2592
Lovell	270[c]	2963
Costain	259	696
McAlpine	200 (1988)	1100
Bovis	*c.*200	1500
Tarmac	60	12,027
Egerton Trust	n/a	300

[a] Includes Canada   [b] Includes substantial lot sales   [c] Excludes substantial lot sales.
Source: Company accounts; author's file notes.

over $60 m. invested in land partnerships over and above the $20 m. invested in housebuilding, totalling some £50 m. of its group capital employed of £160 m. It is not possible to give a comprehensive picture of losses incurred in the recession but to take one of the companies that did survive, in 1991 Barratt made provisions against land values amounting to £24 m. in the USA compared with £49 m. in the much larger UK and it made operating losses every year between 1991 and 1998 totalling a further £20 m. After a period of profitability, Barratt announced the sale of its US business in August 2004.

While there might have been an element of fashion in going to the USA, companies were keen to stress at the time the extent of their market research in choosing their location. It is an interesting reflection on market research to note the almost random nature of their final destination – from Florida to California and from the Texas oil state to the old-economy states of New England. As for explanations used by individual housebuilders, they too varied. The limitations of the home market was a justification open to only a few, and Tarmac and Barratt, then the two largest, both used it. Tarmac's chief executive accepted that the investment in the USA was relatively small and not worth the effort: 'but [Tarmac] had got to the stage where we were nearly up to 10% of the UK housing market so we had to do something and we thought America might be OK on the basis that they speak the same language, but it wasn't a howling success.'[93] Barratt's justification was identical:

[93] Interview with Sir Eric Pountain, Nov. 2000.

'We were producing at that time 10,000 houses a year and there is a limit to how much market share you can take . . . we had always had an eye on the States – it was the closest thing you could get to the UK housing market. Perhaps it was wrong for Barratt to do it at that time but the concept is not wrong.'[94]

However, when firms the size of Charles Church (around 500 units) use the market share argument it is hardly credible to argue that 'we were blocked in the UK and Houston was a boom town.'[95]

Another argument was that the USA would offset the UK housing cycle: as US housing starts fell by 43% between 1973 and 1975 and by 44% between 1986 and 1991, it is hard to understand how this could be taken seriously. 'The idea of [Laing] going to America with the housing division was that they wanted to offset the UK housing cycle . . . we saw it mainly as a financial exercise. There was no belief that it was something which they could do better than the Americans.'[96] Personal preference and ambition should not be ignored. Norman Wakefield, who took Lovell into the USA, had previously enjoyed working in the country. Beazer was expanding on a wide front and bought cement works and aggregate companies in the USA as well as housing: 'Brian had a fascination with the USA and we had decided that we would go into the USA by buying into something we knew best; we wanted to get used in a simple way to what it was like working in the States.'[97] Westbury's owners, the Joiner family, controlled the company (before its flotation) through offshore trusts, and tax planning was critical to the decision.

It is not as easy as in the French case to generalise about the reasons for failure – not forgetting that Taylor Woodrow and, latterly, Wimpey have been successful. Dealing with both a domestic and a distant recession was more than some could manage, and companies failed in consequence. Despite the common language, the development and marketing process was not the same as in the UK. Barratt 'tried to repeat their concentration on the first-time buyer and the part-exchange programme but it didn't work over there.'[98] Looking back, Philip Warner still thought that the USA was a reasonable market for a UK firm to enter but the developer had to recognise that:

---

[94] Interview with John Swanson, Oct. 1999.
[95] Interview with Susanna Church, Aug. 2002.
[96] Interview with Leslie Holliday, Aug. 2000.
[97] Interview with Alan Chapple, Aug. 2000.
[98] Interview with Michael Chapman, April 2001.

'America is an entirely different type of industry. You either buy the land, and develop it, and sell lots off; or buy the lots and build on them. We were just buying the land in developed lots when we started in Atlanta. The trouble with America is that the supply expands to meet demand enormously quickly and if the market turns then you can be caught with a lot of houses partially built. Our timing was not brilliant with hindsight.'[99]

Sometimes the wrong market was chosen, like the booming Houston in the early 1980s. At other times the erstwhile knowledgeable local partners saw the British coming and, to use a colloquialism, took them for a ride. (For obvious reasons this is a difficult topic to document with case studies but my file notes contain more than one such reference.) Buying the wrong company is an error that can be made on either side of the Atlantic, as McAlpine Homes admitted:

'The mistake we made was that you can't buy in small-minded management. We bought companies that were too small. We should actually have looked at spending the $10–15 million that we had allocated on one significant company and grown it. Instead we bought two small companies and ended up having to drive the businesses from the UK.'[100]

Notwithstanding the recent success of Taylor Woodrow and Wimpey, as a generalisation, the UK housebuilders' overseas diversification can be regarded as a failure, totally in France and for most companies in the USA (the two most frequent destinations). The case studies above illustrate a lack of underlying commercial logic and a failure to master the indigenous development culture on equal terms with the local competitors. Rather than acting as a counter-cyclical benefit, the overseas investments also impinged on the ability of the UK housebuilder to weather the domestic recession; in some cases the losses played a critical part in the overall failure of the group, Lovell and Raine Industries in particular. However, losses in another continent were also a considerable distraction in management time in the 1990 recession, a point made by the Barratt company secretary: 'Do not underestimate the extent to which Barratt was distracted by its US operations particularly in view of the fact that executives were going over there frequently.'[101]

---

[99] Interview with Philip Warner, June 2001.
[100] Interview with Philip Davies, Feb. 2000.
[101] Interview with Michael Chapman, April 2001.

Demand and the housing cycle

This book is concerned with the supply side of the speculative housebuilding industry; it is not seeking to explain the factors underlying housing demand, which are extensively covered elsewhere. Nevertheless, it is legitimate to ask whether demand influences supply. At it simplest, the question is ridiculous, for without demand there would be no supply. The question is more properly, to what extent do fluctuations in demand have a material impact on the supply side of the industry? Sustained boom conditions do encourage new entrants into the industry, easily seen in the inter-war period (see Chapter 2), and the heavy investment in private housebuilding by contractors in the 1980s outlined in the first section of this chapter. However, it is not the gradual impact of a steadily rising market which stands out as an agent of corporate change but the major collapse in the marketplace, and it is the latter that is addressed in this section.

Although there have been a number of smaller disturbances to the market, for example 1966–1967, 1980–1981, and the false dawn of 1995, it was the two major housebuilding downturns in the post-war period (for convenience called 1974 and 1990) that played an important role in restructuring the corporate face of the housebuilding industry. There have been corporate failures outside the 1974 and 1990 recessions but typically for reasons specific to the individual company: Morrell Estates (1937) and Howards of Mitcham (1972) both put their sole trading subsidiary into liquidation; Bradley of York, taken over in 1972, and Crouch Group, which collapsed in 1984, both had questionable leadership; while Milbury, which failed the following year, was the victim of fraud. Those apart, there were some 40 quoted companies that either failed completely or left the industry as a direct result of housebuilding losses incurred in those two recessions (see Appendix). The numbers are necessarily imprecise as, at the fringe, there could be debate about whether some companies left the industry because they were forced to, or because they made a strategic decision; if anything, 40 probably understates rather than overstates the case.

The generic explanation for the recessionary failures starts with the preceding booms; in those cases perhaps better described as manias. Kindleberger gives an excellent description of the psychology of manias, disputing that markets act rationally all the time, and referring to 'mob psychology or hysteria.'[102] An essential component of the excessive boom, or mania, is

---

[102] Kindleberger, *Manias, Panics and Crashes*, p. 26.

that the irrational expectations (which of course do not seem irrational to those that hold them) are financed by monetary expansion in its widest sense. For the housebuilding industry, the finance had to be forthcoming both to drive up the price of the end product, the houses, and for the house-builders themselves, so that they could bid up land prices. Thus, in the latter case, not only would the banking system be involved in the supply of credit, but also the land vendors who would offer deferred terms in return for higher prices. Eventually, the bubble breaks, as it always does, and house buyers and housebuilders alike are left to face the financial con-sequences. An inevitable question is why do people not learn from the mistakes of the past, but it is only by participating in a boom that one can fully understand the herd pressures that override all attempts to behave rationally. This author attempted to answer the question in his book on forecasting, pointing out the tendency of the present to exercise a greater psychological influence than the future. 'The memories of the past dimin-ish and the lessons are ignored. The siren call, which tempts all forecasters is "this time it is different", but it rarely is.'[103]

The proximate reasons why housebuilders fail in recessions is the same as in any other industry – they misjudge the level of demand and have insufficient financial strength to survive. The particular characteristic of housebuilding failures is that the development process requires high levels of stock and work in progress, particularly land. The 1974 recession fol-lowed a period of almost unremitting growth since the removal of controls and that had encouraged many developers to acquire land (which, of course, always goes up in value) well in excess of their immediate require-ments; some of this land would have been bought without planning permission and became almost unsaleable. The 1990 recession, which saw owners facing falling house prices for the first time since the war, also had a similar effect on the value of land holdings and, again, there were extensive provisions, estimated at around £3 billion between 1990 and 1992. The contrast with 1974 is that in the 1990s the banks adopted a more far-sighted attitude to debt recovery and tended not to push the larger house-builders into immediate receivership. Although the losses incurred during the recession of the early 1990s did force many firms out of the industry, the process was more orderly and took longer than in 1974.

The companies that failed were not necessarily poor housebuilders in an operational sense. There is no suggestion that they failed because they built poor quality houses; indeed, there are instances of housebuilders

---

[103] Wellings, *Forecasting Company Profits*, p. 77.

providing too much quality. For example, M. Howard (Mitcham) was put into liquidation in 1972 while the housing market was still booming. Donald Howard:

> 'was very much an idealist about housing, how it should be. He wanted to provide the best of everything, provide quality. He thought that commerce would always go hand in hand with providing first class building. As a result, the tower blocks at Wimbledon were superb from the point of view of design and architecture but they weren't necessarily the most commercial thing that one could have put there in terms of the cost of the building. The show flat was opened in 1966 . . . by the time the winding-up order was given they had sold seven out of 106 and three or four of the 29 town houses.'[104]

In all of the literature on individual firms, and in all the interviews and correspondence involved in the original thesis, there has not been one suggestion that firms have declined or failed because they have been left behind technologically, that their product has been the cause of failure. The nearest example is Barratt, which suffered a severe setback as a result of two television documentaries criticising first its timber-framed construction and, second, the value of its starter homes. As recently as 1999, Nicol and Hooper argued that it was difficult to draw any firm conclusions between the trend towards increased concentration and the nature of the housebuilding industry's product.[105] Under 'Economies of scale', it was argued that the benefits of technological change, be they fast or be they slow, came through the suppliers to the industry and were accessible by all firms: within the housebuilding industry, it is management and not technological issues that stand pre-eminent.

It was not a quality or technological issue; housebuilders failed because they misjudged the market and overtraded. More than half of the 40 companies were run by a dominant individual. It is tempting to try to put a more precise number than 'over half'. At each end of the spectrum, it is clear whether there had been a dominant individual, for example Northern Development's Derek Barnes (failed in 1975) or Federated's Peter Meyer (failed in 1990); or whether the housebuilder was a subsidiary with a succession of managing directors and a main board with no feel for the industry, for example, Costain, which sold its housing subsidiary in 1993. In the middle are some companies where the classification would be subjective or, in the earlier period, where insufficient is known about the management

---

[104] Interview with Christopher Blyth, June 2002.
[105] Nicol, 'A Contemporary Change and the Housebuilding Industry', p. 65.

structure. Nevertheless, the approximation is sufficient to emphasise a point made earlier: although housebuilders rarely succeed if they are not focused, the corollary does not apply; many focused housebuilders driven by dominant individuals are perfectly capable of misjudging the market.

The cyclical misjudgements can be recognised after the event by the performance of the individual companies and have been well documented, but occasionally executives have the misfortune to be caught on record. David Charles' optimism ahead of the 1974 recession was quoted in the previous chapter, but another to fail in that recession was Lawdon: its chairman reported in the 1972 accounts, 'I see no break in the growth of the Group . . . we have every confidence that 1972/73 will show a further substantial increase in profits.' Northern Developments was even praised for its high debt strategy:

> 'What Barnes did see early on was that the real profit in housebuilding lay not in the building but in the land that it stood on . . . If you wish to expand rapidly you can generate a certain amount of your finance, but not all of it, from your own profits. Barnes figured – and he was not alone in this – that if the money could be borrowed, the rise in the land value would eventually cover the debt and the interest and still leave him a profit.'[106]

Surprisingly, experience of the 1974 recession did not always enable its participants to anticipate the problems of 1990. For example, Beazer and McLean had the same dominant individual at the helm of their companies in both recessions. They were in good academic company: Ball argued in 1982, some years after the first of the big post-war housing recessions, that 'the major housebuilders are now relatively immune to the housebuilding cycle. A sudden downturn in demand does not threaten the financial existence of these housebuilders as they now have the backing of large corporate enterprises.'[107] However, the passage of time showed that the major housebuilders were far from immune to the housing cycle, and the relevance of the diversification strategy as a means of producing that immunity has been challenged earlier in the chapter. Individual quotations illustrate corporate overconfidence. As the last recession was just starting, Brian Beazer addressed a stockbroker's conference:

> 'From the cradle you are taught that houses are a good investment in this country. While many things you learn from Mummy and Daddy are

---

[106] *Building*, 25th Jan. 1974, p. 108.
[107] Ball, 'The Speculative Housebuilding Industry', p. 39.

untrue, this is not! House prices will not fall because it would be the kiss of death for Mrs Thatcher. People who are even more addicted to self-preservation than I am will have worked that out before me.'[108]

At Tarmac, there also seemed an unwillingness to recognise the reality of the downturn. 'Sam Pickstock's reaction was to carry on regardless. He assumed that the recession would be temporary and encouraged his operating companies to build houses as fast as ever. He also continued to buy land to provide for future building.'[109] And from Hey & Croft at the other end of the size range:

> 'The increase in mortgage rates has inevitably led many people to talk about gloom and doom' in the housing market. So far as the Group is concerned, activity has continued at a high level. Operating primarily as we do in a part of the country that has seen the largest increase in property values, gives the directors confidence that the improved gross margins secured in 1988 will enable the Group to have another good year.'[110]

The quality of entrepreneurial judgement is discussed further in the next chapter.

Chapter 9 argued that there is no economic necessity for housebuilders to become national, and Chapter 12 offers some alternative explanations for why managements wish to grow. That the successful are able to expand to the extent that they have, in a market that has shown no growth, requires that competitors decline or exit the industry. The reasons for failure vary and are not always possible to identify in a simplistic way but this chapter has identified some common themes. Succession was addressed first, and it appears hard to achieve, whether through families or professional management; the entrepreneurial nature of the development process is an important factor. Structurally, the housebuilding firms appear to do best when they, and the highest levels of management, are focused on the mainstream business. The evidence clearly suggests that housebuilders do not combine easily with construction, commercial property or unrelated businesses; and only occasionally are they successful overseas. It may be hard to manage succession but it should be relatively easy for management to ensure that a housebuilder sticks to its last. The third element in the weeding process has been the effect of the 1974 and 1990 recessions that have removed so many housebuilders from the industry. No firm can avoid recession, but

---

[108] *Building*, 10th March 1989, p. 29.
[109] Ritchie, *The Story of Tarmac*, p. 110.
[110] Leonard Hey, Feb. 1989.

the lesson of history for today's housebuilders (and bankers) must be that, after more than ten years of boom and record industry profitability, it makes sense to have a conservative financial policy. By the time this book is read, it may be apparent whether the excesses of recent years are about to prompt another 'weeding process'.

12

An Alternative Explanation of Growth

Introduction

Having rejected the argument that the economies of scale and scope *necessitated* the creation first of regional and then of national housebuilders, and then outlined the causes of decline, the final chapter of this book proposes an alternative explanation of growth. If the economics of speculative housebuilding do not *require* ever larger units, then the explanation for growth must lie elsewhere. This chapter argues that the driving force behind growth and towards consolidation is a complex interaction between financial incentives, stock market pressures, personal motivation and the judgemental qualities of entrepreneurs at critical points in the housing cycle.

The financial incentive for growth is addressed first. To the extent that additional capital (be it retained profits or outside funds) can be profitably invested in the same business, it makes economic sense for the owners of the business to make that investment; as the housebuilders' product cannot be physically delivered to the purchaser, additional investment can only be made by extending geographical coverage. The ability to float on the Stock Exchange has given an added dimension to the financial rationale. The stock market provides an incentive for private companies to grow to a size where they can be floated on a multiple of profits. Once there, the ability to issue shares has allowed companies to finance a faster rate of growth and to make acquisitions. Furthermore, they are not allowed to stop growing: the pressure on quoted company managements is to produce profits growth and the only way that can be done in a static market is by increasing market share.

Rational economic man is no longer assumed to be the standard, and within the literature of the firm personal motivation as a driving force is discussed, although invariably without examples. Even the extensive interviewing underlying this book has produced only the occasional admission of personal ambition, but the behaviour of some of the business leaders is supportive of the proposition that the creation of large businesses can be an end in itself.

Considerable weight is given in this section to the strategies deployed ahead of cyclical downturns. Success in an entrepreneurial environment can occur relative to competitors if firms grow merely because they are the ones that avoid firm-threatening mistakes. In this context, what is important is the quality of judgement that allows some housebuilders, but not others, to avoid over-expansion ahead of a major downturn in the housing cycle. In doing so, they create a 'pool of survivors' that are able to take full advantage of the next upwards phase of the housing cycle, through the opportunistic purchase of cheap land or distressed competitors.

The financial incentive

Hyde put the profit motive succinctly when asking why men pursue particular lines of business activity: 'The answer is that, for the majority, they do what they do simply in order to make the greatest amount of money.'[1] This may seem an obvious, even unnecessary, statement but housebuilders themselves rarely use the expression 'self-interest' in their public documents; nevertheless, other things being equal, larger firms make larger profits. Profits can either be distributed (as excess salaries or dividends) or retained in the business. If profits are retained, the housebuilder has three choices: he can accumulate cash balances, which only defers the distribution/investment decision; he can invest in something he understands, such as more housebuilding; or invest in something he does not understand. Chapters 10 and 11 gave numerous examples of the lack of success in housebuilder diversification and the rational solution is to reinvest within the existing business, which in turn means expansion. Initially, such expansion will be around the housebuilder's head office but as the firm becomes larger and begins to exhaust the local opportunities, a new region must be formed. The incentive to reinvest in the business is exaggerated by the nature of the housing cycle, where rising house prices create stock appreciation, and lead to lengthy periods of above average returns. Before long, it is being assumed that these returns are not abnormal but capable of being sustained, which in turn serves to over-encourage investment – until the crash.

---

[1] Hyde, 'Economic Theory and Business History', p. 1.

Whatever the financial incentives encouraging organic growth, they have been considerably increased by the opportunities offered by the Stock Exchange. The impact of the Stock Exchange on the 'real world' is not a new phenomenon, but it has been a powerful influence on the structure of the housebuilding industry over the last four decades. Prais wrote in the early 1980s that 'Changes in the financial organisation of the economy, such as the growth of the Stock Exchange . . . have perhaps been the most important of recent influences bearing on the optimum size of businesses',[2] an opinion endorsed by this book. The existence of a marketplace for securities, in which annual profits could be capitalised, and shares traded, placed a premium on size in the housebuilding industry from the early 1960s onwards. First, it encouraged companies to grow to a size where they could be floated on the Stock Exchange, for instance, the merger of David Charles and A.H. Taylor prior to the former's flotation in 1963. Second, the existence of a quotation facilitated fundraising for acquisitions or to finance organic growth, and examples are provided below. Third, the presence of institutional shareholders increased the external pressures on management to continue to grow the business; more recently, the institutional pressure has been to encourage mergers so that the investors have fewer, but more marketable holdings.

The public issue of housebuilding securities did not originate in the post-war period. Henry Boot (then only a contractor) and Metropolitan Railway Country Estates both floated on the Stock Exchange in 1919 and, at the height of the inter-war housing boom, between 1933 and 1935, six housebuilders floated – Costain, Ideal, Wimpey, Davis, Taylor Woodrow and Morrell. The first post-war flotation was of John Laing in 1952 but by then Laing was primarily a contractor. The first flotation of a company that was principally a housebuilder at the time of issue was Arthur Wait in 1956. Between 1956 and 1997 (when P&O's sale of Bovis was the last full listing) there were some 105 housebuilding flotations; this excludes flotations of construction companies that, at the time, had little or no housebuilding content but which later became more substantial housebuilders.

Figure 12.1 shows the timing of these issues which are, as would be expected, concentrated in periods when the prospects for the housebuilding industry were considered to be favourable. The largest number were in the 1960s and the peak in 1963–1964 probably reflected taxation fears; the Conservative Government had introduced a short-term capital gains tax in 1962 and there was concern, correctly as it transpired, that an incoming

---

[2] Prais, *The Evolution of Giant Firms in Britain*, p. 23.

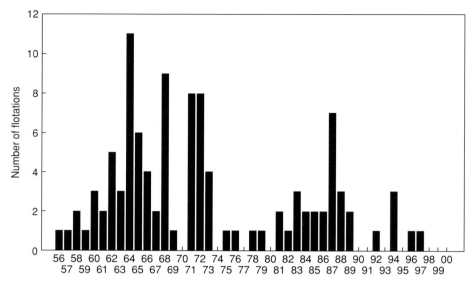

Figure 12.1   Stock Exchange housebuilder flotations, 1956–2000.

Source: Author's analysis of prospectuses.

Labour Government would extend that to long-term gains. There was a pause in new issue activity around 1970 when the housing market dipped, followed by a flurry between 1971 and 1973 as house prices and profits soared: 20 housebuilders were floated in that brief period. The industry was in decline for the rest of the 1970s and there were hardly any new issues, but as activity began to recover in the 1980s new issue activity built up, with the peak once again being at the tail end of the boom: ten companies were floated in 1987–1988 in a testament to investors' hope over experience. The recovery in housebuilders' profitability in the 1990s, in contrast to earlier periods, produced far less in the way of new issue activity; investors were by now reluctant to accord high ratings to housebuilders. By the late 1990s, only one (Bloor) of the top 20 housebuilders was not quoted or part of a quoted group and although this was not dissimilar to the late 1980s or even the early 1970s, the investment institutions were exhibiting an aversion to smaller capitalisation stocks that prevented the flotation of housebuilders from outside the higher reaches of the industry.[3]

Market conditions, by and large, dictated when it was advantageous to float a housebuilding business. The reasons for taking those opportunities were not confined to the needs of the company: they could be personal, as

---

[3] A few small housebuilders did obtain quotations on the AIM.

the examples below indicate. Very substantial fortunes have been created by entrepreneurs who have grown a housebuilding business and then sold it on to another organisation or floated it on the Stock Exchange and realised the proceeds over a period of time. Steve Morgan, who founded Redrow in 1974 and began housebuilding in 1980, was a spectacular example. He floated Redrow in 1994, raising personal capital of £62 m.; further share sales were made in 1998 and again in 2000 when he left the Company, and his wealth is usually estimated as in excess of £300 m. However, rarely is the desire to raise personal capital officially stated as anything more than a secondary reason in a flotation; investors are normally told that the flotation is for the long-term strategic benefit of the company.

Years later, the interview process has found family members more forthcoming, and raising personal cash now features more prominently as an explanation, going back to the very first post-war housebuilding flotation in 1956, A.J. Wait. Arthur Wait's son explained that until the flotation, the family never had any money. Father 'went public so that he could realise cash on a personal basis. The money didn't go back into the Company.'[4] When Iain Bett was asked why Bett Brothers floated in 1967, the answer was: 'One, to raise capital for the family; two, the implications of death duties which could have crippled the firm.'[5] The Green family controlled Bunting Estates which floated in 1964: one of the second generation admitted that they should never have gone public. 'The three brothers had different views about the business and it was a way of crystallising cash.'[6] For more recent flotations, particularly if the companies are still quoted, it is harder to disentangle motives, but two examples were provided by Hey & Croft and Charles Church, both from 1987. For the former, 'The float was mainly to realise capital for the family – the Company did not get much';[7] and Susie Church admitted that the flotation was 'to make some personal money'.[8]

Ascertaining the real reasons behind commercial decisions is not always easy. Official statements are constructed, in part, to say what the audience expects to hear and to exude commercial rationale: 'fashion' or being swept up on the financial tide, was never mentioned. However, the interviews elicited some honest admissions of sheep-like behaviour. The wave of flotations in the 1960s provided encouragement to, for instance, Wardle in 1965: 'Ronnie made the decision on his way into the office having read the

---

[4] Interview with Brian Wait, Aug. 2001.
[5] Interview with Iain Bett, Jan. 2002.
[6] Interview with David Green, Oct. 2001.
[7] Interview with Geoffrey King, Jan. 2002.
[8] Interview with Susanna Church, Aug. 2002.

FT and seen a lot of small housebuilders were going public in anticipation of a Labour victory. Ronnie said "Oh, we'll go as well", made a few phone calls and we were public in about six weeks'.[9] Ben Bailey floated two years later: 'It was the fashion at the time. He had built the business up from nothing and wanted to get some money out.'[10] The early 1970s saw another wave of flotations, including Joviel in 1972: 'Why float? That was what the financial people were suggesting.'[11] And, referring back to the 1987 flotation of Charles Church, Susie Church remembered that, 'Friends were saying that if you want to do it, now is the time.'[12]

Once companies became quoted, they were able to use shares for acquisitions in a way which would not have been possible had they remained private. Hallmark was the first example: it obtained its quotation by 'reversing' into the New Bulawayo Syndicate in 1957; it bought Hesketh Homes in 1958, T.J. Brabon in 1959 and the quoted A.J. Wait in 1963. The rationale for share issues tended to change over time. The late 1960s and early 1970s was a particularly active period and 'doing deals' was fashionable, frequently involving the issue of shares at a high price earnings ratio to buy a company on a lower price earnings ratio. The acquisition mathematics, discussed in the section on conglomerates in the previous chapter, automatically raised earnings per share for the acquirer without either company having to earn a penny more. Perhaps the most blatant use of the stock market was the creation of Orme by Peter Whitfield and Bob Tanner who were looking for new opportunities after the sale of their Clubman's Club to Mecca. According to the 1971 prospectus, they had decided early in 1970 that 'there was scope for rationalisation and expansion in the construction industry, property development and allied activities'. They set about assembling a national housebuilding business but their interest appeared to be in doing the deals, not with the minutiae of housebuilding:

> 'they would say "we've found this business in South Wales. We've bought most of it. We've done a deal with the management. Can you go down and see if its OK? I hope it is because we have already bought the shares off the directors." They used to turn up about once a month, maybe not that.'[13]

In contrast to Orme, Barratt was a prime example of a well managed business using shares to make acquisitions as a means of accelerating its

---

[9] Interview with John Cassidy, March 1999.
[10] Interview with Richard Bailey, Jan. 2002.
[11] Interview with Roy Wright, March 2003.
[12] Interview with Susanna Church, Aug. 2002.
[13] Interview with Rod Mitchell, Jan. 2000.

regional expansion. Its rationale was clearly stated in a 1972 offer document: 'Your Board considers that the acquisition of Bracken . . . constitutes an important step in your Company's planned expansion outside its present area of operations.' Between its 1971 and 1974 financial years it bought seven companies, four of which were for shares; between 1976 and 1979 there were a further five acquisitions, the three largest being for shares. There were also two rights issues during the period to help fund the cash element of the acquisitions and organic growth. During that period, Barratt's share capital almost quadrupled (excluding bonus issues). Other companies preferred to expand organically, issuing shares to provide long-term finance: Berkeley floated in 1985 when its unit sales were 144; by year 2000, output had grown to 3210. There were eight rights issues during this period to finance the growth, increasing share capital by 470%, plus a further couple of share placings. Other housebuilders to use repeated rights issues in the 1980s and 1990s included Bellway, Countryside, McCarthy & Stone and Persimmon.

It was not until the 1980s that managements began to justify publicly their acquisitions by citing the advantages of being a larger housebuilding entity. For instance, Walter Lawrence's 1986 offer document for Poco claimed that its acquisition would 'accelerate significantly the expansion of our housebuilding activities . . . After the acquisition, the enlarged Group will be a national housebuilder and will be in a strong position to take advantage of the growth potential in the housing market.' By the 1990s, it became almost obligatory to bracket rationalisation benefits with size. Alfred McAlpine's 1997 offer document for Raine was typical: 'The enlarged Group will become one of the top ten United Kingdom housebuilders . . . The directors believe that the acquisition of Raine provides a significant opportunity to reduce central overheads and operating costs.'

The market for shares not only facilitated growth but the existence of outside investors, increasingly institutions rather than private individuals, positively encouraged companies to adopt a growth strategy. No company management pleased its investors by saying that it thought it was large enough and had no further plans to grow. The popular managements in the City were those who could deliver growth, and the best rewarded City executives were those that could persuade their clients to make acquisitions. By the late 1990s, institutional shareholder pressure was driving the process of consolidation even further. In the frenzy of the bull market, the share prices of small companies in general were underperforming compared with large companies. Fund managers were increasingly busy people and within the housebuilding industry mergers were being encouraged so that fund managers had fewer but larger companies to monitor.

If the prospect of personal financial gain was the unspoken reason for flotation, then City expectations would sometimes provide the unspoken motivation for growth. As with flotations, the interview process brought forth several admissions that had not been made at the time. Alan Chapple, one-time assistant managing director of Beazer, argued the rationale for being a national housebuilder on the grounds that regional markets give a balance to the business, but when pressed he eventually conceded that 'you do it because you want to crank up your profits.'[14] Philip Warner, long-standing Bovis Homes managing director under P&O ownership, was asked whether he thought that there was any genuine economic rationale in being a large housebuilder: 'If you want to keep the shareholders happy then you've got to keep expanding haven't you – keep the analysts happy.'[15] The advantage of being private was mentioned by a number of public company managing directors. Regalian's David Goldstone referred to the City treadmill: 'you have to go somewhere. You might be able to stand still as private company but not as a public company. We were conscious of the problems; we were more cautious but we had to go ahead.'[16] When Peter Pearce was asked why the first regional expansion (in the late 1960s) was made at Second City his answer was, to grow: 'I think it is why running a private company makes much more sense than running a public company. But you are driven by the need to grow.'[17] John Maunders' 1984 accounts contained the positive statement, 'I consider it essential to expand geographically.' Asked 16 years later why he had thought it essential: 'It was very much the flavour of the month to have a national or quasi-national operation; it was the fashion of the time – why did we grow our hair long and wear flared trousers?' Asked if he had his time again, would he make the acquisitions: 'No, I would just try to be some kind of player in an area I knew well, and where I had the connections.'[18]

Because it is there

The previous section indicated that, once sufficient time had passed, and the participants have left the companies concerned, entrepreneurs will offer different motivation from the received business wisdom of the time, particularly admitting the need for personal capital, the dictates of fashion and investor pressures. Such admissions do not flow easily and it is even

---

[14] Interview with Alan Chapple, Aug. 2000.
[15] Interview with Philip Warner, June 2001.
[16] Interview with David Goldstone, May 2002.
[17] Interview with Peter Pearce, Nov. 2000.
[18] Interview with John Maunders, May 2001.

harder to elicit explanations that have a purely personal rationale, particularly when those people are using someone else's money. Those who wish to grow rarely say, 'I am an empire builder'; their personal aspirations are cloaked in whatever appears to be the business ethos of the day.

Discussion of the role of personal motivation is more prevalent in the literature on management but is still well documented in standard economic works on the theory of the firm; indeed, *The Economist* told its readers that the 2002 Nobel prize winner, Daniel Kahneman, had 'built a career by reminding economists that their idealised subjects are all too human'.[19] The assumption of perfect rationality has been widely criticised as a description of real human behaviour: Myerson commented that 'Experimental studies of decision making regularly find inconsistent and foolish behaviour that violates the predictions of perfect rationality.'[20] For other writers, personal motivation was not necessarily a central tenet. Penrose treated it almost as an afterthought: 'We cannot leave this discussion of the functions and nature of the firm without making a few remarks about the "motivation" of the firm'. She went on to make the important point, albeit one that would be taken as given by anyone brought up in the commercial world, that 'Individuals thereby gain prestige, personal satisfaction in the successful growth of the firm with which they are connected, more responsible and better paid positions, and wider scope for their ambitions and abilities.'[21] Business historian Bill Reader developed the same point with a more personal flavour, stressing the human element. In looking at the way large corporations develop he regarded the economic landscape as one of power politics with businessmen motivated in ways which were not necessarily commercial. 'They seek power. They engage in rivalry . . . The plans they make, although presented, for orthodoxy's sake, as being aimed purely at the maximisation of profits, often have quite other ends in view as well.'[22]

There are, within the literature, other descriptions of personal motivation that could be quoted but what is more interesting is that none are accompanied by any examples. Indeed, out of all the interviews for this book came only occasional admissions of personal motivation. Graham Thorpe ran Hassall Homes during its transition from a small regional housebuilder to a national under the ownership of Raine Industries. Asked why he wanted to be a national, he eventually admitted: 'It was there – why do people climb

---

[19] *The Economist*, 12th Oct. 2002, p. 102.
[20] Myerson, 'Nash Equilibrium and the History of Economic Theory', p. 1069.
[21] Penrose, *The Theory of the Growth of the Firm*, pp. 26, 28.
[22] Reader, 'Personality, Strategy and Structure', p. 108.

mountains? It was a challenge for me rather than any business logic.'[23] Asked why he surrendered his firm's independence to Tarmac, Eric Pountain reflected, 'I don't know why I did it because I could have made a lot more money on my own but I just liked running a bigger company and I couldn't grow McLean fast enough because of the capital constraints.'[24] Redrow was one of the most successful housebuilders of the 1980s and 1990s: as the owner of the business, Steve Morgan's financial motivation would have been high, but he also referred to pressure to grow from the 'City scribblers'. However, at the end of the interview he conceded what must be true for so many business leaders: 'You always want to do better – it's human nature. You strive to drive the business.'[25]

With 40 years of stockbroking experience as support, this author can still do little more than offer confirmation that the corporate actions of those companies he has observed and interviewed cannot be fully explained by sole reference to the economic good of the firm. The excitement, the adrenalin rush, the enhanced sense of self-importance that comes from deal-making, rather than churning out yet another estate of houses, has to be seen to be believed. The role of the dominant character in driving for growth has been mentioned frequently in this book but, for the most part, judgement has to be based on what he does, rather than what he says. A closing example is provided by Beazer, which in its day was one of the most growth-oriented and deal-driven firms in the industry. Brian Beazer became managing director of the small West Country family firm in 1968, when its turnover was under £2 m. and unit sales 150. He led it in an un-paralleled series of acquisitions, many of them fiercely contested, creating not only a national UK housebuilder but taking the Company into building materials, construction, US housing and, biggest of all, the $1.8 billion bid for Koppers, a US aggregates firm with a net asset value of only $0.5 m. With two of the Company's merchant bankers on its Board, Beazer was the largest building company that appeared to be driven by the deal, rather than the product. The criticism of one of his victims was withering, although of little avail at the time:

> 'In my judgement, the Board of Beazer, largely composed of people with an accounting or merchant banking background, does not possess the depth or breadth of industrial management experience and technological attainment necessary to adapt to the diverse demands of a major inter-national construction business'.[26]

---

[23] Interview with Graham Thorpe, April 2001.
[24] Interview Eric Pountain.
[25] Interview with Steve Morgan, April 2003.
[26] John Mott quoted in *Building*, 10th Jan. 1986, p. 15.

The importance of not making mistakes: the pool of survivors

The desire to find a theory for everything may militate against consideration of the random but this section opens with a passing mention of what Hannah referred to as the Gibrat effect, a process of natural selection in which some firms do well and some firms do badly, inducing over time a steady increase in the dispersion of firm sizes; the successful firms increase their share at the expense of the unsuccessful ones and concentration increases. 'Thus, even without any systematic tendency for large firms to experience more rapid growth than other firms, output will become increasingly concentrated in the hands of successful firms.'[27] Prais referred to the dispersion as spontaneous drift, stating that if a group of firms is subject to varying rates of growth then the concentration of the group inevitably increases as time proceeds. In a numerical example, he postulated a group of equal sized firms; every year, half the firms remain unchanged in size, a quarter increase in size and a quarter decrease in size. Over time, firms of ever increasing size emerge, although only small numbers of firms will be in the highest and lowest size groups.

> 'The dispersion of the distribution thus grows inexorably as time proceeds as a result of spontaneous drift; and this increase in dispersion is to be seen whether it is measured in familiar statistical terms . . . or whether it is measured in terms of the share of total activity in the hands of a particular number of largest firms.'[28]

This description, of course, assumes that no new firms are created, a point which Prais later mentions; it also assumes that the firms grow, and continue to grow: the practical evidence is that many firms pass through periods of both growth and decline. It does not seem to present a model for the housebuilding industry but, nevertheless, the dispersion argument is a reminder that concentration can arise without apparent underlying cause. For this book, what it does is to lead into the final observations on growth, namely that the successful firms can only emerge from the pool of post-recession survivors: the survivors are those that do not make firm-threatening mistakes at the onset of recession; and it is the survivors that can acquire the cheap assets, land or competitors, that provide the foundations for the next phase of growth.

Having argued in earlier chapters that there was no economic necessity, no operational requirement, for housebuilders to grow into such large units,

---

[27] Hannah, *The Rise of the Corporate Economy*, pp. 124–5.
[28] Prais, *The Evolution of Giant Firms in Britain*, p. 26.

this final chapter has addressed financial considerations and personal motivation. The third leg of this explanation of growth returns to a recurring theme of the book – the entrepreneur and his judgemental qualities. Nothing stands out so markedly as the role of the entrepreneur – the ability of the dominant individual to create a successful growing business. But to say that successful housebuilders are typically the product of the dominant individual is not, of course, the same as saying that dominant individuals typically create successful housebuilders. As has already been stated, many dominant individuals go on to ruin businesses, sometimes ones they have created themselves, sometimes ones that others have created, and they do so by making strategic mistakes: the ones that do not, form the pool of survivors.

The literature of the firm provides varying approaches to the entrepreneurial or leadership function, and most descriptions give full rein to dynamism, hard work and vision. Maude added an interesting variation with a quotation from an unnamed chief executive of a construction company, citing, 'the ability to make up your mind on insufficient evidence' as a vital leadership characteristic, 'but you have to do it in business, and anybody lacking this ability could scarcely function as a leader.'[29] Indirectly, that leads into perhaps the most important quality for long-term success – judgement. Casson has stressed the role of judgement, defining the entrepreneur as 'someone who specialises in taking judgemental decisions', and he defined these as ones 'for which no obviously correct procedure exists'.[30] In the speculative housebuilding industry, with its long-term vulnerability to the housing cycle, this book argues that it has ultimately been judgement rather than personality that has distinguished the successes from the failures (as one industry leader put it, 'this is a business which just wants to go wrong'). Dominant individuals can still grow a business when the economic background is favourable: paradoxically, these same individuals may also be responsible for its decline, and more often than might be imagined. In particular, it is the judgemental mistakes made at the peak of the cycle which can ultimately cripple their firms.

Archetypal strategic mistakes within the housebuilding industry have been well aired in previous chapters: lack of focus features highly. However, there is one particular judgemental decision that is of pre-eminent importance in the housebuilding industry and that is an ability to anticipate, or sense, a major cyclical downturn in the housing cycle, not with absolute

---

[29] Maude, *Leadership in Management*, pp. 11–12.
[30] Casson, 'Entrepreneurship and Business Culture', p. 31.

foresight, but sufficiently to avoid jeopardising the future of the firm. The previous chapter referred to the large number of firms that had failed because of recession, providing numerous illustrations. The corollary is that entrepreneurs with the judgemental capacity to avoid the strategic mistake of expanding the business into a cyclical downturn, create a pool of survivors; those survivors improve their position in the industry, not necessarily absolutely, but relative to their competitors. This facilitates their corporate growth in the next cyclical upswing: those least affected by the crashes of 1974 and 1990 were able to profit at the expense of those most affected, either by buying their competitors at distressed prices if they were acquisitive (for example Persimmon/Ideal, Redrow/Costain, Westbury/Clarke, Wilson Bowden/Trencherwood), or being in the best position to buy land at cyclically depressed prices if they favoured organic growth (for example Berkeley, Bellway and the companies above). Readers may remember David Calverley using the term 'tragedy' to describe Trafalgar's financial inability to buy land at the depressed prices of the time; it was this that so weakened the firm relative to its competitors. As Devine et al. put it,

> 'analysing growth of firms is not a separate activity from analysing their decline and death. Growth and decline are complementary aspects of the competitive process in the economy as a whole; and understanding of one contributes to an understanding of the other.'[31]

It would be a satisfying conclusion to this book if it could detail just how this judgement was exercised and, even better, how to identify in advance which entrepreneurs possess it. In practice, few entrepreneurs claim that they lack judgement; it is only after the event that one can identify those that had it and even then it is hard to ascertain how that judgement came to be formed. When successful housebuilders, in the sense that they had 'read the cycle' better than their contemporaries, were asked to rationalise their judgemental skill, it was the answers that they did not give that were illuminating. No interviewee referred to the benefits of his own education, nor the role of his firm's economist or business strategist, nor even to collective board decisions, and certainly not to City advice: instead, the responses were always of a personal nature and, despite their underlying growth ambitions, contained a strong cautionary element. David Wilson, one of the most successful post-war housebuilders, was reflective on the subject:

> 'We have always been fairly cautious and aware of what can happen in this industry. On the one hand you've got to be dynamic and ambitious

---

[31] Devine, *An Introduction to Industrial Economics*, p. 135.

but on the other hand you've got to be very aware of what can happen. Saying no is hard to do; I don't know why. It takes a lot of courage and intuition – and intuitive management can be very irritating for the people around you who like to have decisions explained clearly.'[32]

Redrow's founder specifically credited his instinct: 'Steve denies carrying a crystal ball in his pocket. The decision to pull out of the south-east was based on instinct.'[33]

Those who 'saw the recession coming' may have exaggerated their fore-sight after the event, but contemporary evidence does exist. Fairview had warned in its 1971 Annual Report (published in spring of 1972) that 'The vast inflationary tendency in house prices . . . cannot continue for ever'. Its strategy differed from most other housebuilders but the key to its survival was its judgement of the housing cycle. 'We said that the only way for us to survive is to liquidate our stock and go for cash, as quickly as possible, selling at whatever price you could. So we doubled our production . . . and whatever price we could get for them we would sell them.'[34] He did the same again in the 1990 recession. Private companies were in a position to take even more radical steps and use their judgement to sell the whole business, as the founders of Poco did at the end of 1986: 'We thought, if you pay double what it is worth then you can have it'.[35]

There is no doubt that some managements went into the 1990 recession in a more defensive mode. Bellway's Howard Dawe claims to have seen the recession coming a year early: 'We stopped buying land for 12–18 months. We went aggressively for sales via part-exchange and sold as hard as we could.'[36] It was in this recession that the foundations were laid for the 1990s, Bellway's most successful decade. The story of Tony Pidgley deciding to 'go liquid' as the market peaked has entered into housebuilding folk-lore. Looking back from the 1992 Annual Report, 'Berkeley recognised the weakness of the market at an early date and by February 1989 had already started to turn for home by aggressively converting completed or nearly completed houses back into cash.' The founders' view ten years on was that the signs were clear: 'The reality is that in 1988 it was not difficult to see what was happening. The money we were making was outrageous. Jim [Farrer] and I sat down and decided we would go liquid; we did give up the

---

[32] Interview with David Wilson, March 2001.
[33] Burland, *The Redrow Group*, p. 67.
[34] Interview with Dennis Cope, Sep. 1999.
[35] Interview with Roy Dixon, Aug. 2001.
[36] Interview with Howard Dawe, Nov. 2001.

profit chase to go for cash.'[37] It is this strategic decision, based on what its proponents would typically refer to as instinct, that critically marks the successful firms and creates the pool of survivors from which the next generation of growth emerges.

There is nothing original in pointing out that business success is intimately related to the quality of a firm's leadership, or that entrepreneurial behaviour did not always lend itself to rational economic analysis. Some 40 years ago, Hyde drew attention to 'the range of difficulty confronting the business historian in his endeavour to explain behaviour and motives and draw forth conclusions from his observations.'[38] More recently, Casson proposed a theory of the firm centred on the entrepreneur, and his description of the entrepreneur fits the people that have been discussed in this book:

> 'the nature of the firm is most naturally explained in terms of the qualities required of the successful entrepreneur . . . The key to the firm's success lies not in specific business strategies . . . nor in specific ownership advantages . . . It is the quality of entrepreneurial judgement, as reflected in the correctness of these decisions, which holds the key to long run success.'[39]

The study of the housebuilding industry is of particular value to the proponents of an entrepreneurial theory of the firm, not because other industries do not possess entrepreneurial characteristics but because, in lacking recognisable economies of size, the growth of speculative housing firms can be ascribed to little more than the talents and ambitions of the man in charge. That one cannot always give rational economic explanations for their business decisions only serves to emphasise the difficulty of drawing too precise conclusions from any given sample of businesses. John Kay in his 'Beware the pitfalls of over-reliance on rationality', warned that 'The world is usually too complicated for classical decision theory to be of much practical value. Often we don't have all the information we need, and there is too much uncertainty for us to attach probabilities to different outcomes.'

A final observation refers to chance. Davies structured an intriguing corporate history around the role of chance, arguing in his opening paragraph that 'as people tend to be unpredictable, the role of chance becomes very

---

[37] Interview with Tony Pidgley, May 2001.
[38] Hyde, 'Economic Theory and Business History', p. 2.
[39] Casson, *Information and Organisation*, pp. 114–15.

significant'.[40] Many of the housebuilding industry's leaders have arrived in random ways. Berkeley's Tony Pidgley was adopted by gypsies, thereby gravitating towards earth-moving; Crest's Bryan Skinner had a house built for him and worked out how profitable it was; Leon Roydon (Carlton and Comben) gave up medical studies because he was too squeamish. Dennis Cope (Fairview) went to work for the BBC and broke his ankle playing football: 'my sister was at that time working for a surveyor in north London who said, "if your brother is sitting at home with his leg in plaster why doesn't he come up here and answer the telephone?"' Derek Barnes (Northern Developments) started as an apprentice with Blackburn Rovers; presumably, if his footballing skills had been better, there would have been a different number two in the industry in the early 1970s. There were temporary jobs that became permanent careers: Alan Cherry (Countryside) had secured a job in the borough architects' department but took a temporary job with the local estate agent while waiting to start. Duncan Davidson (Persimmon) took his temporary job on a construction site before his army commission and enjoyed it so much that he later joined Wimpey. The industry might not have looked any different if these men had gone in different directions, but the corporate analysis would surely not have been the same. It is from such raw material that theories are constructed.

This book has sought to address a major gap in the understanding of the twentieth-century private housebuilding industry by determining the corporate structure of the industry, from the emergence of localised firms operating on large sites in the inter-war period, through the growth of regional firms from the 1960s, to the creation of the national housebuilders in the closing decades of the century. Thus, Part I established which were the leading firms of their time, what was their size, and (one of the surprising unknowns in the corpus of the literature) how market share increased through the century. Part II examined why the firms grew and why they declined. It rejected the economies of scale, in their broadest sense, as necessitating increased size; physical economies of scale were of little advantage and, anyway, were outside the control of the housebuilder, and economies of scope, while pertinent, appeared to be matched by the diseconomies inherent in the large-scale duplication of local operations and the loss of entrepreneurial flair.

Instead, for an explanation of why housebuilding firms have grown, this book has turned to the prosaic explanations of money and ambition, and the simplistic concept of not making mistakes. Under the catch-all heading of

---

[40] Davies, 'Business Success and the Role of Chance', p. 208.

money is included the reinvestment of profits into the business, as larger capital tends to mean larger entities. However, the opportunity to obtain a Stock Exchange quotation has provided a much greater money motive. In part, it dictated expansion to the minimum size necessary to float, but thereafter the requirement of the investment community was for growth, and the housebuilders provided it, frequently via acquisitions, even though the anecdotal evidence after the event did not indicate that the business leaders always believed in the underlying economic logic. Interlinked with the institutional encouragement to grow is, of course, personal ambition; business leaders are competitive and one should not overlook the fact that larger financial rewards accrue to those running larger companies.

Not making mistakes is as useful a piece of advice as 'buying at the bottom' if one is not told when the bottom is reached; no one makes mistakes for the fun of it. However, there appear to be strategic mistakes in the speculative housebuilding industry that are firm-threatening and, with the benefit of a historical perspective, potentially avoidable. Focus has been extensively discussed in Chapter 11 and, whereas being a focused housebuilder is no guarantee of success, it would appear that mixing the housebuilding business with any other form of activity invariably ends in failure, relative or absolute. Within the focused firms, what seems to characterise the difference in long-term success is the quality of entrepreneurial judgement that enables the firm to anticipate the major cyclical downturns in the industry, not to avoid them but to position the firm, financially and operationally, so that the impact is minimised. This creates what was earlier described as 'a pool of survivors', best able to benefit from weakness of others: it is these firms that, 'by avoiding mistakes' have been able to grow at the expense of their competitors.

It is hoped that the material contained in this book will provide a framework for those engaged in the analysis of specific aspects of the national industry. It should also enable local historians to set their findings in an appropriate context; there is much that could still be done at a local level to improve our knowledge of the smaller firms, particularly those active in the inter-war period. For those whose interest lies more with the theory of the firm, this book should assist inter-industry studies, particularly those concerned with entrepreneurship, for the speculative housebuilder surely encapsulates the entrepreneurial spirit at its most raw.

Appendix
Quoted Company Departures, 1937–2004

Quoted company	Type	Outcome	Probable cause
Morrell Estates	F	Failed 1937	Poor financial performance
Davis Estates	F/G	Taken over 1957	Succession
A.J. Wait (Holdings)	F	Taken over 1963	Attractive offer
R.J. Barton	F/G	Taken over 1967	Offer from larger company – possible succession
Ideal Homes	F	Taken over 1967	Succession
E. Fletcher Builders	F	Taken over 1969	Attractive offer
Comben & Wakeling	F	Reverse takeover 1970	Succession and contracting losses
Hallmark	G	Housing sold 1971	Followed acquisition
Eldon R. Gorst	F	Taken over 1971	Attractive offer
Chansom	F	Taken over 1971	Followed poor financial performance
Daniel T. Jackson	F	Reverse takeover 1971	Weakened by construction losses
Arthur Wardle	F	Taken over 1972	Succession, attractive offer
Norman C. Ashton	F	Taken over 1972	Received good offer at retiring age
Tudor Jenkins	F	Taken over 1972	Attractive offer
Bardolin	F	Taken over 1972	Financial amalgamation
Ashworth & Steward	F	Taken over 1972	Attractive offer
W.A. Hills	F	Taken over 1972	Attractive offer
Page-Johnson	F	Taken over 1972	Attractive offer
H. Kay (Buildings)	G	Taken over 1972	Attractive offer, recession
Howards of Mitcham	F	Failed 1972	Losses in early 1970s
Drury Holdings	F	Taken over 1972	Weakened by construction losses
Bradley of York	F	Taken over 1972	Weakened by financial problems late 1960s
MRCE	G	Taken over 1972	Rationalisation
Varney Holdings	F	Taken over 1973	Attractive offer
Hart Builders	G	Taken over 1973	Attractive offer
John McLean	F	Taken over 1973	Attractive offer, succession
Dean Smith	F	Taken over 1973	Received attractive offer
Ellsworth Estates	F	Reverse takeover 1973	Poor financial performance
Budge Brothers	F	Failed 1974	Recession
Galliford Estates	F	Taken over 1974	Recession
Bovis	F	Taken over 1974	Recession and banking crisis
James Harrison	F	Taken over 1975	Attractive offer, succession
Greensquare Properties	F	Failed 1975	Recession

Quoted company	Type	Outcome	Probable cause
Lewston	G	Failed 1975	Recession, diversification
Fell/Bacal	F	Failed 1975	Construction losses and recession?
Northern Developments	F	Failed 1975	Recession
H.C. Janes	F	Taken over 1976	Succession
Lawdon	F	Failed 1976	Recession
Joviel	F	Failed 1976	Recession
Greaves Organisation	F	Failed 1976	Recession
David Charles	F	Failed 1977	Recession
Orme	F	Taken over 1978	Attractive offer
Algrey	G	Sold 1979	Recession, diversification
Dares Estates	F	Run down in 1970s and 1990s	Construction losses, succession and repeated financial failures?
Francis Parker	G	Run down in 1970s	Followed near failure
Bunting Estates	F	Run down in 1970s	Diversification problems
Burns Anderson	G	Run down in 1970s	Poor financial performance in mid 1960s
Five Oaks Investments	F	Run down in 1970s	Construction losses and repeated financial difficulties
Davis Estates (2)	G	Run down late 1970s	Diversification
Rush & Tompkins	G	Run down late 1970s	Diversification
Bernard Sunley	G	Run down from 1978	Concentration on property
M.P. Kent	F	Run down late 1970s /early 1980s	Concentration on property
Scottish Homes	F	Taken over 1980	Attractive offer
Gough Cooper	F	Taken over 1980	Succession contracting losses
Federated Land	F	Taken over 1982	For its property assets
Finlas/Lowe & Brydone	F	Taken over 1982	Attractive offer
Fairview	F	Housing MBO 1982	To focus on property
Second City Properties	F	Taken over 1983	Attractive offer
William Whittingham	G	Taken over 1983	Succession, diversification
Crouch Group	F	Failed 1984	Followed speculative property development in USA
Comben Group	F	Sold 1984	Extraneous to engineering parent
C.H. Pearce	G	Taken over 1985	Attractive offer
Milbury	G	Failed 1985	Fraud
William Leech	F	Taken over 1985	Succession
London & Northern	G	Taken over 1987 and housing sold 1988	Diversification
Kentish Property	F	Failed 1989	Recession
Rowlinson	F	Run down in early 1980s	Concentration on property

Quoted company	Type	Outcome	Probable cause
Percy Bilton	G	Run down in 1980s & 1990s	Industrial property development preferred
Federated Housing (2)	F	Failed 1990	Recession
Arncliffe Holdings	F	Sold 1991, virtual collapse	Recession
Beazer	G	Taken over 1991	Diversification and overconfidence
Tern Group	G	Failed 1991	Housing diversification never successful, recession
Colroy	F	Taken over 1991	Succession – controlling shareholder in 1980s
James Crosby	F	Taken over 1991	Succession and recession
McInerney Properties	F	Failed 1991	Abandoned by Irish parent
Egerton Trust	F/G	Failed 1991	Recession and diversification
Erostin	G	Failed 1991	Commercial property losses
Fairbriar	F	Bank rescue 1991	Recession, overconfidence
Hey & Croft	F	Failed 1992	Recession – flotation encouraged larger projects
Walter Lawrence	G/F	Rescue bid 1992	Recession
Costain Homes	G	Sold 1993	Succession and diversification
Galliford Sears	G	MBO 1993	Focus on retailing
Wiggins (Allison)	G	Financial reconstruction 1993	Recession
F.J.C. Lilley	G	Failed 1993	Recession, diversification
English China Clays	G	Run down and sold early 1990s	Focus on main activity
Rawlings Bros	G	Sold 1994	Diversification
Anglia Secure Homes	F	Sold 1994, virtual collapse	Recession
Royco	F	Failed 1994	Succession
Mowlem Homes	G	Sold 1994	Recession, concentration on construction
Birse Homes	G	Sold 1995	Recession, diversification
Clarke Homes	G	Sold 1995	Recession, focus on main business
Allied Residential	F	Taken over 1995	No consistent leadership
London & Clydeside	F	Taken over 1995	Lost direction
Trencherwood	F	Taken over 1996	Succession and recession
McLean (2)	G	Sold 1996	Diversification
Charles Church	F	Bank rescue, taken over 1996	Followed financial collapse and death of founder
Ideal Homes (2)	G	Sold 1996	Recession
Britannia Group	G	Sold 1996	Diversification into housing failed
Raine	G	Rescue bid 1997	Recession

Quoted company	Type	Outcome	Probable cause
Bovis Homes	G	Sold 1997	Focus on main business
Maunders	F	Taken over 1998	Attractive offer
Bellwinch	F	Taken over 1998	Impact of recession and succession
Amey Homes	G	Sold 1998	Focus on construction
Banner Homes	F	MBO 1999	Retiring controlling shareholder
CALA	F	MBO 1999	Dissatisfaction with stock market rating
Cussins Property	F	Taken over 1999	Received attractive offer
Wainhomes	F	Taken over 1999	Attractive offer from one director
Lovell Homes	G	Sold 1999	Delayed effect of recession
Fairclough Homes	G	Sold 1999	Impact of recession; concentration on construction
Allied London Properties	F	Run down in 1990s	Possible succession
A. & J. Mucklow	G	Run down mid-1990s	Concentration on property
Avonside	G	Run down late 1990s	To concentrate on merchanting
Try Group	G	Merged 2000	To enlarge size of company
Regalian	F	Sold 2000	Succession
Ward Homes	F	MBO 2000	Succession
Morrison Construction	G	Group taken over 2000	Attractive offer
Allen Homes	G	Sold 2000	Overconfidence, group underperformance
Linden	F	MBO 2000	Dissatisfaction with stock market rating
Tilbury Homes	G	Run down and sold 2000	Concentration on construction
Beazer	F	Taken over 2001	Lost direction
Bryant	F	Taken over 2001	Lost direction
Fairview	F	MBO 2001	Dissatisfaction with stock market rating
McAlpine Homes	G	Sold 2001	Focus on construction
Tay Homes	F	Taken over 2002	Financial underperformance
Prowting	F	Taken over 2002	Financial underperformance
Laing Homes	G	Sold 2002	Parent financially weak
Henry Boot Homes	G	Sold 2003	Parent focusing on construction
Bett Homes	F	Sold 2003	Succession
Wilson Connolly	F	Taken over 2003	Financial underperformance
Swan Hill	F	Taken over 2003	Financial underperformance

F = Focused on speculative development   G = More general mix of group business

Bibliography

Abbott, A.W. *A Short History of the Crown Agents and their Office* (London, 1959).

Adams, D. and Watkins, C. *Greenfields, Brownfields and Housing Development* (Oxford, 2002).

Anon. 'Initiative and Progress shown by Private Enterprise in Attempting to Solve Oxford's Housing Problem', *Oxford Monthly*, Aug. 1932, p. 6.

Anon. *Nash Houses: T.F. Nash Limited* (London, c.1933).

Anon. *Tarmac: 50 Years of Progress 1903–1953* (n/p, 1953).

Anon. *The Way Forward: a Résumé and a Record of Building and Construction during 75 Eventful Years* (London, c.1954), (Sir Lindsay Parkinson).

Anon. *Howard Farrow: a Story of 50 Years 1908–58* (London, 1958).

Anon. *The A.J. Wait Group* (n/p, c.1960).

Anon. *Wates Have a Way with Them* (London, 1963).

Anon. 'Richard Costain Centenary 1865–1965', *Bulletin, Staff Journal of the Costain Group* (June, 1965).

Anon. *McAlpine: the First Hundred Years* (London, c.1969).

Anon. *Walter Lawrence 1871–1971: a History of the Family Firm of Walter Lawrence* (n/p, 1971).

Anon. 'Higgs & Hill 1874–1974', *The Crown Journal*, Centenary Issue, No. 178, 1974.

Anon. *Comben Homes Celebrate their 75th Anniversary* (Bristol, c.1975).

Anon. *Wilson (Connolly) Holdings Ltd: the first 75 years* (Northampton, c.1980).

Anon. *Bradley: Building on a Name* (n/p, c.1983).

Anon. *Balfour Beatty 1909–1984* (London, 1984).

Anon. *Tilbury 100 Years Onward: Tilbury Centenary 1884–1984* (Horsham, 1984).

Anon. *Bovis Centenary 1885–1985* (n/p, c.1985).

Anon. *Prowting 75* (Uxbridge? 1987).

Anon. *Work is Fun: the Ward Holdings Story* (Chatham, c.1990).

Anon. 'One Hundred Not Out: the First Century of Hilbery Chaplin 1894–1994', c.1994 (unpublished typescript).

Anon. *Miller: Celebrating the Miller Group's Diamond Jubilee* (Edinburgh, 1994).

Anon. 'Economics Focus: All too Human', *The Economist*, 12th Oct. 2002, p. 102.

Arora, A. 'Williams & Glyns vs. Barnes – Overview', *The Company Lawyer*, Vol. 2, No. 1, 1981, pp. 23–25.

Ashworth, H. *The Building Society Story* (London, 1980).

Ashworth, W. *The Genesis of British Town Planning* (London, 1954).

Aspinall, P. 'The Internal Structure of the Housebuilding Industry in Nineteenth-century Cities' in Johnson, J.H. and Pooley, C.G. (eds) *The Structure of Nineteenth-century Cities* (London, c.1982), pp. 75–105.

Attenburrow, J.J. *Some Impressions of the Private Sector of the Housing Market*, Building Research Station Current Paper 57/68, July 1968.

Ball, M. 'The Speculative Housebuilding Industry' in *The Production of the Built Environment*, Proceedings of the Third Bartlett Summer School 1981 (London, 1982), pp. 1, 31–51.

Ball, M. *Housing Policy and Economic Power* (London, 1983).

Ball, M. *Rebuilding Construction: Economic Change and the British Construction Industry* (London, 1988).

Ball, M. *Housing and Construction: a Troubled Relationship* (Bristol, 1996).

Ball, M. 'Chasing a Snail: Innovation and Housebuilding Firms' Strategies', *Housing Studies*, Vol. 14, 1999, pp. 9–21.

Ball, M., Harloe, M. and Martens, M. *Housing and Social Change in Europe and the USA* (London, 1990).

Barker, K. *Review of Housing Supply, Final Report* (London, 2004).

Baron, T. 'Design and Marketing in the Eighties', 1980 (unpublished transcript).

Beaverbrook, Lord. *Courage: the Story of Sir James Dunn* (London, 1962).

Beazer, C.H.G. *Random Reflections of a West Country Master Craftsman* (Bath, 1981).

Becker, A.P. 'Housing in England and Wales During the Business Depression of the 1930s', *Economic History Review*, 2nd Series, Vol. 3, 1951, pp. 321–41.

Betham, E. (ed.) *Housebuilding 1934–36* (London, 1934).

Boot, C. *Post-war Houses* (Sheffield, 1944).

Bornat, J. 'A Second Take: Revisiting Interviews with a Different Purpose', *Oral History*, Spring 2003, pp. 47–53.

Bossom, A.C. 'The Building Industry since the War' in *Britain in Depression: a Record of British Industries Since 1929* (London, 1935).

Boswell, J. *The Rise and Decline of Small Firms* (London, 1973).

Bowen, I. 'Building Output and the Trade Cycle (UK 1924–38)', *Oxford Economic Papers*, Vol. 3, 1940, pp. 110–30.

Bowley, M. 'Some Regional Aspects of the Building Boom 1924–36', *Review of Economic Studies*, 5, 1938, pp. 172–86.

Bowley, M. *Housing and the State 1919–1944* (London, 1945).

Bowley, M. 'The Housing Statistics of Great Britain', *Journal of the Royal Statistical Society, Series A*, Vol. 113, 1950, pp. 397–411.

Bowley, M. *The British Building Industry: Four Studies in Response and Resistance to Change* (Cambridge, 1966).

Bramley, B., Bartlett, W. and Lambert, C. *Planning, the Market and Private Housebuilding* (London, 1995).

Broakes, N. *A Growing Concern* (London, 1979).

Brown, J. and Rose, M.B. (eds.) *Entrepreneurship, Networks and Modern Business* (Manchester, 1993).

Bundock, J.D. 'Speculative Housebuilding and Some Aspects of the Activities of the Suburban Housebuilder within the Greater London Outer Suburban Area 1919–1939', M. Phil., University of Kent, 1974.

Burland, M. and Whitehouse, J. *The Redrow Group* (Flintshire, 1999).

Burnett, J. *A Social History of Housing 1815–1985*, 2nd ed. (Cambridge, 1985).

Buzzelli, M. 'Firm Size Structure in North American Housebuilding: Persistent Deconcentration 1945–98', *Environment and Planning A*, 2001, pp. 533–50.

Capie, F. and Collins, M. *Have the Banks Failed British Industry?* (London, 1992).

Carlisle, H. and Lickiss, M. *Milbury plc Westminster Property Group Investigation Under the Companies Act* (London, 1988).

Carr, M.C. 'The Development and Character of a Metropolitan Suburb: Bexley, Kent' in Thompson, F.M.L. (ed.) *The Rise of Suburbia* (Leicester, 1982), pp. 212–67.

Casson, M. 'Entrepreneurship and Business Culture' in Brown, J. and Rose, M.B. (eds) *Entrepreneurship, Networks and Modern Business* (Manchester, 1993), pp. 30–54.

Casson, M. *Enterprise and Leadership* (Cheltenham, 2000).

Casson, M. *Information and Organisation: a New Perspective on the Theory of the Firm* (Oxford, 2001).

Casson, M. and Rose, M.B. 'Institutions and the Evolution of Modern Business: Introduction', *Business History*, Oct. 1997, pp. 1–6.

Catherwood, F. *At the Cutting Edge* (London, 1995).

Catherwood, H.F.R. 'Development and Organisation of Richard Costain Ltd' in Edwards, R.S. and Townsend, H. (eds) *Business Growth* (London, 1966), pp. 271–83.

Central Housing Advisory Committee. *Private Enterprise Housing. Report of the Private Enterprise Sub-committee of the Central Housing Advisory Committee of the Ministry of Health* (London, 1944).

Chandler, A.D. *The Visible Hand: the Managerial Revolution in American Business* (Cambridge, Mass., 1977).

Chandler, A.D. *Scale and Scope: the Dynamics of Industrial Capitalism* (Cambridge, Mass., 1990).

Channon, D.F. *The Strategy and Structure of British Enterprise* (London, 1973).

Channon, D.F. *The Service Industries: Strategy, Structure and Financial Performance* (London, 1978).

Chick, M. 'British Business History: a Review of the Periodical Literature for 1991', *Business History*, Vol. 35, Jan. 1993, pp. 1–16.

Church, R. 'The Family Firm in Industrial Capitalism: International Perspectives on Hypotheses and History', *Business History*, Vol. 35, Oct. 1993, pp. 17–43.

Clark, D.G. *The Industrial Manager: His Background and Career Pattern* (London, 1966).

Cleary, E.J. *The Building Society Movement* (London, 1965).

Coad, R. *Laing: the Biography of Sir John W. Laing (1879–1978)* (London, 1979).

Coase, R.H. 'The Nature of the Firm', *Economica New Series*, Vol. 4, 1937, pp. 386–405.

Cole, G.D.H. *Building and Planning* (London, 1945).

Coleman, D.C. 'The Uses and Abuses of Business History', *Business History*, Vol. 29, April 1987, pp. 141–56.

Colli, A. and Rose, M.B. 'Families and Firms: the Culture and Evolution of Family Firms in Britain and Italy in the Nineteenth and Twentieth Centuries', *Scandinavian Economic History Review*, No. 47, 1999, pp. 24–47.

Collins, J. and Porrass, J. *Built to Last: Successful Habits of Visionary Companies* (London, 1998).

Connor, L.R. 'Urban Housing in England and Wales', *Journal of the Royal Statistical Society*, Vol. 99, 1936, pp. 1–66.

Cooper, P. *Building Relationships: the History of Bovis 1885–2000* (London, 2000).

Cooper, R. and Clarke, D. *3i Fifty Years Investing in Industry* (Oxford, 1995).

Corley, T.A.B. 'The Entrepreneur: the Central Issue in Business History?' in Brown, J. and Rose, M.B. (eds) *Entrepreneurship, Networks and Modern Business* (Manchester 1993), pp. 11–29.

Costain, Sir Albert. *Reflections* (Cirencester, 1987).

Cox, Dr R.C.W. 'Urban Development and Redevelopment in Croydon 1830–1940', PhD thesis, University of Leicester, 1970.

Crane, W.H. 'A Dynamic Model of the UK Private Sector (owner occupied) Housing Market', PhD thesis, University of Liverpool, 1980.

Craven, E. 'Conflict in the Land Development Process: the Role of the Private Residential Developer', PhD thesis, University of Kent, 1970.

Cullen, A. 'An Analytical Account of Takeovers, Acquisitions and Joint Ventures by Building Capital During the 1970s' in *The Production of the Built Environment*, Proceedings of the Bartlett Summer School 1979 (London, 1980), pp. 120–5.

Davies, P.N. 'Business Success and the Role of Chance: the Extraordinary Phillips Brothers', *Business History*, Vol. 23, No. 2, July 1981, pp. 208–32.

Davis, M. *Every Man his own Landlord: a History of Coventry Building Society* (Coventry, 1985).

Devine, P.J., Jones, R.M., Lee, M. and Tyson, W.J. *An Introduction to Industrial Economics*, 4th ed. (London, 1985).

Dunaway, D. 'Method and Theory in the Oral Biography', *Oral History*, Autumn 1992, pp. 40–5.

Dyos, H.J. 'The Speculative Builders and Developers of Victorian London', *Victorian Studies*, Vol. 11, 1968, pp. 641–90.

Eccles, R. 'The Quasi Firm in the Construction Industry', *Journal of Economic Behavior and Organization*, Dec. 1981, pp. 335–57.

Eichler, N. *The Merchant Builders* (Cambridge, Mass., 1982).

Elsas, M.J. *Housing Before the War and After* (London, 1942).

Erdman, E.L. *People and Property* (London, 1982).

Evans, A.W. *Economics, Real Estate and the Supply of Land* (Oxford, 2004).

Feinstein, C.H. *National Income, Expenditure and Output of the UK 1855–1965* (Cambridge, 1972).

Fielding, N. 'The Volume Housebuilders', *Roof*, Nov./Dec. 1982.

Fleming, M.C. and Nellis, J.G. 'The Interpretation of House Price Statistics for the United Kingdom', *Environment and Planning A*, Vol. 13, 1981, pp. 1109–24.

Ford, W.K. *The Story of the Haywards Heath Building Society 1890–1990* (Haywards Heath, 1990).

Fox, W. *London's Speculative Builders*, Labour Research Department (London, 1934).

Furnell, M. *The Diamond Jubilee of Ideal Homes* (West Byfleet, 1989).

Gent, J.B. (ed.) *Croydon, the Story of a Hundred Years*, Croydon Natural History and Scientific Society (Croydon, 1970).

Gerald, E. *The Relationship between House Prices and Land Supply* (London, 1992).

Gibb, K., McGregor, A. and Munro, M. 'Housebuilding in Recession: a Regional Case Study', *Environment and Planning A*, Vol. 29, pp. 1739–58.

Gillen, M. *An Introduction to the Private Housebuilding Industry*, Working Paper No. 1, Centre for Residential Development (Nottingham, 1994).

Gillen, M. *Volume Housebuilding Companies: Identification and Taxonomy*, Working Paper No. 5, Centre for Residential Development (Nottingham, 1994).

Gillen, M. *Sectoral Restructuring: in the Private Housebuilding Industry*, Working Paper No. 10, Centre for Residential Development (Nottingham, 1995).

Gordon, C. *The Cedar Story: the Night the City was Saved* (London, 1993).

Gourvish, T. 'British Business and the Transition to a Corporate Economy: Entrepreneurship and Management Structure', *Business History*, Vol. 29, 1987, pp. 18–45.

Gourvish, T. 'Business History: in Defence of the Empirical Approach?' *Accounting Business and Financial History*, Vol. 5, 1995, pp. 3–16.

Granovetter, M. 'Economic Activity and Social Structure: the Problem of Embeddedness', *American Journal of Sociology*, Vol. 91, 1985, pp. 481–510.

Gray, T. *The Road to Success: Alfred McAlpine 1935–1985* (London, 1987).

Grebler, L. *Large Scale Housing and Real Estate Firms: Analysis of a New Business Enterprise* (New York, 1973).

Hall, P., Thomas, R., Gracey, H. and Drewett, R. *The Containment of Urban England* (London, 1977).

Hallett, G. *Housing and Land Policies in West Germany and Britain* (London, 1977).

Hamnett, C. and Randolph, B. *Cities, Housing and Profits* (London, 1988).

Handy, C. *Understanding Organizations*, 4th ed. (London, 1999).

Hannah, L. (ed.) *Management Strategy and Business Development* (London, 1976).

Hannah, L. *The Rise of the Corporate Economy*, 2nd ed. (London, 1983).

Harloe, M., Issacharoff, R. and Minns, R. *The Organisation of Housing: Public and Private Enterprise in London* (London, 1974).

Hart, E. and Clarke, R. *Concentration in British Industry 1935–75* (Cambridge, 1980).

Harvey, C. 'Business Records at the Public Record Office', *Business Archives*, No. 52, Nov. 1986, pp. 1–18.

HMSO. *Report of the Inter-departmental Committee on the Rent Restriction Acts*, Cmd. 3911, 1931.

HMSO. *Fourteenth Annual Report of the Ministry of Health 1932–3*, Cmd. 4272.

HMSO. *Housing Policy Technical Volume Part I (Housing Policy: a Consultative Document)* Cmnd. 6851, 1977.

Hobson, O.R. *A Hundred Years of the Halifax* (London, 1953).

Hodge, Major W.J. 'The Mulberry Invasion Harbours', *The Structural Engineer*, March 1946, pp. 125–98.

Holmans, A.E. *House Prices: Changes through Time at National and Sub-national Level*, Government Economic Service Working Paper No. 110 (London, 1990).

Horsey, M. 'London Speculative Housebuilders of the 1930s: Official Control and Popular Taste', *London Journal*, Vol. 11, No. 2, 1985, pp. 147–59.

House, F.H. *Timber at War: an Account of the Organisation and Activities of The Timber Control 1939–1945* (London, 1965).

Hudson, K. *The History of the English China Clays* (Newton Abbot, *c.*1968).

Humphries, J. 'Inter-war House Building, Cheap Money and Building Societies: the Housing Boom Revisited', *Business History*, Vol. 29, 1987, pp. 325–345.

Hyde, F.E. 'Economic Theory and Business History: a Comment on the Theory of Profit Maximisation', *Business History*, Vol. 5, 1962, pp. 1–10.

Ive, G. and McGhie, W.J. 'The Relationship of Construction to other Industries and to the Overall Labour and Accumulation Process' in *The Production of the Built Environment*, Proceedings of the Third Bartlett Summer School 1982 (London, 1983), pp. 3–12.

Jackson, A. *Semi-detached London* (London, 1973), 2nd rev. ed. (Didcot, 1991).

Jenkins, A. *On Site 1921–71* (London, 1971).

Jenkins, A. *Built on Site* (London, 1980).

Jeremy, D.J. *A Business History of Britain 1900–1990s* (Oxford, 1998).

Jeremy, D.J. and Shaw, C. (eds) *Dictionary of Business Biography*, 6 Vols (London, 1984–1986).

Jeremy, D.J. and Farnie, D.A. 'The Ranking of Firms, the Counting of Employees and the Classification of Data: a Cautionary Note', *Business History*, Vol. 43, July 2001, pp. 119–34.

John, A.H. *A Liverpool Merchant House: Being the History of Alfred Booth and Company 1863–1958* (London, 1959).

Johnson, J.H. 'The Suburban Expansion of Housing in London 1918–1939' in Coppock, J.T. and Prince, H.C. (eds) *Greater London* (London, 1964).

Johnson, J.H. and Pooley, C.G. (eds) *The Structure of Nineteenth-century Cities*, (London, *c*.1982), pp. 142–66.

Jones, E. *Accountancy and the British Economy 1840–1980* (London, 1981).

Jones, S.R.H. 'Transaction Costs and the Theory of the Firm: the Scope and Limitations of the New Institutional Approach', *Business History*, Vol. 39, 1997, pp. 9–25.

Jordan, S. 'Regional Newspapers and Prosopography', *Business Archives*, No. 69, Nov. 1995, pp. 13–26.

Kay, J. *Foundations of Corporate Success* (Oxford, 1993).

Kay, J. 'Beware the pitfalls of over-reliance on rationality', *Financial Times*, 20th Aug. 2002, p. 9.

Kellett, J.R. *The Impact of Railways on Victorian Cities* (London, 1969).

Kemp, P. 'The Transformation of the Urban Housing Market in Britain 1885–1939', PhD thesis, University of Sussex, 1984.

Kennett, D. 'A Provincial Builder', Unpublished typescript, Luton Library, *c*.1970.

Keynote Publications. *Housebuilding* (London, 1985).

Kindleberger, C.P. *Manias, Panics and Crashes: a History of Financial Crises*, 4th ed. (New York, 2000).

Lambert, C. *New Housebuilding and the Development Industry in the Bristol Area*, SAUS Working Paper 86 (Bristol, 1990).

Lee, C.H. 'Corporate Behaviour in Theory and History: I', *Business History*, Vol. 32, Jan. 1990, pp. 17–31.

Lee, C.H. 'The Evolution of Theory: II. Corporate Behaviour in Theory and History', *Business History*, Vol. 32, April 1990, pp. 163–79.

Littlewood, J. *The Stock Market: 50 Years of Capitalism at Work* (London, 1998).

Livesay, H.C. 'Entrepreneurial Dominance in Business Large and Small, Past and Present', *Business History Review*, Vol. 63, 1989, pp. 1–21.

MacIntosh, R.M. 'A Note on Cheap Money and the British Housing Boom, 1932–37', *Economic Journal*, Vol. 61, 1951, pp. 167–73.

Madden, L.W. 'Builders and their Businesses 7: John McLean & Sons Ltd of Wolverhampton', *Building*, 18th April 1969.

Madden, L. 'The Volume Housebuilders', *Building*, 16th April 1982, pp. 26–31.

Manchester and District Housebuilders' Association. *Housebuilding by Private Enterprise: a Plea for the Housebuilder* (Manchester, *c*.1950).

Marriott, O. *The Property Boom* (London, 1967).

Marshall, J.L. 'The Pattern of Housebuilding in the Inter-war Period in England and Wales', *Scottish Journal of Political Economy*, XV, 1968, pp. 184–205.

Martens, M. 'Owner Occupied Housing in Europe: Post-war Developments and Current Dilemmas', *Environment and Planning A*, Vol. 17, 1985, pp. 605–24.

Massey, D. and Catalano, A. *Capital and Land* (London, 1978).

Matthews, D. 'British Business History: a Review of the Periodical Literature for 1989', *Business History*, Vol. 33, April 1991, pp. 185–202.

Matthews, D. 'The Business Doctors: Accountants in British Management from the Nineteenth Century to the Present Day', *Business History*, Vol. 40, July 1998, pp. 72–103.

Maude, B. *Leadership in Management* (London, 1978).

Menary, S. 'The Pursuit of Excellence', *Housebuilder*, April 2002, pp. 32–4.

Merrett, S. *Owner Occupation in Britain* (London, 1982).

Minkes, L. *The Entrepreneurial Manager* (Harmondsworth, 1987).

Monk, S. *The Speculative Housebuilder: a Review of Empirical Research* (University of Cambridge, Dept. of Land Economy, 1991).

Monk, S., Pearce, B.J. and Whitehead, C.M.E. 'Land-use Planning, Land Supply and House Prices', *Environment and Planning A*, Vol. 28, 1996, pp. 495–511.

Moran, M. *The Politics of Banking: the Strange Case of Competition and Credit Control* (London, 1984).

Morgan, N. *A History of the NHBC and Private Home Building* (Carnforth, 1987).

Morton, R.R. 'The Speculative Housebuilding Industry in the Nineteen Seventies', PhD thesis, University of Liverpool, 1982.

Mumford, M.J. 'Chartered Accountants as Business Managers: an Oral History Perspective', *Accounting, Business and Financial History*, Vol. 1 No. 2, 1991, pp. 123–40.

Murie, A., Miner, P. and Watson, C. *Housing Policy and the Housing System* (Birmingham, 1975).

Myerson, R.B. 'Nash Equilibrium and the History of Economic Theory', *Journal of Economic Literature*, Vol. 37, Sep. 1999, pp. 1067–82.

Needleman, L. *The Economics of Housing* (London, 1965).

Nevin, E. *The Mechanism of Cheap Money: a Study of British Monetary Policy* (Cardiff, 1955).

NHBC. *New House-Building Statistics* (Amersham), Quarterly.

Nicol, C. and Hooper, A. 'Contemporary Change and the Housebuilding Industry: Concentration and Standardisation in Production', *Housing Studies*, Vol. 14, Jan. 1999, pp. 57–76.

Norris, K. *Small Building Firms: Their Origins, Characteristics and Development Needs*, Chartered Institute of Building Occasional Paper No. 32 (London, 1984).

O'Carroll, A. 'The Reshaping of Scottish Housing 1914–39' in Watters, D. *Mactaggart and Mickel and the Scottish Housebuilding Industry* (Edinburgh, 1999), pp. 211–23.

Parry Lewis, J. *Building Cycles and Britain's Growth* (London, 1965).

Payne, P.L. 'Family Business in Britain: a Historical and Analytical Survey' in Rose, M.B. (ed) *Family Business* (Aldershot, 1995), pp. 69–104.

Pearson, P. and Richardson, D. 'Business Networking in the Industrial Revolution', *Economic History Review*, Vol. 54, 2001, pp. 657–79.

Penrose, E.T. *The Theory of the Growth of the Firm*, 3rd ed. (Oxford, 1995).

Perry, G. *Movies from the Mansions: a History of Pinewood Studios* (London, 1986).

Pollard, S. *The Development of the British Economy 1914–1980*, 3rd ed. (London, 1983).

Powell, C. *The British Building Industry Since 1800: an Economic History*, 2nd ed. (London, 1996).

Prais, S.J. *The Evolution of Giant Firms in Britain: a Study of the Growth of Concentration in Manufacturing Industry in Britain* (Cambridge, 1981).

Price, S.J. *Building Societies: Their Origin and History* (London, 1958).

Ramsey, S.C. 'Speculative House Building', *Journal of the Royal Institute of British Architects*, April 1938, pp. 529–41.

Raw, C. *Slater Walker: an Investigation of a Financial Phenomenon* (London, 1977).

Reader, W.J. 'Personality, Strategy and Structure: some Consequences of Strong Minds' in Hannah, L. (ed.) *Management Strategy and Business Development* (London, 1976).

Reader, W.J. *To Have and to Hold: an Account of Frederick Bandet's Life in Business* (Hitchin, 1983).

Redding, S.G. *The Working Class Manager: Beliefs and Behaviour* (Farnborough, 1979).

Redwood, J. 'The UK Housing Market', *Quarterly Review*, National Westminster Bank, Nov. 1974, pp. 52–64.

Reid, M. *The Secondary Banking Crisis, 1973–75: its Causes and Course* (London, 1982).

Richardson, H. and Aldcroft, D. *Building in the British Economy between the Wars* (London, 1968).

Richmond, L. 'The Records of the Registrar of Companies', *Business Archives*, Nov. 1992, pp. 43–50.

Ricketts, M. *The Economics of Business Enterprise: an Introduction to Economic Organisation and the Theory of the Firm*, 2nd ed. (London, 1994).

Ritchie, B. *The Abbey National Story: a Key to the Door* (London, 1990).

Ritchie, B. *The Good Builder: the John Laing Story* (London, 1997).

Ritchie, B. *The Story of Tarmac* (London, 1999).

Rose, J. *Dynamics of Urban Property Development* (London, 1985).

Rose, M.B. (ed.) *Family Business* (Aldershot, 1995).

Ross, D.M. 'The Unsatisfied Fringe in Britain', *Business History*, Vol. 38, July 1996, pp. 11–26.

Royal Institution of Chartered Surveyors. *The Property Boom 1968–73 and its Collapse. A Supplementary Memorandum of Evidence to the Committee to Review the Functioning of Financial Institutions* (London, 1978).

Rydin, Y. 'Housebuilders as an Interest Group. The Issue of Residential Land Use Availability', *Geography Discussion Papers New Series*, No. 6 (London, 1983).

Sadtler, D., Campbell, A. and Koch, R. *Break up! When Large Companies are Worth more Dead than Alive* (Oxford, 1997).

Salt, R. *A Good Job Well Done: the Story of Rendel, A West Country Builder* (Amersham, 1983).

Saul, S.B. 'Housebuilding in England 1890–1914', *Economic History Review, 2nd Series*, 1962–1963, pp. 119–37.

Scott, P. *The Property Masters: a History of the British Commercial Property Sector* (London, 1996).

Shiller, R.J. *Macro Markets: Creating Institutions for Managing Society's Largest Economic Risks* (Oxford, 1998).

Short, J., Fleming, S. and Witt, S. *Housebuilding Planning and Community Action* (London, 1986).

Simon, H. *Administrative Behaviour: a Study of Decision-making Process in Administrative Organisation*, 2nd ed. (New York, 1965).

Slaven, A. and Checkland, S. (eds) *Dictionary of Scottish Business Biography* (Aberdeen, 1986).

Smith, K., Ferrier, W. and Grimm, C. 'King of the Hill: Dethroning the Industry Leader', *Academy of Management*, Vol. 15, No. 2, 2001, pp. 59–70.

Smith, M.E.H. *Guide to Housing*, 3rd ed. (Cambridge, 1989).

Smyth, H. *Land Banking, Land Availability and Planning for Private Housebuilding*, SAUS Working Paper 23 (Bristol, 1982).

Smyth, H. *Property Companies and the Construction Industry in Britain* (Cambridge, 1985).

Spender, J.A. *Weetman Pearson, First Viscount Cowdray* (London, 1930).

Storey, D. *The Performance of Small Firms: Profits, Jobs and Failure* (London, 1987).

Stratton, M. and Trinder, B. *Twentieth Century Industrial Archaeology* (London, 2000).

Swenarton, M. and Taylor, S. 'The Scale and Nature of the Growth of Owner-occupation in Britain Between the Wars', *Economic History Review*, Vol. 38, 1985, pp. 373–92.

Thompson, F.M.L. *Chartered Surveyors: the Growth of a Profession* (London, 1968).

Thompson, F.M.L. (ed.) *The Rise of Suburbia* (Leicester, 1982).

Thorns, D.C. *Suburbia* (London, 1972).

Toms, S. and Wright, M. 'Corporate Governance, Strategy and Structure in British Business History, 1950–2000', *Business History*, Vol. 44, July 2002, pp. 91–124.

Tucker, K.A. (ed.) *Business History: Selected Readings* (London, 1977).

Vipond, M.J. 'Fluctuations in Private Housebuilding in Great Britain 1950–1966', *Scottish Journal of Political Economy*, 16, 1969, pp. 196–211.

Wardley, P. 'The Anatomy of Big Business: Aspects of Corporate Development in the Twentieth Century', *Business History*, Vol. 33, April 1991, pp. 268–96.

Wardley, P. 'The Emergence of Big Business: and the Largest Corporate Employers of Labour in the United Kingdom, Germany and the United States *c.*1907', *Business History*, Vol. 41, Oct. 1999, pp. 88–116.

Wardley, P. 'On the Ranking of Firms: a Response to Jeremy and Farnie', *Business History*, Vol. 43, July 2001, pp. 119–24.

Watters, D. *Mactaggart and Mickel and the Scottish Housebuilding Industry* (Edinburgh, 1999).

Weber, B. 'A New Index of Residential Construction and Long Cycles in House Building in Great Britain 1838–1950', *Scottish Journal of Political Economy II*, 1955, pp. 104–32.

Wellings, F. *Construction Equities: Evaluation and Trading* (Cambridge, 1994).

Wellings, F. *The History of Marley* (Cambridge, 1994).

Wellings, F. *Forecasting Company Profits* (Cambridge, 1998).

Wellings, F. 'The Rise of the National Housebuilder: a History of British Housebuilders through the Twentieth Century', PhD thesis, University of Liverpool, 2005.

Wellings, F. *A Dictionary of British Housebuilders* (Beckenham, 2006).

Wellings, F. *Private Housebuilding Annuals* (see below).

White, V. *Wimpey: the First Hundred Years* (London, 1980).

Whitehand, J.W.R. 'Makers of British Towns: Architects, Builders and Property Owners *c.*1850–1939', *Journal of Historical Geography*, Vol. 18, No. 4, 1992, pp. 417–38.

Williamson, O.E. and Winter, S.G. (eds) *The Nature of the Firm: Origins Evolution and Development* (Oxford, 1991).

Wilson, J.F. *British Business History 1720–1994* (Manchester, 1995).

Zhang, Y. and Rajagopalan, N. 'When the Known Devil is Better than an Unknown God: an Empirical Study of the Antecedents and Consequences of Relay CEO Successions', *The Academy of Management Journal*, Vol. 47, No. 4, 2004, pp. 483–500.

The Private Housebuilding Annual

The *Private Housebuilding Annual* was a stockbroking publication between 1980 and 2002; the name of the broker reflected changes in ownership. In 2003 and 2004 the *PHA* was published by *Building* magazine and in 2005 by the author.

Laing & Cruickshank

Private Housebuilding: an Investment Strategy, Aug. 1980.

Private Housebuilding, Oct. 1981; Nov. 1982; Dec. 1983; Nov. 1984; Jan. 1986.

Alexanders, Laing & Cruickshank

Private Housebuilding, May 1987.

C.L. Alexanders, Laing & Cruickshank
   Private Housebuilding, Dec. 1988.
Laing & Cruickshank
   Private Housebuilding, June 1990.
Credit Lyonnais Laing
   Private Housebuilding, Sep. 1991; Aug. 1992–Aug. 1997.
Credit Lyonnais Securities Europe
   Private Housebuilding Annual, Aug. 1998–Aug. 2002.
Building Magazine
   Private Housebuilding Annual, Aug. 2003; Sep. 2004.
Fred Wellings
   Private Housebuilding Annual, Aug. 2005.

Company Minute Books

Henry Boot Minute Book 1931 onwards
Comben Minute Book 1971 onwards
Comben AGM Minute Book
New Ideal Building and Land Development Minute Book No. 1, 1934 onwards
New Ideal Homesteads Minute Book No. 3, 1941–1967
John Laing & Sons Minute Books 1920 onwards
John Laing & Sons Minute Book 1928 onwards
John and David Martin Minute Book
MRCE Minute Book No. 1, 1919 onwards
Taylor Woodrow Minute Book 1931 onwards
Taylor Woodrow Minute Book 1948–1951
Taylor Woodrow Estates Minute Books 1943 onwards
Taylor Homes Minute Book No. 1, 1946 onwards
Alfred Booth Minute Book 1973 onwards
Whelmar Minute Book 1977 onwards
Wimpey Minute Book No. 2, 1931–1934 (subsequent minutes in loose-leaf book)
Wimpey Board of Management Minute Books 1937 onwards
Files of Wimpey correspondence and early minute books are held in the CIRCA+ WICCAD archive at Kimmins Mill, Stroud

Index

General

accountants, 116, 127, 129, 131–4
accounting, 19–20, 27, 30, 168
acquisitions, 8, 20, 27, 66, 74, 81, 89,
    95, 97, 100–103, 117, 137, 152,
    163, 173, 180–81, 190, 194, 215,
    227–8, 249, 251, 254–6, 265
advertising, 154, 156–7
architects, 9, 123, 126, 129
archives, company, 21–2

Bank of England, 83, 184
banking, 96, 138, 149–51, 184, 186–8,
    244
    secondary, 83–5, 95–6, 149, 194
bankruptcies, 21, 93, 95–6, 183, 186,
    194, 244
Barker Report, 10, 143–4
Borders case, 43, 179
brands, 65, 101, 155–7, 162, 173, 236
building controls, 5–6, 55, 59–67,
    69–70, 73, 75–6, 106, 154, 175–6,
    193, 208, 244
building licences, 60, 75
building materials, 171

capital
    personal, 253, 256
    resources, 11, 63, 117, 122, 136,
        138–42, 149, 152–3, 173, 188,
        210, 221, 225, 235, 250
    return on, 11–12
    sales–capital ratio, 11, 29, 138, 168
    working, 11, 136, 139, 149
chance, 264–5
Companies House, 19–20, 25–6, 164
concentration, 5, 13, 21, 28, 69, 82,
    91, 93, 108, 111, 136, 147, 168,
    189, 245, 259
conglomerates, 7, 195–6, 131, 216,
    225–36
consolidation, 6–7, 82, 93, 100–101,
    105–6, 136, 152, 173, 249, 255

construction, 4–5, 7–8, 10–12, 29,
    51–2, 56–9, 64–5, 71–2, 143, 176,
    193, 195, 208–22, 247
    fixed-price, 183–4, 210–12
contractors, 4, 8–11, 32, 55–9, 63–5,
    90, 93, 107, 142–3, 176, 186, 194,
    210, 202–22, 243

Defence Regulation 56A, 56, 59,
    61
diseconomies of scale, 7, 137,
    159–66, 173, 264
diversification, 4, 55, 208–43, 246,
    250
dominant individual, 6–7, 27, 73,
    116–23, 125–33, 135, 177–8, 181,
    183–5, 191–2, 195–6, 198, 202–5,
    207, 245–6, 258, 260

ease of entry, 136–41
economies of scale, 5, 7, 106, 136–59,
    167–9, 172–3, 226, 236, 245, 249,
    264
education, 27, 115–16, 124, 131–2,
    261
entrepreneurs, 6–8, 12–13, 65, 79,
    115–22, 125, 131, 137–8, 140–41,
    148, 151, 159–61, 173, 199, 201,
    203–4, 207, 215, 221, 228, 231,
    234, 247, 249–50, 253, 256,
    260–61, 263–5

family firms, 78, 115–17, 119, 185,
    197, 199
finance for housebuilders, 8, 83, 93,
    108, 116, 138, 140–41, 148–53,
    173, 244, 246, 249–55
focus, 7, 176, 186–7, 189–91, 195,
    208–43, 247, 260, 265
founders, 5–7, 7–9, 115–16, 119, 121,
    124, 126–8, 131–3, 176, 178, 191,
    193, 198–9

People

If there are two family members in the same company, both are identified in the same line; if more, then shown as 'et al.', as in Gallaghers and Laings. Where the name is synonymous with the company, it is worth checking in the company index.